An Illustrated History of Nova Scotia

Harry Bruce

Co-published by
NIMBUS PUBLISHING LIMITED
and
THE PROVINCE OF NOVA SCOTIA

Co-published by the Province of Nova Scotia
and Nimbus Publishing Limited.
Sponsored by: Communications Nova Scotia
A product of the Nova Scotia Government
Co-publishing Program

Design: Arthur B. Carter, Halifax
On the cover: Two panels from the Fort Anne Heritage Tapestry, on display at Fort Anne National Historic Site in Annapolis Royal. The four-panel tapestry was completed in 1995, by volunteers, and its total size is 18' wide x 8' high, (5.5 m x 2.5 m).

Cover film: Maritime Photo Engravers
Printed and bound by Transcontinental Printing Inc.

Canadian Cataloguing in Publication Data
Bruce, Harry, 1934–
An illustrated history of Nova Scotia
Co-published by the Province of Nova Scotia.
Includes bibliographical references and index.
ISBN 1-55109-219-0
1. Nova Scotia—History.   I. Nova Scotia.   II. Title.

FC2311 B78   1997   971.6   C97-950184-9
F1038.B78   1997

Printed In Canada

For my father, Charles Bruce
1906–1971

PREFACE

It was the Information and Communications division of the Nova Scotia government's Department of Supply and Services that hired me to write a history of the province, and the assignment came to me from Sandy Phillips. She has since retired from her job as Director, information services, but I am still grateful to her. Every writer should be lucky enough to get such an assignment.

Before plunging into the research, I knew Nova Scotia's story was interesting, but failed to appreciate the number of amazing characters who walked its roads, sailed its vessels, drank its rum, fought in its political arenas, excelled at warfare and in the professions, and helped make the province the unique and spirited corner of Canada it remains to this day. Nor had I grasped how powerfully international forces, and decisions in London, Paris, Versailles, Boston, New York, and Washington, had influenced the destiny of this cold and frequently turbulent corner of the British Empire. It was a revelation to me, too, that if Nova Scotia had not refused to join the rebel states during the American Revolution, Canada might never have been born.

I hope readers of this book will find it half as fascinating to read as I found it to write. They'll discover no original research. The idea was not to make historical breakthroughs, which I am ill-equipped to do, but to milk as many published sources as I could find for the sake of creating a book that almost everyone—native, visitor, come-from-away, or expatriate Bluenoser—might enjoy and, from time to time, want to consult.

My father, the poet, novelist, and newspaperman Charles Bruce, spent most of his life in Toronto, and treated his homesickness with books by Nova Scotians and about Nova Scotians. I grew up surrounded by these volumes, and after I'd moved to Nova Scotia for good, inherited them. To expand the collection, I haunted used bookstores in Halifax. By the time Sandy Phillips accepted my bid to write the book under contract, which was more than twenty years after I'd moved from Toronto to Halifax, I had so many books about Nova Scotia and Canada on my shelves that, to do my research, I scarcely had to leave my home.

The province hired my friend Marjory Whitelaw to provide extra research—notably on the Acadians, Scots, Mi'kmaq, blacks, and women of the province, and for the the final chapter on postwar Nova Scotia—and this is a better book for her contribution. Thank you, Marjory. And thank you Susan Lucy, coordinator of editorial services at Communications Nova Scotia, for your intelligent editing.

Whatever the quality of my work here, this book was long overdue. One of the volumes I inherited from my father was "The History of Nova Scotia" by G. G. Campbell. This new book is one of the first to wrap up the entire history of the province in one volume for adults since Campbell's came out—and that was half a century ago.

Harry Bruce
Port Shoreham
September 1997

CONTENTS

An 1837 R. Petley print titled "Indian of the Mic Mac Tribe." At the time of European contact, the Mi'kmaq occupied what are now coastal areas of the Gaspé Peninsula, Nova Scotia, Prince Edward Island, northern and eastern New Brunswick—territory their ancestors had occupied for at least 2,000 years.

CHAPTER 1

THE ICE LEAVES. HUMANS ARRIVE

Perhaps 10,000 or 11,000 years ago, when the population of the entire world amounted to about five million, families of nomadic hunters, dressed to survive icy winds, were spending the bitter winters at an encampment of bark and hide-covered dwellings near what is now Debert in Colchester County, Nova Scotia.

The first humans to inhabit North America probably crossed the Bering Strait from northeast Asia to Alaska in waves of migration, which started as early as 25,000 years ago and gradually spread across the whole continent. What distinguished the Paleo-Indian culture was their tools, which were made by chipping and flaking stone, and especially a style of spearhead that archaeologists call "fluted points."

At that time what has become Prince Edward Island was linked to the mainland by a low plain that spread across much of the future Gulf of St. Lawrence. Off Nova Scotia's Atlantic coasts, the famous fishing banks of millenniums hence were still islands or peninsulas. The last invasion of glaciers from the Ice Age, which had squashed Nova Scotia as a curling stone might squash a wet sponge, had retreated fewer than 2,000 years before. Indeed, the Ice Age was so recent that the Debert settlement may well have been "the earliest dated occupation in North America in a truly periglacial environment."[1]

If the Debert people who made fluted points were like their Paleo-Indian relatives to the south and west, they were expert at hunting in packs. They or their forebears had probably come up from New England in pursuit of game, though some scholars suspect the first humans in Nova Scotia migrated from land that is now beneath the Atlantic Ocean. As trees, bushes, and grass replaced the vanishing ice, grazing mammals followed the vegetation, and small bands of hunters pursued them into the new territory. Winter was fierce. While the continental lid had disappeared, ice caps, snow fields, and glacier chunks may still have lingered in the local highlands. The snowfall was heavier than now, and the subsoil never thawed.

In this subarctic climate, the prey of the Debert hunters may have included the last of the mastodons, but more plentiful were creatures that now live further north—Arctic foxes and hares and, crucial to the survival of these humans, caribou. The herds likely spent the warm weather grazing near

Cobequid Bay and in winter moved up to the exposed slopes to the north, where high winds kept snow from burying their forage. The Debert people set up camp where they could intercept the northbound herds as the first snow fell, when plummeting temperatures enabled them to freeze meat, and the animals' new winter coats were thick and glossy. In the spring they intercepted the southbound herds.

The range of the mastodon included Nova Scotia. This was confirmed when the preserved remains of two mastodons were discovered by miners—one in 1991 and partial remains of another in 1993—at National Gypsum Quarry (Canada) at East Milford. The remains are estimated to be 70,000 years old.

The hunters brought down the caribou with fluted points. They had stone knives to cut the skin, meat, and tendons; stone cleavers to dismember the carcasses; and stone hammers for breaking bones to extract marrow. With stone scrapers, they removed fat and flesh from skins, and with stone awls they made holes for the sewing of clothes and coverings for their dwellings. With stone tools they fashioned other implements, as well as weapons and ornaments, out of bones, antlers, wood, and bark. They could not have survived without stone and caribou.

The Debert people dressed in shirts, snug leggings or pants, and fitted jackets, all sewn from skin and furs. Either the jackets had hoods, or people wore hats thick enough to protect their heads from the knifing winter winds. It is likely, too, that these northern Paleo-Indians decorated their clothing with stains extracted from plants or rocks and used the teeth, claws, and bones of their prey to make pendants and amulets. They would have believed that wearing such charms would help make them superb hunters.

For several decades, small bands lived at Debert for at least part of every winter. They may have been groups of families who joined forces to kill caribou and then dispersed in the spring to go their separate ways—to forest and tundra for smaller game, or to seacoasts for seals, walrus, waterfowl, and their share of millions of salmon.

The wealth of artifacts recovered from the Debert site made it archaeologically spectacular, but there is also evidence of Paleo-Indian gatherings at Kingsclear on the St. John River, Quaco Head on the New Brunswick side of the Bay of Fundy, Cape Blomidon in Nova Scotia's Minas Basin, and in eastern Prince Edward Island. While these people probably had the same dark hair, eyes, and skin colour as native bands in the Maritimes 10,000 years later, they vanished about 8000 BC.

Archaeologists have found scant evidence of human life in the Maritimes between 8000 and 3000 BC, but some scholars believe that throughout this 5,000-year "Great Hiatus" descendants of the Paleo-Indians lived in coastal settlements whose remains the rising ocean later obliterated.

While peoples from the northwest (the Shield Archaic tradition), the west (Laurentian), and the southwest (Susquehanna) may all have moved into the Maritimes as far back as 5,000 years ago, archaeologist James A. Tuck has argued that, "The Maritime Archaic tradition was the dominant Late Pre-Ceramic [5,000 to 2,500 years ago] culture along the coast of the Maritimes. Moreover, I believe it to be a very old tradition, with its roots ... perhaps as far back as Paleo-Indian times. At some unknown time, the Maritime Archaic people became adjusted to life along the coast and developed a technology for harpooning seals, walrus, perhaps even small whales, and ... swordfish."[2] They fashioned lances and barbed harpoons with whale bones, swordfish bills, and polished and chipped stone, and also made carvings of birds and fish.

When French explorers reached the Maritimes, the native population consisted of the Malecite and Passamaquoddy peoples of southwestern New Brunswick, and the Mi'kmaq, who ranged over almost all of the Maritimes as well as Quebec's Gaspé Peninsula. The precise origin of these peoples remains uncertain. All three spoke dialects of the Algonquian tongue—as did the Blackfoot of the prairies, more than 3000 kilometres inland—but they lived much as the Maritime Archaic people had lived on these same coasts.

As soon as river ice broke up, the Mi'kmaq abandoned their inland hunting camps and hurried down to the sea. At traditional locations on bays, coves, and estuaries, they gathered in bands of up to 200 people, fished for winter flounder, and built weirs to exploit the coming runs of herring, smelt,

A Mi'kmaq petroglyph (rock carving) of two natives wearing ceremonial hats as they participate in a dance. Many carvings were discovered at sites in Queens County in the 1800s.

gaspereaux, salmon, and sturgeon. With hook and line and multi-pronged spears, they took cod, striped bass, sea trout, and plaice. They also ate clams, mussels, scallops, and oysters.

During late winter and early spring, hunters with clubs and spears stalked harp and hooded seals on fields of ice. In summer, harbour seals, grey seals, and probably walruses hauled themselves onto beaches to become easy prey. To get dolphins and whales, however, the Mi'kmaq used seagoing canoes, some as long as eight metres. It must have taken near-miraculous ability and courage to challenge the ocean in a paper-thin, birchbark canoe, hurl spears and harpoons at a whale, stab and hack the thrashing giant till it died, and then haul it back to shore.

Spring and fall, the seacoasts offered the Mi'kmaq an amazing number of birds. Nicolas Denys, a seventeenth-century trader from France, wrote that at one spot in Nova Scotia he saw an unbelievable number of geese and ducks, and that other birds rose in flocks so thick they blotted out the light of the sun.

The Mi'kmaq trapped beaver. They also lowered water levels at ponds till they exposed the animals' lodges and then shot them with bows and arrows. As winter approached, families laid in supplies of smoked fish and eels, and hunters went after bear, otter, muskrat, and whatever caribou lingered in the region. In deepest winter, deer and moose were easy to track, and Mi'kmaq hunters, wearing expertly crafted snowshoes, drove the creatures through deep

A nineteenth-century print by R. Petley of Mi'kmaq women working.

snow till they toppled from exhaustion, killed them with stone-pointed lances, and butchered them on the spot.

The dangerous weeks occurred just as winter ended and spring began. The melting snow made land travel difficult, ice still gripped lakes and rivers, birds and animals were scarce, and in this "starving time" native peoples could only hope their frozen meat and smoked fish would last till the season of plenty returned.

The natives who met the Europeans exploring the Maritimes in the sixteenth and seventeenth centuries were descendants of the Mi'kmaq of roughly 2,000 years ago. Through all the centuries, their wigwams, covered in bark and housing a central fireplace, had remained the same; so had their cycles of fishing and hunting, their starving times, joyful greetings of spring, and even their clothing and some of their games.

They used antlers, bone, and stone to make tools and weapons. From birch bark they fashioned everything from bowls, boxes, and baskets to canoes, wigwams, moose-calls, and waterproof capes. They had awls, beaver-incisor knives, bark-peelers, and needles for weaving mats and making snowshoes. They turned the teeth of animals into pendants, and bones into beads, and believed the ornaments they wore were magical.

The chief difference between the Mi'kmaq of the time when Christ was born and their descendants in 1643–when the boy king, Louis XIV, began his seventy-two-year reign over France–was that the later ones were getting to know Europeans, and the seemingly irresistible goods that white men kept bringing from their unknown empire beyond the ocean's horizon. For the native peoples of Nova Scotia, this new relationship would prove all but fatal.

Mi'kmaq basketry (top) and quillwork (bottom) remain a practiced art to this day.

13

In 1496 John Cabot presented his plan to King Henry VII of England, mapping his route towards what he anticipated would be the spices and treasures of the Far East, to conquer lands yet unknown.

On March 5, 1496, Henry VII of England granted the letter of patent for Cabot's voyage, but no funding for the explorations.

CHAPTER 2

A MAN FROM VENICE FINDS THE SHORES OF CANADA

Some argue that Egyptians, Phoenicians, or Romans reached North America in ancient times, while others insist that, little more than five centuries after Christ's death, a party of Irish, led by St. Brendan, sailed to Canada in a leather boat. What is more certain is that, a thousand years ago, Norsemen built a settlement on the Great Northern Peninsula of Newfoundland, and that one of their leaders, Leif (The Lucky) Ericsson, explored the coasts of Baffin Island, Labrador, and a balmier neighbourhood further south. With his crew of thirty-five, he wintered there, in what would one day become legendary as "Vinland."

Norse sagas celebrated Vinland as a country with seaside grapevines, dew that was sweet to the tongue, and the biggest salmon anyone had ever seen. Centuries later, Cape Breton Islanders would claim that such a haven must surely have been their island, but while certain historians have argued that Vinland was indeed in Nova Scotia, no evidence has ever proved them right. In any event, the Norse made the first-known exploration of Canada by Europeans and thus set an ancient precedent for the great age of transatlantic exploration.

A woodcut of St. Brendan—the patron saint of sailors—and crew en route to their earthly paradise. The whale, Jasconius, surrounds their boat.

Nearly 500 years passed before John Cabot sailed into the same neighbourhood to officially "discover" mainland North America for western Europe. Yet right up until the mid-fourteenth century, Greenland Norsemen had continued to visit Labrador to get timber. Moreover, some students of transatlantic exploration have built a compelling case suggesting that, in 1398, a Scottish knight, Prince Henry Sinclair, spent an entire winter among hospitable Mi'kmaq in Nova Scotia. Various scholars have also claimed that seafarers from Ireland, England, Brittany, Normandy, Portugal, and the country of the Basques truly deserved credit for having rediscovered North America before Columbus. One can't help wondering how many European seafarers, before 1492, made unofficial, unsung, or unintentional journeys to Nova Scotia.

The first European known to have reached North America was a Viking, Bjarni Herjolfsson. Blown off course on a voyage from Iceland to Greenland, he and his oarsmen probably reached the coast south of Nova Scotia in the year 986. About fifteen years later, another Viking, Leif Ericsson, landed somewhere south of the St. Lawrence and named the land Vinland.

Some of the earliest transatlantic voyages may well have started in Bristol, which among British cities was second in size only to London. Long before Columbus saw the Bahamas, merchants of this bustling port were backing voyages of exploration to mysterious lands beyond the Atlantic's western horizon. As early as 1480, Bristol fishermen may already have visited Newfoundland. It was from Bristol that in 1497 John Cabot sailed to North America and did what Columbus had failed to do: set foot on the mainland. News of his finding a new continent shot through Europe so fast that, as R. A. Skelton explained in the "Dictionary of Canadian Biography," he later earned fame for having achieved "the intellectual discovery of North America."[1]

Five centuries after Cabot's voyage he remains an enigma. Was he short, tall, fat, or thin? No portrait of him exists, nor a scrap of his handwriting. Even the spelling of his name shifts like the wind. He has been Giovanni, Joanes, Johannes, and Zoane. He has been Caboto, Kaboto, Cabbotto, Chabato, and Caboote. He was born around 1450 in Genoa, a major trading centre since Roman times. Genoa was where Columbus, some four years older than

Cabot, grew up. Cabot's father was a trader and moved his family to Venice when John was a boy.

For a future explorer, the world offered no better town. As western headquarters for the "silk road"—the overland trade route between Europe and Asia—Venice owed its prosperity to places few Europeans had ever seen. A contemporary of Cabot's called Venice "the most beautiful and wealthiest [city] in the world, for indeed merchandise gushes through it as does water through a fountain."[2]

An illustration by C. W. Jefferys of Cabot sighting land.

Like his father, Cabot was a trader. His business took him to Mecca, where he quizzed leaders of camel caravans about the Far Eastern origins of spices and other treasures. He mastered navigation and astronomy, made maps, and, since he knew the world was round, fashioned globes. Cabot believed the quick way to the riches of Cathay and Cipango (Japan) lay across the western ocean, but he was sure the islands Columbus had found were not in Asia. The true route, Cabot argued, lay much farther north. In both Spain and Portugal, he failed to get the backing he needed to cross the Atlantic. He therefore decided to try his luck in England, and on March 5, 1496, he received from King Henry VII the letters patent for his voyage. They have been called "nothing less than the founding document of Canadian discovery"[3] and begin like this:

"Be it known and made manifest that we have given and granted ... to our well-beloved John Cabot, citizen of Venice, and to Lewis, Sebastian, and Sancio, sons of the said John ... full and free authority, faculty and power to sail to all parts, regions, and coasts of the eastern, western, and northern sea, under our banners, flags and ensigns, with five ships or vessels ... and with so many and with such mariners and men as they may wish to take with them ... to find, discover, and investigate whatsoever islands, countries, regions, or provinces of heathens and infidels, in whatsoever part of the world placed, which before this time were unknown to all Christians."

Henry VII also authorized Cabot and his sons "to set up our aforesaid banners and ensigns in any town, city, castle, or mainland whatsoever, newly found by them," and, on behalf of England, to conquer any strange people they met. The king did not tap his royal coffers for so much as one penny of investment in the expedition. For financial support, Cabot turned to men who knew all about gambling on seagoing business experiments, the capitalists of Bristol's Society of Merchant Venturers. He was as good a salesman as he was mariner. After hearing him explain why Cathay surely lay beyond the western sea on a round world, an Italian diplomat in London said he was overwhelmingly persuasive.

John Cabot's son Sebastian is believed to have accompanied him on his second expedition.

In 1496 Cabot set out with one ship, but disagreements with his crew, bad weather, and a shortage of food forced him to turn back. When he sought further funding in Bristol after this fiasco, historian Leslie F. Hannon wrote, "He must have argued brilliantly, marshalling all his evidence from Ptolemy to Polo. He managed to procure a ship, though it represented a big comedown from the five-ship squadron specified in the letters patent."[4]

The ship was the Matthew, possibly named after Cabot's wife Mattea. In "The White and the Gold," Thomas Costain called it "a ratty little caravel."[5] It had a tubby hull, a high bow and stern, square-rigged sails on two forward masts, and a triangular sail on the aftermast. No bigger than a modern tugboat, it was small enough to row. Since discovery voyages were dangerous, and the Matthew would sail unescorted into unknown waters in a cold climate, Cabot could round up a crew of only eighteen or twenty, not all of them sailors. Some were Bristol merchants. One was a barber from Genoa. All in all, Cabot had both an inadequate crew and, in Costain's opinion, "surely the meanest of equipment with which to make such a hazardous and important venture."

But make it he did. The Matthew probably followed the ancient path of the Norsemen, stopping at Iceland and Greenland, pushing on to Baffin Island, and then breezing down the coasts of Labrador and Newfoundland. It took fifty-two days to sail from Ireland to the spot where Cabot went ashore. Unfortunately, experts still can't agree on whether that was in Labrador, Newfoundland, or Cape Breton Island.

Around dawn on June 24, 1497, Cabot spotted what may have been western Cape Breton Island. Carrying the royal banner, his party went ashore, and the man all England would know as "the Great Admiral" claimed the country in the name of Henry VII. He thought he had reached the outskirts of Asia.

Cabot saw no castles to confiscate or strange peoples to conquer. He found snares set for animals, bone needles, and axe-notched trees, but no natives. It is possible, however, that Mi'kmaq silently watched the arrival of the Matthew, the landing of the men with pale faces, and the fluttering of the royal banner. The Europeans did not linger. Having declared North America a British possession, the Venetian agent of the king of England sailed away to explore more coasts. It remains the clearest proof of Cabot's skills as a mariner that, after he turned for home, at the "cape of the mainland nearest to Ireland," the tubby Matthew zipped across the Atlantic in fifteen days.

The news of his discovery turned him into a national hero. The excitement infected even the king, who helped arrange Cabot's second expedition in the spring of 1498, this time with five ships. Cabot revelled in his brief fame. Venetian diplomat Lorenzo Pasqualigo wrote, "vast honour is paid to him and he goes dressed in silk, and these English run after him like mad ... "[6]

In 1997, the year marking the 500th anniversary of Cabot's landing in North America, a modern replica of Cabot's ship Matthew visited Halifax and other eastern Canadian ports.

The second expedition was a disaster. Writing a dozen years later, one Polydore Vergil said Cabot sailed first to Ireland, and then further west, and was "believed to have found the new lands nowhere but on the very bottom of the ocean, to which he is thought to have descended together with his boat."[7]

Cabot gave England its first excuse for claiming it owned North America and started a seagoing stampede to the Grand Banks. While some fishermen already knew about the fabulous cod stocks there, Cabot's descriptions of his voyage through huge schools of fish turned a semi-secret into an international scoop. The cod off Newfoundland, he reported, were so abundant his men caught them by lowering weighted baskets into the sea. As early as 1522, the British fishing fleet on the Grand Banks was so big the government assigned a man-of-war to protect it, and in the 1530s, when Jacques Cartier made the voyages that introduced the crown of France to the history of Canada, cod fishermen from Brittany were already old hands off the coasts of both Newfoundland and Nova Scotia.

A modern portrayal of the French explorer Jacques Cartier. He mapped his travels to North America in the 1500s and was the first to chart the St. Lawrence River —an invaluable discovery that enabled France to colonize the North American interior.

CHAPTER 3

THE MAN FROM SAINT-MALO WHO MAPPED AN INLAND SEA

The Renaissance produced a gang of explorers so bold they changed the world forever. Four years before Columbus found the Caribbean islands that he believed were part of Asia, Bartolomeu Dias of Portugal became the first European to round the tip of Africa; and in 1498 another Portuguese, Vasco da Gama, established a sea route to India. By 1500, Portuguese adventurers had sailed their chunky caravels to Labrador and Brazil. Spaniards would soon find Florida, march in the jungles of Puerto Rico, and gaze at the Pacific Ocean from a Panama peak.

In 1520, while the Spanish crew of Portuguese captain Ferdinand Magellan endured the first voyage around the world, Joao Alvares Fagundes, also of Portugal, investigated the south coast of Newfoundland and probably Cape Breton Island and Chedabucto Bay in Nova Scotia. The Portuguese had already set up Newfoundland fishing stations. Basque, Breton, and English fishermen also led the way for the explorers. As early as 1504, French fishermen used Canso, N.S., as a summer base, and when Jacques Cartier of Saint-Malo made the first of his epic voyages to Canada in 1534, he was greeted in the Gulf of St. Lawrence by French fishermen.

Cartier was forty-three, but ever since his boyhood he had watched fishing boats return from the Grand Banks, and he may well have visited the banks himself. Saint-Malo was a mariners' town, and long before Cartier's adventures on the St. Lawrence River, he had put in time before the mast.

He spoke Portuguese and may have seen Brazil. In 1524, when Giovanni da Verrazzano, an adventurer from Florence, sailed under the French flag to explore coastal North America from the Carolinas all the way up to Cape Breton, Cartier was probably with him. The man from Saint-Malo may also have witnessed the Florentine's end; Caribs killed Verrazzano and ate him.

Verrazzano's voyages occurred because King François I of France refused to recognize a treaty in which Spain and Portugal divided between themselves all the new lands that any discoveries revealed. The king insisted that France, too, exploit whatever riches the New World offered and, with respect to the treaty, sneered, "I should very much like to see the clause of Adam's will which shuts me off from my share of the world." To continue Verrazzano's mission to secure for France a share of what lay across the Atlantic, King François hired Cartier.

A royal command in March 1534 instructed the explorer "to discover certain islands and lands where it is said that a great quantity of gold, and other precious things, are to be found." Like so many others, however, Cartier also dreamed of finding a route to Asia.

An engraving of Giovanni da Verrazzano. He explored the coast of Nova Scotia without making a landing. His descriptions of this voyage, although not detailed, were glowing and probably stimulated further French exploration efforts.

Once described as "a man of open countenance with kindly eyes and obstinate chin," he probably sported a master mariner's trim beard. While he never sat for a portrait, modern author Thomas B. Costain decided he had "the face of a man who finds philosophic calm in contemplation of the sea but can be roused easily to violent action ... A sober man ... fair in his dealings, capable and without fear ... and with a hint of power in his steady eyes."[1]

Cartier's expedition did not receive the blessing of his spirited hometown. Fishing-vessel owners in Saint-Malo did not want local sailors serving other masters, and they feared that news about whatever lay beyond the Grand Banks would lure still more competitors to the fishing grounds. To round up a crew, Cartier had to turn to the courts. With the help of Baron Philippe Chabot, High Admiral of France, and 6,000 livres from the royal treasury, however, he was ready to sail in the spring of 1534. He had a crew of sixty aboard two fully decked caravels. Each vessel carried muskets, cannons, and enough food to last six months.

The expedition left Saint-Malo on April 20 and, running before steady winds, reached Newfoundland in only twenty days. After cruising up the northeast coast and waiting for ice to clear from the Strait of Belle Isle, the vessels sailed along the coast of Labrador toward the Gulf of St. Lawrence. On June 11, just across what is now the Quebec border, Cartier led his men ashore at Brest, already familiar to hundreds of European fishermen as a good source of wood and water. The explorer and his crew now knelt at the first recorded Christian religious service in Canada. Cartier was so affected by the glowering and rocky terrain that he entered in his journal a famous denunciation of Canada's subarctic wilderness: "I am inclined to believe that this is the land God gave to Cain ... "

King François I of France encouraged France's exploration of North America and hired Cartier to meet that end.

Cartier veered towards some mountains to the south and, in stormy weather, sailed down Newfoundland's west coast. He then headed for the Magdalen Islands and on to Prince Edward Island. While not knowing that Newfoundland, too, was an island, he shrewdly guessed the existence of Cabot Strait: "I am inclined to think ... there is a passage between Newfoundland and the Breton's land. If this were so, it would prove a great saving both in time and distance."

"In these lines," Toronto writer Leslie F. Hannon said in 1971, "one can see Canada taking shape."[2]

Cartier explored coastal Prince Edward Island and liked what he found: "the best-tempered region one can possibly see, and the heat is considerable." Indeed, the island already seemed the haven its inhabitants would one day tout as "The Garden of the Gulf."

Leaving a scarf and a knife hanging from a branch for a wary Mi'kmaq they had seen running on a beach, Cartier and his men sailed northward beside New Brunswick and, full of giddy hope that they had found a northern route to Cathay, up Chaleur Bay. It was here that he had his first face-to-face dealings with North American natives. They were almost certainly Mi'kmaq, and their behaviour, as recorded in his journal, indicated that they were no strangers to trade with Europeans.

"We caught sight of two fleets of Indian canoes that were crossing the bay—in total, about forty or fifty canoes. When one of the fleets reached this point, a large number of Indians sprang out on the beach and set up a great noise, waving us to come ashore, and holding up furs on poles. But as we had only one boat we decided not to risk it, and rowed away.

"They now launched two of their largest canoes to follow us, and these were joined by five more from the second fleet. All came after our longboat, showing signs of excitement and happiness, and of their wish to be friends with us ... We did not care to trust them, and waved them back. But they surrounded our longboat with their seven canoes.

"Since they would not go back, we ordered two small cannon to be fired over their heads and this at first sent them paddling back toward the point. However, they proceeded to come on as before and we shot off two fire-lances which frightened them so much that they paddled away as fast as they could and did not follow us any more."

Cartier's cannons may have been the first guns ever to go off in Canada, but a time would come when the sound of firearms would no longer scatter the Mi'kmaq. They would have guns of their own.

The French sailed up Chaleur Bay to the mouth of the Restigouche River. Disappointed that they had not found a route to Asia and gloomily heading back down the bay, they again met the Mi'kmaq, who seemed frantic to trade and offered them cooked seal meat. This time, Cartier was more businesslike. The French gave the Mi'kmaq beads, knives, and hatchets in exchange for furs.

"[They] showed a marvellously great pleasure in possessing and obtaining these iron wares and other commodities, dancing and going through many ceremonies and throwing salt water over their heads with their hands," Cartier wrote. Some of the women stood in the bay up to their knees, swaying and singing, while others stroked the arms of the sailors from Brittany. The Mi'kmaq felt so relaxed with the strangers "that at length we bartered with them, hand to hand for everything they possessed, so that nothing was left to them but their naked bodies."

Cartier now sailed north to Gaspé, where he met and feasted with Chief Donnacona of the Laurentian Iroquois; sailed away with two of the chief's sons; just missed discovering the St. Lawrence River; explored the coast of Anticosti Island; and in early September arrived home in Saint-Malo.

What had he accomplished? He was not the first European to reach the

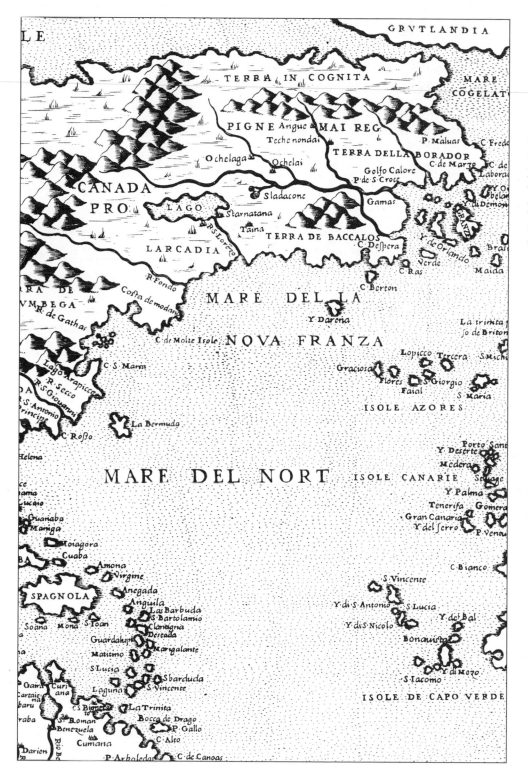

A detail of the map engraved in 1566 by Bolognino Zaltieri. The area that would later become known as Acadia is referred to as "Larcadia."

Gulf of St. Lawrence, nor even the first Frenchman. But he was the first explorer to investigate its coasts in what would one day be Prince Edward Island, New Brunswick, Quebec, Newfoundland, and Labrador. He wrote about the gulf, mapped it, sniffed the vast hinterland beyond it, showed off his borrowed Iroquois (who were learning French), and made the New World sound so intriguing that, even though he had found neither treasure nor a route to the Indies, King François promptly gave him money and authority for a second voyage.

In 1536 Cartier returned to the port of Saint-Malo, France, with 12 Iroquois on board and reports of the St. Lawrence River— what he believed was the passage to the Indies.

Unfortunately, Cartier's exploration of the gulf marked the effective beginning of the destruction by Europeans of a Mi'kmaq culture that went back thousands of years. What followed, wrote Alfred G. Bailey, was "an era of almost steady infiltration of European traits into the cultural areas of the Atlantic provinces."[3]

In May 1535, with three ships and 110 men, Cartier once more sailed for the Gulf of St. Lawrence, and this time Indians showed him the way to the mouth

of St. Lawrence River and the path towards Canada. The river was so long that they had heard of no one who had ever seen its source. Cartier, again believing he had found the passage to the Indies, pushed inland to Hochelaga (Montreal). Having spent the winter at Stadacona (Quebec), where scurvy killed many of his men, and having used trickery to kidnap a dozen Iroquois, all of whom would die in France, Cartier arrived in Saint-Malo in July 1536. On the return voyage he had discovered Cabot Strait, which separates Newfoundland and Cape Breton Island, thus completing his vision of the inland sea that washes the shores of half the provinces in Canada.

Cartier's last transatlantic voyage occurred in 1541. King François I had named Jean-François de la Rocque de Roberval "lieutenant-general in the country of Canada" and ordered him to found the first French colony in America, complete with fortified towns, churches, and priests to convert Indians to the Roman Catholic faith. With five ships and a crew that a Spanish spy estimated at 1,500 men, Cartier sailed as Roberval's fleet captain, guide, and subordinate. He built fortifications for the colonists at the mouth of a St. Lawrence tributary near Stadacona and spent one winter there; but believing he had found gold and diamonds, left for France before Roberval and the main body of colonists showed up.

When they met at St. John's, Newfoundland, Cartier disobeyed Roberval's orders to accompany him back up the St. Lawrence and, in the dark of night, sailed for France. He became a businessman, and in 1557, at the age of sixty-six, he expired. His gold had turned out to be iron pyrites, and his jewels mere quartz; in France one still hears the expression "false as Canadian diamonds."

Jacques Cartier's arrival in Quebec, 1534.

There was nothing false, however, about the St. Lawrence River, or its gigantic entranceway. Cartier discovered for Europeans one of the greatest rivers in the world. He began France's occupation of three-quarters of a continent. That occupation would dominate the history of Nova Scotia for generations, and colours its character to this day.

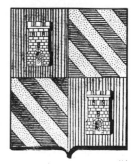

Jean-François de la Rocque de Roberval and his shield.

Pierre Du Gua de Monts was appointed lieutenant general and was granted a trading monopoly in New France. Among de Monts' recruits for his 1604 expedition were Samuel de Champlain and his friend and backer, Jean de Biencourt de Poutrincourt, both of whom were instrumental in establishing a permanent settlement at Port-Royal and securing Acadia as a French colony.

CHAPTER 4

THE BIRTH OF ACADIA

After Cartier and Roberval failed to find gold, a passage to Cathay, or the fabulous kingdom of the Saguenay touted by certain Iroquois, and after Roberval's colony in Quebec disintegrated under the weight of winter, famine, disease, rebellion, and his own blundering cruelty, official France lost interest in Canada. For decades, the kings and nobles of France could think of little but the Wars of Religion racking their homeland. More than half a century passed before the native peoples of the future Acadia witnessed a single French attempt to found a colony.

Throughout all this time, however, Bretons and others continued to exploit the fishing grounds off the New World, and by the 1590s at least 150 French vessels were in the cod trade. As a sideline, some fishing skippers gave European goods to Indians in exchange for furs, and when beaver hats became the rage among affluent Europeans, the sideline blossomed as a major industry. In 1588, King Henri III of France considered giving fur-trade monopolies to entrepreneurs in exchange for their agreeing to launch colonies.

While Henri III never acted on this idea, Henri IV did. Gallant, witty, and popular, this first of the Bourbon kings triumphantly concluded the Wars of Religion in 1598 and promptly named the Marquis de La Roche lieutenant-general of the territories of Maine, Canada, Labrador, and Newfoundland. With the appointment came title to the whole enormous region, a monopoly of its fur trade, and a duty to plant a settlement. La Roche persuaded authorities in Rouen to entrust him with 250 beggars and tramps, chose forty of the sturdiest and, with ten soldiers to keep the peace, dumped them on Sable Island off southeast Nova Scotia.

Some forty kilometres long, Sable Island was a crescent of surf-smashed sand that lurked like a booby trap amid what would one day be major transatlantic shipping lanes. Seafarers would curse it for centuries as "the Graveyard of the Atlantic," and even in 1598 its reputation was already sinister. Fifteen years earlier, during the island's first recorded shipwreck, a vessel under the command of Elizabethan swashbuckler Sir Humphrey Gilbert had foundered there, drowning 100 men. Sable Island would bring death to most of La Roche's settlers, but not in the sea.

Leaving them tools, food, clothing, and hastily built living quarters, he sailed for Newfoundland to find fish and furs. He meant to return in September, but storms drove his two ships back to France. In 1599, 1600, and 1601, subsidies from Henri IV enabled La Roche to send clothing and wine to the Sable Islanders. They ate fish, fowl, seal meat, vegetables from their own gardens, and the descendants of cattle that the Portuguese explorer Joao Alvares Fagundes had probably put on the island eighty years earlier.

Sir Humphrey Gilbert's tragic shipwreck in 1583 was the first to be recorded at Sable Island. As a result of the numerours casualties throughout the centuries, Sable Island gained the reputation as "Graveyard of the Atlantic."

In 1602, however, La Roche failed to send his usual shipment, an oversight that may have caused despair and fury among the men on the spooky sand bar. Their rage exploded in the winter of 1602–03, and it was as deadly as any thundering surf. The rebels at first butchered only two administrators, but the urge to kill spread like ship fever. Fifty men had settled on the island in 1598, but when Captain Thomas Chefdostel arrived in the spring of 1603, only eleven remained. Chefdostel took them home, where they sold their animal pelts at a good profit, and with their tales about the horrors they had endured, so touched Henri IV that he gave them rewards. "Instead of their being hanged for their misdeeds," La Roche complained, "they have been given money."

Some writers have suggested the fate of La Roche's settlement proved he was a fool, but others defend him. Trying to establish an outpost on Sable Island was not as bizarre in 1598 as it would later seem. From so strategic a spot, La Roche might have monitored the main entrance to the Gulf of St. Lawrence and the mighty river beyond, as well as the coastal waters that tempted outlaw fur traders to poach on his territory. While 1602–03 was hideous on Sable Island, and the whole venture seemed futile, some of La Roche's street people did survive there for five years. Not since the Vikings had any Europeans lived for so long at an official settlement within the boundaries of the future Canada. La Roche established a French claim in North America by right not just of discovery but of occupation, and France regarded Sable Island as part of Acadia even before the founding of Port-Royal in western Nova Scotia.

It was in 1605 that Samuel de Champlain had a hand in establishing Port-Royal. By then the word "Acadia" had found its home. Back in 1524, when Giovanni da Verrazzano cruised the east coast of North America for France, he named the Virginia countryside "Arcadia," after a part of ancient Greece legendary for its rustic charm. By the time Englishmen were struggling to survive in Virginia, almost a century later, Arcadia had lost its "r" and moved north. When Champlain and friends first cruised the Bay of Fundy in 1604, they were sailing in what various documents called "Lacadie," "La Cadie," or "Accadie." Some argue that "Acadia" actually comes from the Mi'kmaq "quoddy," meaning land, while others believe its origin lies in "aquoddie," an Indian word for the pollock fish. Whatever its roots, Champlain already knew it covered the Gaspé region of Quebec, eastern Maine, and the Maritime Provinces.

A detail from a 1612 map by Champlain depicting a sailing vessel.

Soldier, sailor, map-maker, explorer, commander, colonizer, author, and empire-builder, Champlain was born around 1570 in Saintonge, the cognac district on the Bay of Biscay. He was the son of a naval captain, Anthoine de Complain, and of Dame Marguerite Le Roy, but that is all anyone knows about the ancestry of this supreme figure in early Canadian history. His hometown, Brouage, was a Huguenot stronghold, but while Champlain may have been born a Protestant, he was a Catholic when he crossed the Atlantic.

The art of navigation, he once recalled, attracted him from the days of his "tender youth," but at about thirty, he was not a sailor but a sergeant in the army of King Henri IV. He saw military service in Spain and, while accepting a pension at Henri's court, received an intriguing invitation from Aymar de Chaste, the new owner of the trade monopoly for New France. De Chaste had hired Captain François Gravé Du Pont to lead a fur-trading expedition up the St. Lawrence River, and would the young army veteran like to go along for the ride? Champlain would sail merely as a passenger, but as historians would gratefully discover, he would prove to be a superb travel writer.

On March 15, 1603, Champlain boarded La Bonne Renommée at Honfleur near the mouth of the River Seine. Six months later, he was back in France to deliver to the king his map of the "rivière de Canada" (St. Lawrence), and a report on everything he had not only seen, but—from natives as far up the St. Lawrence as Montreal—had also heard. Before 1603 was out, Champlain published the first of his descriptions of Canada, "Des sauvages," and began to promote a trip to Acadia.

During the previous July, Gravé Du Pont's expedition, homeward bound from the St. Lawrence, had lingered at Gaspé, where Champlain heard about the tantalizing Acadia. It was said to have silver and copper mines and to offer a gateway to the eternally elusive path to Asia. Nor was Champlain the only French adventurer with Acadian dreams. Aymar de Chaste had died, and the dominant figure in the development of New France was now Pierre Du Gua de Monts. De Monts may well have sailed to Canada several times in the 1590s and, like Champlain in 1603, had reached Tadoussac. Its location where the Saguenay flowed into the St. Lawrence made it a trading centre for Quebec tribes. He now wanted to find a warmer country and may have been susceptible to Champlain's alluring talk of Acadia.

King Henri IV of France saw the end of the Wars of Religion in 1598 and revived France's interest in establishing colonies in North America by granting fur-trade monopolies to entrepreneurs in exchange for their making new settlements there.

De Monts' expedition of 1604 resulted from a revival of the French monarchy's long-dormant interest in Canada. When Henri IV settled the Wars of Religion and united France, he enabled it to launch an era of penetration across the Atlantic. Despite the fate of the Sable Island outpost, the king decided that, since the treasury of old France had been depleted by war, he would continue to encourage private investment in the building of New France. Thus, in 1603 de Monts, a Protestant who had excelled while fighting for Henri, received both a trading monopoly and an appointment as lieutenant-general "of the coasts, lands and confines of Acadia, Canada, and other places in New France." The post carried obligations to establish sixty colonists a year and to convert natives to Christianity.

By early 1604, de Monts had already founded a powerful trading company and rounded up not only ships and supplies for a colonizing expedition to Acadia, but also carpenters, masons, stonecutters, architects, soldiers, vagabonds, and his backer and friend, Jean de Biencourt de Poutrincourt. Dreamer, adventurer, and another Protestant champion of the king, Poutrincourt yearned to build a great agricultural colony across the Atlantic. Other noblemen joined the expedition simply to find treasure or claim land. There was a priest to look after the spiritual needs of the Catholics and a minister to serve the Protestants. Champlain would make maps, keep notes, and help search for mines. The voyagers totalled about 120.

After a two-month crossing against terrifying headwinds, around menacing ice floes, and past Sable Island, where their ship narrowly escaped foundering, de Monts and his settlers reached the South Shore of Nova Scotia on May 8 The ecstatic crew named the first land they spotted Cap de la Hève (Cape Haven), a name that survives as LaHave. "From this day on," Hannon wrote in "The Discoverers," "as Champlain immediately set about his given task with compass, protractor, pencil, and chart paper, the coastline of the Maritimes and of New England begins to take clear shape."[1]

De Monts, his men, and his flagship waited on the South Shore for François Gravé Du Pont (with whom Champlain had sailed on the St. Lawrence a year earlier) to arrive with the expedition's other vessel, La Bonne Renommée, whose hold held food supplies for the coming winter. Meanwhile, the new lieutenant-general of Acadia stumbled on Jean Rossignol filling up the Levrette with Mi'kmaq pelts, arrested him for illegal trading, and confiscated his vessel. De Monts called the scene of the crime Port du Rossignol (later Liverpool), and the name of Lake Rossignol, thirty kilometres inland, remains a link to this clash between Frenchmen some four centuries ago. Nearby Port Mouton got its name when a sheep ("mouton") fell off de Monts' ship, and drowned. The crew retrieved it for dinner.

While still at Port Mouton, de Monts dispatched a party northeast in a small boat to search for La Bonne Renommée, and Champlain southwest to look for a settlement site. Charting every island, bay, cove and promontory of this strange coast, naming Cape Sable, whose sandy beaches were covered with seals, Cape Fourchu (forked), Cape Negro (near a black rock), and Cormorant Island (plenty of eggs), and compiling the first list of Nova Scotia seabirds, Champlain sailed right around the end of Nova Scotia and into the long, skinny St. Mary's Bay. Within three weeks, he rejoined de Monts.

After the search party found La Bonne Renommée at Canso, the vessel delivered its cargo of food to Port Mouton. Gravé Du Pont sailed for the St. Lawrence in pursuit of furs, and de Monts, relying on Champlain's freshly gained information, took his own ship and Rossignol's captured vessel to St. Mary's Bay. There, at the entrance to the Bay of Fundy, the two ships dropped anchor, and de Monts and Champlain, sailing a longboat before a summer breeze, romped through the surging tides of waters totally unknown to them.

The Annapolis Basin delighted them, and de Monts soon gave the whole neighbourhood to Poutrincourt. This gift would shortly include the most famous French outpost in Nova Scotian history, Port-Royal. It would enrapture, obsess, and torment Poutrincourt. It would break both his heart and his fortune.

A likeness of Samuel de Champlain, known as the "Father of New France," whose detailed travel writings and maps of his exploration are historical treasures. He founded a settlement at Quebec in 1608. After the English occupation there (1629–32), he returned, this time appointed governor by Richelieu. He died just two years later.

CHAPTER 5

PORT-ROYAL: A FOOTHOLD FOR FRANCE

E asy to guard by cannon, a natural channel linked the Bay of Fundy to the Annapolis Basin, a saltwater lake ringed by trees. This, Champlain decided, was "one of the finest harbours I had seen ... where two thousand ships could lie in safety. [It] was the most suitable and pleasant for a settlement ... " De Monts, however, insisted on leading the expedition well up the Bay of Fundy towards the neighbourhood of the world's highest tides. While he never found the rumoured mines he sought, the names of Minas Basin, Minas Channel, and New Minas are descendants of the French for "Bay of Mines."

After exploring the steep coast between Advocate Harbour and Cape Chignecto—it was in this countryside, some argue, that the Scot, Prince Henry Sinclair, spent the winter of 1398 among the Mi'kmaq—de Monts and his men sailed back down the Bay of Fundy and on June 24, 1604, St. John's Day, found and named the St. John River. Further down the coast, they entered the St. Croix River and built a temporary settlement on Île Sainte-Croix, where they hoped to ride out the coming winter. On September 2, Champlain sailed south, returning a month later with enough information to write the first precise description of Maine's Penobscot region.

The French mounted cannons on the island in the St. Croix so they could blast enemies out of the water and erected what looked like a fortified manor house from Normandy. Fear of the natives had inspired them to hunker down midstream, but winter and disease were worse threats. As early as October 6, snow fell on what were probably the only Europeans living north Florida in North America. The island's small spring froze solid. By December, the ice floes in the river made it extremely dangerous to cross to the mainland in search of food and firewood. Seventy-nine men had settled on the island in 1604. By the following spring, which further tortured the survivors by arriving late, thirty-five had died, probably of scurvy, and twenty more were so feeble they could barely move.

In early June, none of de Monts' ships had arrived from France. He was ready to call off the whole adventure and to set out in longboats to find

The habitation at Port-Royal as drawn by Champlain. The enclosed courtyard afforded some protection from the harsh winters.

rescuers among the fishing fleets of the Gulf of St. Lawrence. But on June 15, Gravé Du Pont, already a veteran skipper in North American waters, showed up in a longboat of his own. He had anchored his ship, loaded with supplies, only a few kilometres away, and a second supply vessel was on the way from Saint-Malo. Cannons roared a greeting. Trumpet fanfares echoed in the wilderness. "He was welcomed to the joy of all," Champlain wrote.

Champlain and de Monts promptly set sail for points south. It was on this voyage that Champlain drew the maps that made him New England's first cartographer and, fifteen years before the Mayflower arrived, charted Plymouth Harbour. It was also on this voyage that de Monts rejected Boston Harbour as a potential capital of Acadia. After Indians murdered one of his crew on a Cape Cod beach, he may have decided this whole neighbourhood, heavily populated by native peoples, was too dangerous for any outpost inhabited by a handful of French.

Some authorities suggest Gravé Du Pont and Champlain now founded Port-Royal, but their commander was still de Monts, and it was he who transported his colony across the Bay of Fundy to the Annapolis Basin. In 1904, 300 years after de Monts and his men first saw the neighbourhood, the Canadian government installed a statue of him at Annapolis Royal (formerly Port-Royal) and a tablet declaring that here he had established "the first settlement of Europeans north of the Gulf of Mexico." If de Monts founded Port-Royal, however, Gravé Du Pont and Champlain chose the exact site: a slope near fresh water at the head of the basin, where hills offered protection from the ferocious winter nor'westers that Champlain had endured on Île Sainte-Croix.

From the island, 120 kilometres away, the French shipped to Port-Royal all the planks, joinery, and furniture they had brought from France the previous year and built another habitation. Of the survivors of the winter, however, only three, including Champlain, volunteered to face another one at Port-Royal. They, and the forty newcomers who had arrived with Gravé Du Pont in June, would be the first year-round residents of North America's earliest permanent settlement of Europeans north of Florida. The cruel lesson of Île Sainte-Croix inspired de Monts to order the construction at Port-Royal of a four-sided dwelling that enclosed a courtyard, and this time his settlers actually enjoyed a certain amount of comfort. Built of huge timbers, and lined with palisades, the habitation boasted four brass cannons out front. The rear walls had loopholes for muskets.

After de Monts sailed for France, the chief at Port-Royal was not Champlain, still only an observer and map-maker, but Gravé Du Pont. Champlain didn't mind. He built a workroom for himself in the trees and, before winter set in, revisited the St. John River and made another futile search for copper mines at the head of the Bay of Fundy.

The colonists quickly befriended Henri Membertou, the chief or sagamo, as well as the medicine man, or shaman, of the local Mi'kmaq. He proved intensely loyal to the little band of Frenchmen. Other sagamos were so jealous of Membertou's being a host to Europeans, with all their merchandise that, according to Champlain, they slandered him as "the most evil and treacherous among all those of his nation." The French, however, saw him as noble and amazing.

The Order of Good Cheer was instituted in the winter of 1606-7. North America's first social club, it served as a diversion from the long winter. Each member would take his turn as Grand Master, charged with directing the preparation and service of the banquet.

He appeared no more than 50 years old, but the poet Marc Lescarbot, who arrived at Port-Royal from France in 1606, believed he was at least 100. The chief himself claimed that when he had met Jacques Cartier, some seventy years before, he was already old enough to be a husband and father. Yet in 1607, he led his warriors into Maine to avenge the murder of his son-in-law. Father Pierre Biard, a Jesuit priest at Port-Royal, called him "the greatest, most renowned and most formidable savage within the memory of man; of splendid physique, taller and larger-limbed than is usual among them; bearded like a Frenchman, although scarcely any of the others have hair upon the chin; grave and reserved; feeling a proper sense of dignity for his position as commander."

On June 24, 1610, Membertou and his family became the first Indians to receive solemn baptism in New France. Port-Royal claims several other "firsts." The forty-odd colonists in 1605, Champlain wrote, "began to make gardens. I, also, made one which I surrounded with ditches full of water, wherein I placed fine trout. The seeds throve well." The field where, it is thought, Champlain made his garden is still there, near the new habitation. The gardens amounted to North America's first experimental farm, and the ditches may well have been both its first irrigation system and first waters stocked with game fish. In 1605, Port-Royal was home to the first resident surgeon on the continent, and the first continuing church services in the New World's northland.

Jean de Biencourt de Poutrincourt, soldier, scholar, and composer, was North America's first landed proprietor to foster practical cultivation, and the first land-owner who hoped to build in the New World both a family dynasty and a great agricultural colony. De Monts had given the Annapolis Basin to Poutrincourt in 1604 and then sent him back to France with a cargo of furs. As lieutenant-governor of Acadia, Poutrincourt returned in 1606 with his son Charles, a young cousin, Charles La Tour, several friends, and skilled workmen.

The newcomers revelled in a strange freedom. In France, the joys of the chase were open only to the nobility, but everyone at Port-Royal was free to fish for trout in the streams, hunt deer, and dig for clams on the tidal flats.

Poutrincourt arrived just in time to join North America's first social club. While William Shakespeare, Ben Jonson, and other playwrights were meeting over dinner at the Friday Street Club in London's Mermaid Tavern, Champlain was founding "l'ordre de bon temps." Its purpose was to banish gloom among men spending the coldest winter they had ever known, under threat of disease and without French women, in a dark forest 5000 kilometres from home. In 1865, historian Beamish Murdoch explained how the club worked:

"There were fifteen guests, each of whom, in his turn, became steward and caterer of the day. At the dinner, the steward, with napkin on shoulder, staff of office in hand, and the collar of the order around his neck, led the van. The other guests in procession followed, each bearing a dish. After grace in the evening, he resigned the insignia to his successor, and they drank to each other in a cup of wine. It was the steward's duty to look to supplies, and he would go hunt or fish a day or so before his turn came, to add some dainty to

Lescarbot reading his play

A drawing of playwright Marc Lescarbot by C. W. Jefferys. Lescarbot wrote and produced the first theatre performance in North America.

Louis Hébert the Apothecary

C. W. Jefferys' drawing of apothecary Louis Hébert, who treated both European settlers and Mi'kmaq inhabitants.

the ordinary fare. During this winter they had fowl and game in abundance, supplied by the Indians and by their own exertions. These feasts were often attended by Indians of all ages and both sexes, sometimes twenty or thirty being present ..."[1]

Marc Lescarbot, the first poet and lawyer to winter in North America, and the first European to record the sighting of a ruby-throated hummingbird, brought to Port-Royal the continent's first library and described the arrival of the first European pets. As his ship approached Nova Scotia in 1606, he wrote, "Our dogs thrust their noses over the side the better to sniff the land breezes and could not refrain from showing their joy ... "

In honour of de Monts, Poutrincourt, Champlain, and Membertou, the high-spirited Lescarbot wrote and produced "Théâtre de Neptune." On November 16, 1606, as Poutrincourt returned to Port-Royal from an expedition to Cape Cod, where Indians had killed several of his crew, a boat that Lescarbot had decorated to look like a huge seashell went out to greet him. Riding the shell was the great god Neptune, accompanied by Tritons (demigods of the sea) and Mi'kmaq. In the French and Mi'kmaq tongues, the court recited verse praising Port-Royal's leaders, and then, with trumpets blaring and cannons booming, sang a hymn to the glory of the king of France. The performance was the first European theatrical presentation in North America. It predicted Acadia would become "un florissant" empire for France.

Among those who came to Port-Royal with Poutrincourt in 1606 was Louis Hébert. The first apothecary to live in North America, Hébert treated both settlers and Mi'kmaq. He was also an ardent gardener. Poutrincourt planted grain and vegetables almost the moment he arrived, and Hébert helped him. When Poutrincourt, Champlain, and Hébert sailed for Cape Cod in August, Lescarbot stayed behind and continued the gardening, often hoeing

C. W. Jefferys' illustration of the performance of "Neptune"—the first European theatrical presentation in North America.

by moonlight. Before the year was out, Port-Royal boasted the first grain crops that white men had ever grown in North America, and Poutrincourt ordered the construction of the continent's first water-driven mill to grind wheat into flour.

He had brought to Port-Royal carpenters, masons, stonecutters, locksmiths, and tailors. They worked only one three-hour shift per day, and John Quinpool, writing in 1936, described this arrangement as the "first minimum work week in America."[2] Quinpool decided Port-Royal also boasted Canada's first baker's bread, which Lescarbot judged as good as any baked in Paris; first daily wine allowance for workmen (three quarts per man); first distillation of tar and turpentine; first graded highway; first weekly bible classes, led by the busy Lescarbot; and first lime kiln, smith's forge, and Canadian-made knife. The weather was freakishly warm on January 14, and

Champlain's map of Port-Royal, 1613.

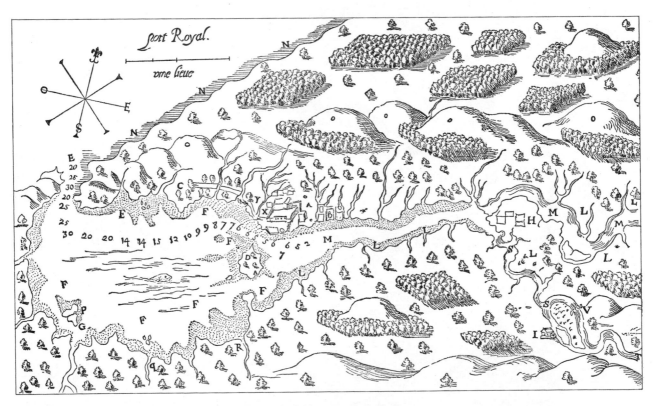

Les chifres montrent les braſſes d'eau.

A Le lieu de l'habitation.
B Iardin du ſieur de Champlain.
C Allée au trauers les bois que fit faire le ſieur de Poitrincourt.
D Iſle à l'entrée de la riuiere de l'Equille (1).
E Entree du port Royal.

F Baſſes qui aſſechent de baſſe mer.
G Riuiere ſainct Antoine (2).
H Lieu du labourage où on ſeme le blé.
I Moulin que fit faire le ſieur de Poitrincourt.
L Prairies qui ſont innondées des eaux aux grandes marées.

M Riuiere de l'Equille.
N La coſte de la mer du port Royal.
O Coſtes de montaignes.
P Iſle proche de la riuiere ſainct Antoine.
Q (3) Ruiſſeau de la Roche (4).
R Autre Ruiſſeau.

S Riuiere du moulin.
T Petit lac.
V Le lieu où les ſauuages peſchent le harang en la ſaiſon.
X Ruiſſeau de la truitiere.
Y Allée que fit faire le ſieur de Champlain.

Champlain's "Port des mines" map of the Advocate Harbour area, engraved in 1613, indicates the results of some mineral exploration. On a commercial level, however, mining never occurred.

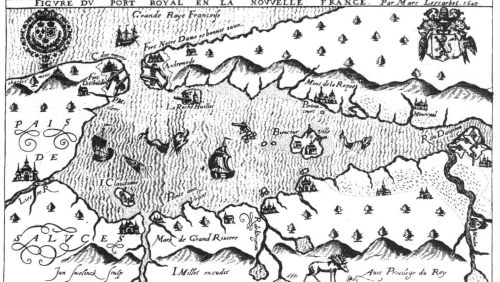

Lescarbot's map of Port-Royal appeared as an illustration in his "History of New France," published in 1609. The map's information is highly exaggerated and would have been used as propaganda.

Champlain's map of New France, published in 1632, portrays Acadia in reasonably accurate detail as compared to works by other cartographers of that time. The map that was published as a part of Champlain's "Les Voyages de la Nouvelle France," includes results of his exploration from 1603 to 1629.

Lescarbot wrote, "We sported ourselves with singing and music on the river and in that same month we went to see the corn and did dine merrily in the sunshine." Surely, Quinpool insisted, this was the "first agricultural picnic in America."

Events on both sides of the Atlantic shattered de Monts' business in the New World and Poutrincourt's dream of an agricultural empire. Poachers sabotaged de Monts' trade in fish and furs, and his backers grew leery of sinking more money into Acadia. Norman and Breton merchants reviled his monopoly, and the Paris hatters' corporation intrigued against him. Moreover, France now seemed less interested in colonization than in evangelizing the native people and reaping quick fur-trade profits. In 1607, Henri IV revoked de Monts' ten-year monopoly, and the settlers abandoned Port-Royal. Leaving it in Membertou's hands, Poutrincourt sailed for France with a cargo of cod and, to prove Port-Royal was promising, samples of minerals, corn, and wheat, as well as Canada geese.

Champlain's future now lay up the St. Lawrence. There, he would become a national hero of the future Canada. His three years in Acadia had seasoned him for his life's work in Quebec. And Poutrincourt? From Port-Royal, he had organized a fur business which had often taken him to the mouth of the St. John River, the best trading spot in Acadia. He befriended many Indians. They trusted him. He treated them with none of the cruelty that the Spanish inflicted on native peoples further south. Many Mi'kmaq, including Membertou, would ecstatically welcome Poutrincourt back to Port-Royal.

The twentieth-century replica of the Port-Royal habitation was constructed in the 1930s by the Canadian Parks Service.

Other views of the habitation at Port-Royal reveal its austere enclosed structure and the view to Annapolis Basin.

This panel from the Fort Anne Heritage Tapestry depicts Port-Royal during the French regime.

By receiving land grants from James I, Sir William Alexander, the Earl of Stirling, also received the right of creating baronets of Nova Scotia to entice settlers to North America.

Baronetage Badge granted to the Baronets of Nova Scotia.

CHAPTER 6

ENGLISH RAIDS, FRENCH INTRIGUES, SCOTTISH HEARTBREAKS

Poutrincourt refused to abandon his New World dream. After showing Henri IV "fruits of the earth" from Acadia, he won a renewal of his monopoly and, to gain influential support for his third expedition, promised to convert the Mi'kmaq to Roman Catholicism. With the pope's blessing, a ship filled with food, furniture, and munitions, and Father Jessé Fléché on board, Poutrincourt returned to Acadia in 1610. Also with him came his sons Jacques and Charles (whom historians call Biencourt), fortune-seeker Claude de Saint-Étienne de La Tour, and La Tour's son Charles. As youngsters in 1606 Biencourt and his cousin and future lieutenant, Charles de La Tour, had first seen Port-Royal. Now they were back; Biencourt was eighteen, La Tour seventeen.

When the French reached Port-Royal, the Mi'kmaq, who had been loyal caretakers of the habitation for three years, greeted them rapturously. Within days, Poutrincourt had Father Fléché baptize Membertou and twenty of his family. It was to please the most pious of Poutrincourt's wealthy backers—and to convince the king it was unnecessary to impose Jesuit missionaries on Port-Royal—that he ordered Fléché to create these instant Catholics. Poutrincourt distrusted Jesuits and promptly sent his son Biencourt back to France not only with a cargo of furs but with instructions to report the news of the baptism of the Mi'kmaq.

While breezing past the Grand Banks, however, Biencourt learned from fishermen that a madman had stabbed Henri IV to death. The king had been the supreme Acadian ally of the Poutrincourts. Queen Marie de Medici, regent for the nine-year-old Louis XIII, had less religious tolerance than her late husband, and less interest in colonial expansion. While Biencourt's news of the Mi'kmaq baptisms pleased her, it did not dampen her zeal for Jesuits. When Biencourt sailed back to Port-Royal in the "Grâce de Dieu" in early 1611, he had with him not only supplies and thirty-six colonists, but two Jesuit priests, Pierre Biard and Enemond Massé.

King Louis XIII of France inherited the throne at age nine.

The priests quickly discovered that the supposedly converted Membertou and his relatives knew virtually nothing about their new faith. As André Vachon explained the situation in the "Dictionary of Canadian Biography," "The learned theologians of the Sorbonne moreover disapproved of this speedy fashion of conferring baptism."[1] Father Fléché went home to France. In late June, Poutrincourt appointed Biencourt acting commander of Port-Royal and sailed for France himself. He desperately needed money. To raise enough to send one small boat to Port-Royal with essential provisions, he agreed to send over a third Jesuit, Gilbert Du Thet.

By the summer of 1612, relations between the Jesuits at Port-Royal and Biencourt, still only twenty, had deteriorated till they threatened to destroy the colony. When Membertou had died the previous September, Biencourt and Father Biard had clashed over where to bury him: with his pagan ancestors, as Biencourt insisted, or in a Catholic cemetery, as Biard demanded. The priest had triumphed, and he and Biencourt had been feuding ever since. Each sent to Paris poisonous missives about the other.

Queen Marie de Medici of France was regent for her son, King Louis XIII, after her husband's murder.

At the royal court of France, Biencourt and his father were no match for the Jesuits, and Poutrincourt, now in disgrace, found it harder than ever to raise money. He endured debtors' prison for a while, emerging sick and defeated. At Port-Royal, things went from bad to disastrous. Fed up with tales of Biencourt's treachery, the Marquise de Pons—first lady-in-waiting to the queen and rich backer of Jesuits—decided to set up her priests in a more important colony. In 1613, her agent, René Le Coq, arrived at Port-Royal with a load of settlers, took Fathers Biard and Massé aboard his ship, and sailed south to build fortifications near the mouth of the Penobscot River.

England, however, regarded Maine as its territory. The redoubtable Samuel Argall came north from Jamestown in Virginia in the Treasurer, captured Le

Coq's two vessels, rounded up all the French, released some in a small boat, and took fourteen, including Father Biard, back to Jamestown as prisoners. In this assault, seven years before the Mayflower arrived at Plymouth Harbour, Argall led the first English expedition to violently contest the French occupation of Acadia. The bloody rivalry would continue for another century and a half.

Argall's next target was Port-Royal. On October 31, 1613, with his prisoner Father Biard along for the ride, the Treasurer and the two French ships that the English had captured slipped into Annapolis Basin. The next morning, they found Port-Royal deserted. Some settlers were upriver at "the great meadow," while others were off in the woods cutting fuel. Argall's raiders piled ashore, confiscated the habitation's best animals and slaughtered the rest. They looted food, furniture, and munitions, burned down everything but the grist mill and some barns, and claimed the territory for England.

Argall now sailed to the nearby farmland where his prisoner, Father Biard,

In the name of England, Argall and his raiders sacked Port-Royal in 1613.

urged the people of Port-Royal to join the English. But even with their food and houses gone and winter looming, the colonists refused to become

turncoats. At a meeting with Biencourt, Argall blamed the Jesuits for inspiring the governor of Virginia to order the attack. The young Frenchman, who believed Biard had guided the English to Port-Royal, demanded they turn the priest over to him to be hanged. Argall, however, apparently believed Virginians were perfectly capable of executing a Jesuit. Biard was lucky. The ship taking him to Virginia, probably to be hanged, was pushed right across the Atlantic by a storm, and he reached France in April 1614.

Nova Scotia was the first British colony to possess its own flag. Its origin is traced to the granting of the Charter of New Scotland in 1621.

Meanwhile, some Port-Royal settlers had starved to death, others were living among the Mi'kmaq, and still others had made their way to French settlements on the St. Lawrence. Quite a few, however, including Biencourt and young La Tour, stayed in the neighbourhood of Port-Royal, barely surviving on a diet of roots and lichens. They were still alive on March 27, 1614, when Poutrincourt sailed into the Annapolis Basin for the last time and

found the charred ruins of all his dreams. He gave his holdings in Acadia to Biencourt—who remained the commander of what was left of Port-Royal—and took most of the surviving colonists back to France. A year later, during a dispute with one of his military officers, Poutrincourt died of bullet wounds.

Biencourt, backed by shipowners in the Protestant stronghold of La Rochelle and working out of the wreckage of Port-Royal with Charles de La Tour and perhaps twenty other Frenchmen, pursued the fishing and fur-trade businesses. Despite competition from English, Dutch, and other French traders, whom he fought with guns and lawsuits, his ventures were profitable. As the Acadian fur trade slackened in the early 1620s, however, and as France ignored his warnings about the growth of New England and the deterioration of Port-Royal, Biencourt spent more and more time with the Mi'kmaq. By the time of

King James VI of Scotland was also James I of England.

his death, probably in 1623, when he was thirty-one or thirty-two, he and Charles de La Tour, now thirty, had spent half their lives in Acadia. It was their home. Biencourt named La Tour his heir.

"Without the ruinous rivalry of the Jesuits, the destruction caused by the Argall raid, and with even a slight amount of support from the Crown to establish the colony," the "Dictionary of Canadian Biography" says, "the accomplishments of the Poutrincourts–father and son–might have been of a far higher order."[2] They might even have done for Acadia what Champlain did for Quebec.

While Biencourt and La Tour were learning to live like the Mi'kmaq they admired, Sir William Alexander, the Earl of Stirling, was persuading King James I of England to let him found a New Scotland. James was the son of Mary, Queen of Scots, and became James VI of Scotland in 1587 after she was beheaded. When his cousin Elizabeth I died in 1603, he became also King James I of England. Alexander was a prominent figure at the Scottish court, a highly regarded poet, chosen by the king as a collaborator in translating the Book of Psalms. In 1615 Alexander became a member of the Scottish Privy Council, and in this position he won the king's complete confidence.

Jean de Biencourt de Poutrincourt in a detail from an engraving. He served as lieutenant-governor of Acadia.

Through the establishment and sale of knight baronetcies, James had already created the plantation of Ulster in Northern Ireland. With this in mind, Alexander, an advocate of colonial emigration, persuaded him that the only way to get Scots to emigrate was to give them a New Scotland comparable to New France and New England. The king, in 1621, granted Alexander the huge territory of today's three Maritime Provinces, plus the Gaspé Peninsula of modern Quebec. Unfortunately, this was the very territory the French occupied as Acadia.

James offered knight baronetcies for sale, and imposed on the purchasers various tiresome responsibilities with respect to settlers. Membership in the new order of Baronets of Nova Scotia pleased some of the nobility and gentry, but the last thing most of them wanted was actually to go there.

Soon after Biencourt died, Charles de La Tour began to conduct and protect his fur trade from a fortified post near Cape Sable at the southwestern tip of Nova Scotia. In Britain, meanwhile, after James I died in 1625, Sir William Alexander enjoyed the patronage of Charles I. Thanks to the new king, Sir William's colonization effort continued to receive funding through the sale of knight-baronetcies, and Nova Scotia got its armorial bearings. (It is to this royal commission of 1626 that the province still owes its flag and coat of arms.) The Scots, however, still did not rush to settle Nova Scotia, and it was not until 1629 that about seventy showed up at the deserted Port-Royal led by Alexander's son, Sir William the Younger. Among the Scots was none other than Charles de La Tour's father Claude.

War had broken out again between England and France in 1627, and an English expedition under the command of the adventurer David Kirke had captured a squadron of French vessels off Gaspé. Among the prisoners Kirke took to England was the mercurial Claude de La Tour. Promoter, lobbyist, and courtier, the twice-married French careerist soon charmed English noblemen and palace ladies alike and made a special friend of Sir William.

Armorial achievement of Nova Scotia was granted by King Charles I in 1625.

The English now controlled all of Acadia except Charles de La Tour's outpost near Cape Sable, and Claude, never one to let patriotism preclude gain, may have felt that the last, best chance for the La Tours lay with the enemy. Whatever his motives, he sailed to Acadia with the Scots in the spring of 1629; probably stayed with them all summer at Port-Royal; returned to England in the fall to become a baronet of Nova Scotia; and the following spring, accepted a second baronetcy for his son Charles.

In exchange for the titles, Claude apparently promised to persuade his son to swear allegiance to Britain, surrender the fort at Cape Sable, and give control of Acadia to Sir William. To complete a busy schedule in England, Claude took as his third wife a Scottish-born lady-in-waiting to Queen Henrietta Maria. In the summer of 1630, he arrived at Cape Sable with his new wife, fresh colonists, and two English men-of-war, but his son Charles gave him what must have been the shock of his life. Although the baronetcies promised the La Tours an enormous chunk of Nova Scotia, and France's neglect of Acadia had often infuriated Charles, he refused to betray his king and country.

Claude begged and threatened him, then tried to conquer him. With soldiers and sailors from the English warships, he attacked Charles' fort. The battle between father and son lasted two days and according to historian George MacBeath, "has no parallel in the history of the New World."[3] The son won. The English withdrew. Claude and his wife, who valiantly assured him she had married for better or worse, withdrew to Port-Royal, but he had lost face with the French, who saw him as a traitor, and with the Scots and English, who saw him as a failure. As his disgrace grew, his happiness vanished. Charles finally extended to him enough forgiveness to allow his return to Cape Sable, but not enough to let him live inside the fort. The older La Tours dwelt in a house outside the palisades.

By now, the English had forced Champlain to surrender Quebec, and thirty Scots had died during their first winter at Port-Royal. The Scottish colony was doomed. Barely launched, it was being scuppered by the King of England, Charles I. During peace negotiations with France, his relations with Parliament were rancorous, his unpaid army and navy hostile, and his treasury bare. He had married the sister of King Louis XIII, and his dowry was only half-paid. One of the concessions he made to get payment in full was to return Acadia to France. He ordered Sir William to withdraw all colonists from Nova Scotia and make sure they demolished everything they had built.

When news of the deal reached the colony in September 1632, it so enraged the remaining Scots that twenty-five of them, under Andrew Forrester, sailed across the Bay of Fundy to overpower the French at the first European settlement on the St. John River. Charles de La Tour, now governor of Acadia for Louis XIII, had built the sturdy trading post only the year before, but when the raid occurred he was in France. Forrester's men ransacked the fort, vandalized its chapel, toppled its wooden cross, and sailed away with booty and prisoners.

King Charles I of England reigned 1625–49. His unwavering belief in the Divine Right of Kings to rule contributed to his downfall and subsequent execution.

In mid-December, however, Isaac de Razilly, lieutenant-general of all New France, anchored his St. Jehan in the Annapolis Basin, accepted the peaceful surrender of Alexander's colony, and shipped Forrester and forty-one other Scots back to Britain. Not for more than 140 years would Scots again try to found a permanent settlement in Nova Scotia.

Sir William Alexander never did get to see New Scotland. His passion to people it with his countrymen plunged him so deeply in debt that, as he lay dying in London in 1640, creditors crowded around him like vultures. Claude de La Tour spent his last years at Cape Sable as a contented husband, proud father, ardent gardener, and genial host to the giants of Acadian history who occasionally dropped by. He died sometime after 1636. He was a traitor and opportunist, to be sure, but also one of the most colourful characters in the early history of Acadia.

His son Charles turned out to be even more colourful and came to hate a certain Frenchman more than any English, Dutch, Scot, or Bostonian he ever met. Perhaps no feud in Canadian history has been as savage as the one between frontiersman Charles de La Tour and aristocrat Charles de Menou d'Aulnay.

C. W. Jefferys depicted the meeting between Françoise-Marie Jaquelin and Charles de La Tour. She became his second wife and full partner in business at the fort on the St. John River.

CHAPTER 7

THE FEUD BEGINS

In 1627, Charles de La Tour advised both Louis XIII and the real ruler of France, the ruthless, devious Cardinal Richelieu, that he had had no help from his motherland since Biencourt's death in 1623. The English were planning to seize New France; he was being "pursued to death" by French trespassers on his trading territory; and while greedy men kept hauling riches out of Acadia, no one was investing anything in its protection. With his "little band of resolute Frenchmen," his allies among "the people of the country" (Mi'kmaq), and his three small ships, he would carry on, but could he please have a formal commission authorizing him to defend Acadia?

In that same year, Richelieu founded the Company of New France to build a French empire stretching from the Arctic to Florida, and from the Atlantic deep into the unknown west. France had previously left its North American trade largely in the hands of merchants, but now Richelieu yanked this opportunity away from the fur traders. It was the first supply fleet of the Company of New France that the English had captured when, on the outbreak of war, they had arrested Charles de La Tour's father.

By 1630, when the older La Tour arrived at Cape Sable with the Scottish baronetcies in his pocket, three tense years had passed since Charles had sent his entreaties to Louis XIII and Richelieu. He had received no reply. Shortly after he repelled his father, however, two ships arrived with enough tradesmen and supplies for him to construct his fort at the mouth of the St. John River. The vessels also brought Récollet fathers, one of whom blessed Charles' earlier marriage to a Mi'kmaq and baptized their three daughters. A letter from a director of the Company of New France urged La Tour not to collaborate with the English, as some good-for-nothing Frenchmen had done. Wry thoughts of his father must have crossed La Tour's mind.

While his fort on the St. John was still under construction, La Tour, at thirty-eight, received news that probably made the summer of 1631 the supreme season of his life. Richelieu had nominated him the king's lieutenant-general of Acadia, and Louis XIII had confirmed the appointment in language that heaped praise on him. La Tour had first arrived at Port-Royal as the fourteen-year-old son of a disreputable adventurer, but now he was not only an associate of the mighty Company of New France, but also the king's man in Acadia.

Cardinal Richelieu, founder of the Company of New France, nominated Charles de La Tour the king's lieutenant general of Acadia.

The treaty of St-Germain-en-Laye, signed on March 29, 1632, settled the war, gave New France and Acadia back to France, and enabled Richelieu to startle Britain with an Acadian coup. He named Isaac de Razilly head of a colonizing expedition, and in September, this naval commander—with three vessels, and "300 'hommes d'élite,' " including soldiers, sailors, tradesmen, six

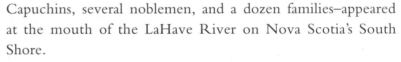

Capuchins, several noblemen, and a dozen families—appeared at the mouth of the LaHave River on Nova Scotia's South Shore.

The settlement of Acadia had started in 1604, stopped in 1607, resumed in 1610, and collapsed in 1613. The population had shrunk to a few dozen scattered farmers and itinerant fur traders who owed their allegiance first to Biencourt and then to Charles de La Tour. Help from France had been virtually nonexistent. With the arrival of Razilly in 1632, however, the settling of Acadia began with a new sense of purpose and both encouragement and money from the mother country.

An able commander, scion of a distinguished military family, and cousin of Richelieu, Razilly was among the cardinal's most trusted advisers. In 1626, he had recommended to Richelieu that France strive for mastery of the sea and, with the formation of the Company of New France, mastery of North America as well. Now, he arrived at the LaHave as lieutenant-general of all New France. Preferring to leave Champlain in charge at Quebec, he planned to establish his headquarters in Acadia. Only a year before, however, the king had named Charles de La Tour lieutenant-general of Acadia. Immediately after Razilly's arrival, a troubled La Tour sailed for France to investigate the new meaning of his own royal commission. Where did it begin? Where did Razilly's end?

Across the LaHave from today's Riverport, Razilly built Fort Sainte-

Marie-de-Grâce, a storage depot, chapel, houses, and barracks. Before 1632 was out, he rid Port-Royal of its Scots and, in the following three years, arranged the clearing of farmland for forty settlers at Petite Rivière at the mouth of the LaHave River; joined explorer-trader-entrepreneur Nicholas Denys in the establishment of an inshore fishery at Port du Rossignol (Liverpool); encouraged Denys to start a timber-exporting business; and built a fortified port at Canso to extend his fur trade.

Like Poutrincourt a quarter-century earlier, Razilly not only loved Acadia but yearned to make it a colonial empire. He called it "a blessed land," which promised a good life for France's poor and miserable. All he wanted to do, Denys wrote, was "people this land, and every year he had brought here as many people as he possibly could." Although Razilly lived in Acadia little more than three years, he had a powerful impact on the country. Many of the first Acadians in the Maritimes, whose descendants now number some 300,000, arrived under his direction. Champlain called him "prudent, wise, laborious, and impelled by a holy desire to increase the glory of God, and carry his courage to the country of New France, there to unfurl the standard of Jesus Christ and cause the lilies [of France] to flourish."

By 1635, Razilly had the satisfaction of knowing he had restored French interests in Acadia, and that the development projects he had launched were thriving. But in November, at the age of only forty-eight, he died at his settlement on the LaHave. His passing "proved a disastrous blow which had a lasting effect on the country."[1]

The blow proved especially disastrous for La Tour. In early 1633, he and the Company of New France had agreed that, in return for the right to share the Acadian fur trade with Razilly, he would maintain settlements on the St. John and at Cape Sable. "In order to facilitate the said trade," the agreement stipulated, "the said Sieur de la Tour is to have one or two clerks attached to the said Commander de Razilly or his habitations, who are to have one of the keys to the warehouse where the goods are stored ... " Razilly had the same rights at La Tour's posts. The idea was to guarantee an equal division of the trade in pelts, but in reality, the deal turned the men into watchdogs over each other.

The two watchdogs liked each other. With La Tour working from the mouth of the St. John and Razilly from the mouth of the LaHave, they made their tricky division of Acadia's fur-trade work. In 1634, Razilly and his associates founded a private trading company, Razilly-Condonnier, while La

Tour served as the Company of New France's top man in Acadia. As heads of rival operations, their friendship remained firm. When Razilly died, however, his brother Claude put the thirty-one-year-old Menou d'Aulnay in charge of Razilly-Condonnier. D'Aulnay was a watchdog who neither liked nor respected La Tour, his senior by a dozen years. Indeed, it is unlikely that any two characters in the history of Canada loathed each other more than d'Aulnay and La Tour.

Like Razilly, d'Aulnay was a cousin of Richelieu's. His father, diplomat and warrior René de Menou, served on both Louis XIII's private council and Richelieu's council of state, and his ancestors included knights, crusaders, an admiral, and an officer who had served with Joan of Arc. D'Aulnay had

probably studied fencing, tilting, and horsemanship. Intelligent, strong-willed, and despotic, he was every inch an aristocrat. In late 1632, after reaching New Rochelle with lumber and pelts, he haughtily ordered a senior court official to take inventory of his cargo, authorize its unloading, and be quick about it. The man's spirited refusal enraged d'Aulnay, particularly since the fellow had performed legal services for La Tour.

"Whether or not [La Tour and d'Aulnay] had already clashed, it would have seemed wrong to d'Aulnay that a man of inferior birth from the colonial backwoods should have more influence with high officials than he ... himself," historian M. A. MacDonald has speculated. "Years later, La Tour's descendants would trace the roots of the war between the two men to d'Aulnay's jealousy, claiming that d'Aulnay [could hardly bear] the fact that La Tour had wielded the authority of a King's governor and lieutenant-general in Acadia."[2]

D'Aulnay regarded Charles de La Tour as his arch rival. He worked to discredit La Tour at France's court in the course of their ongoing clashes, which culminated in d'Aulnay gaining La Tour's fort at the mouth of the St. John River.

In 1636, however, the Company of New France gave d'Aulnay a better reason than envy or snobbishness to hate La Tour. Razilly had sent a raiding party, led by d'Aulnay, into the Penobscot region of Maine to oust New Englanders from Fort Pentagouet. Not wanting to serve under the young nobleman, La Tour had refused to bolster the attack. Without him, d'Aulnay risked his life at Fort Pentagouet and captured it with style, but the company awarded the fort to none other than La Tour's father, Claude.

Under the authority of the company, Charles de La Tour was chief of the outposts at Cape Sable and the St. John, while d'Aulnay had absolute authority at Port-Royal and the settlement on the LaHave. Each still had the right of inspection in his rival's territory, and each got half the revenues from the trading concession. This arrangement hid enormous potential for conflict, and in 1638 ministers of the king made it even worse. They were trying to make peace between the two rivals in Acadia, but were so ignorant of the region's geography that they gave d'Aulnay New Brunswick but not the fort on the St. John, and La Tour peninsular Nova Scotia but not Port-Royal. To turn Port-Royal into the capital of Acadia again, d'Aulnay had already begun to move settlers from LaHave to the Annapolis Basin. This would establish him just across the Bay of Fundy from La Tour's fortified post at the mouth of the St. John River.

It was also in 1638 that Louis XIII named d'Aulnay lieutenant-general of Acadia and, with Claude de La Tour probably dead, gave him Fort Pentagouet. D'Aulnay married Jeanne Motin, the devout young daughter of a wealthy investor in the Razilly-Condonnier company. Her dowry may have included shares in the business, giving d'Aulnay added incentive to make it thrive. His having a wife in Acadia killed whatever hope La Tour had that the man he saw as an intolerable interloper would return to France for good.

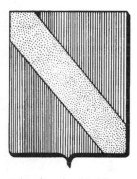

D'Aulnay's shield. He was every inch an aristocrat.

In the spring of 1640, La Tour, too, married a Frenchwoman. The Mi'kmaq mother of his three daughters had died, and he now wed Françoise-Marie Jacquelin at Cape Sable. Probably the daughter of a country doctor in France, she had met La Tour in Paris eight years earlier. She may have been an actress, and d'Aulnay would later call her disreputable. La Tour, however, knew her as an able, competent woman, and she lived with him at their wooden fort on the St. John not only as his spouse but as a full partner in his business.

When she set up house there, relations between her husband and d'Aulnay had already turned violent. Increasingly desperate, La Tour seems to have incited some Mi'kmaq to murder two of d'Aulnay's men on the St. John River, and in 1639 he intercepted a small vessel his rival had sent to Fort Pentagouet and imprisoned its nine crew members.

Shortly after their marriage in 1640, La Tour and his wife sailed to Port-Royal, apparently to exercise their right to inspect pelts, and found themselves in a skirmish with d'Aulnay on the Annapolis Basin. Each side killed men, but La Tour's lost. D'Aulnay threw the La Tours and their surviving crew into the prison at Port-Royal, where Françoise might have been forgiven for wishing she had never left Paris. Capuchin friars arranged the release of La Tour's people, but war between the king's two lieutenants in Acadia was now inevitable. It would kill men on both sides, generate endless legal action and useless negotiation, squander the energy of two remarkable leaders, and almost ruin them both.

C. W. Jefferys renders a proud and courageous
Madame de La Tour defending the fort on the St. John.

CHAPTER 8

THE WOMAN WARRIOR OF FORT LA TOUR

Only five years passed between the marriage and death of Françoise-Marie Jacquelin, but in that short time she proved herself the first heroine in the history of Canada. She was loyal, eloquent, resourceful, and courageous under deadly gunfire. She gave La Tour a son, restored his reputation, and died in his service.

D'Aulnay used his influence at court to brand her husband a traitor (though La Tour had refused the pleas of his own father to transfer his loyalty to Britain). In the first springtime after the skirmish on Annapolis Basin, La Tour received orders to return to France and face d'Aulnay's charges, but knowing he might never leave the mother country alive, he stayed on the St. John. In late 1642, however, his wife evaded d'Aulnay's naval blockade of the La Tour fort and headed for France. She arrived just as Cardinal Richelieu died, successfully appealed royal rulings that her husband be arrested and charged with disloyalty, and returned to Acadia aboard the Saint-Clément. She brought food, munitions, soldiers, and settlers.

When the ship approached the La Tour fort in the spring of 1643, d'Aulnay, who had been trying to starve La Tour into submission, used his fleet to chase the Saint-Clément back out to sea. There, it sat. After word got to La Tour, he waited for an inky night, then sneaked out in a shallop for a shipboard reunion with the wife he had not seen for eight months. The Saint-Clément weighed anchor and sailed to Boston. In this burgeoning capital of a coastal colony, which already boasted more than 11,000 settlers, La Tour, desperate for markets and supplies, had previously wooed New England merchants. Now, he chartered four English vessels, returned to the St. John, chased d'Aulnay back to Port-Royal, burned down a mill, killed three soldiers, and vanished with a longboat full of pelts.

La Tour's collaboration with Englishmen made it easy for d'Aulnay to undo everything Françoise-Marie had done to restore her husband's reputation. On her return to France in 1643, she found him utterly disgraced. He was an outlaw. A royal decree barred her from leaving France, on pain of death. But she borrowed money, escaped to England, chartered the Gillyflower, loaded it with supplies, and in late March 1644, again sailed for Acadia. Off Cape Sable, a French ship, under the command of d'Aulnay

Françoise-Marie Jacquelin de La Tour was the first heroine in Canadian history. She attempted to defend her husband's fort in his absence.

himself, intercepted the Gillyflower. He would have relished preserving La Tour's wife for the gallows, but when he came aboard, she hid successfully among the cargo in the vessel's bowels.

After reaching Boston, she successfully sued the Gillyflower's captain for taking six months to cross the Atlantic and failing to deliver her to the St. John River. With the proceeds of the settlement, she hired three ships and then ran d'Aulnay's blockade, reaching home near Christmas of 1644.

In February 1645, d'Aulnay suffered heavy losses during an unsuccessful attack on the La Tour fort. From La Tour deserters, however, he learned in April not only that his arch-enemy was again seeking help in Boston, but that La Tour had left his wife on the St. John with only forty-five men. D'Aulnay sailed across the Bay of Fundy with 200 men and demanded that Mme de La Tour surrender the fort. She chose to fight.

Led by her, the outnumbered defenders withstood d'Aulnay's bombardments from the sea for three days, but by the fourth morning, Easter Sunday, the pounding had smashed down part of the fort's parapet, and many of his soldiers clambered ashore with cannons. As the story goes, Françoise-Marie and her men were worshipping when a traitor, a Swiss mercenary, helped d'Aulnay's force penetrate the fort. In the hand-to-hand clash that followed, both sides suffered heavy casualties. But Mme de La Tour—in the thick of the smoke, screams, clanging of swords, and spattering of gore—refused to give up her husband's fort. It was only after d'Aulnay promised to spare all the survivors that she capitulated.

While historians have not been unanimous about what happened next, it seems that, when d'Aulnay discovered that a mere handful of Mme de La Tour's men had managed to kill or maim so many of his own, his rage got the better of his honour. He ordered the hanging of every La Tour soldier who had survived the battle, except the one who agreed to be their hangman, and Mme de La Tour was forced to watch the executions with a rope around her neck. Three weeks later, there at the wooden fort where she had lived such a short time with her husband, she expired. Some said sorrow killed her, others that she died of rage, and still others that d'Aulnay had her poisoned. One thing was certain: as his prisoner and a woman who had disobeyed a royal command to remain in France, she had little left to live for.

Marie-Françoise Jacquelin de La Tour was ordered to watch the execution of her fellow captives after their valiant efforts were defeated by d'Aulnay's forces.

La Tour was still in Boston, preparing to relieve his fort, when he heard it had fallen and his wife had died. He had friends in New France, however, and from 1646 to 1650, he ran a trading business out of Quebec City. He backed the work of Jesuit missions and fought with the Huron against the Iroquois. In

Acadia, d'Aulnay was master. Letters patent from the French court confirmed him as governor of Acadia, which France claimed stretched from the St. Lawrence to Virginia, and awarded him a monopoly of its entire fur trade. Even before then, however, he was seizing the vessels of French rivals in the pelt business, some as far from Port-Royal as the Gulf of St. Lawrence, and thereby infuriating the Company of New France.

On May 24, 1650, d'Aulnay's canoe capsized off Port-Royal and, after clinging to it for ninety minutes, he died. The death of this capable bully doubtless struck La Tour as the best news in two decades. Before the year was out, he popped up in France and pleaded for an inquiry into both his own conduct and the many complaints against the dead man. The inquiry blamed d'Aulnay for the bloodshed in Acadia during the 1640s, and La Tour again basked in royal favour.

La Tour's meeting with Governor Winthrop of Massachusetts, seeking support for his impending battle with d'Aulnay.

He was soon back in possession of his Acadian property and his governorship and, with several families of colonists, arrived at Port-Royal in 1653. He presented d'Aulnay's widow, Jeanne Motin, with a royal order to give him back the St. John River fort he had started to build more than twenty years before. Since they were both deeply in debt, they ended the La Tour-d'Aulnay feud and started a new Acadian dynasty. At sixty, La Tour married his late enemy's widow, then in her mid-thirties. By d'Aulnay, she had had eight children, and though historians would call her arrangement with La Tour a marriage of convenience, she gave him five more. Jeanne Motin may well have held the motherhood record for mid-seventeenth-century Acadia.

One year after La Tour's third marriage, Acadia fell to New Englanders. Forces under Robert Sedgwick, a Puritan major-general from Massachusetts, plundered the French forts on the St. John, at Port-Royal, and on the Penobscot River. With La Tour as their star prisoner, they returned to Boston. From there, he went to jail in England, and eventually reached an agreement. La Tour would pay his debts in Boston and certain costs of the recent conquest of Acadia; as well he would swear allegiance to England. In return, England would recognize his right, as his father's heir, to be a baronet of Nova Scotia.

What drove him to accept these terms may have been despair over both the downfall of Acadia and the huge debts he and his third wife owed to French merchants. History forced him to accept an English deal that derived from the very one he had rejected a quarter-century earlier. (Posterity did not judge him harshly; long after La Tour's death, King Louis XIV recognized the rights of his children in Acadia.).

To rid himself of liabilities, La Tour sold certain Acadian rights to two English gentlemen, but kept a small share of the revenue for himself. He seems to have retired to Cape Sable, where he and Jeanne Motin raised their youngsters. As M. A. MacDonald wrote in "Fortune & La Tour," "the underdog who would never accept defeat, became the ultimate survivor." He died in the spring of 1666 at seventy, probably at Port-Royal, which he had first seen as a lad of fourteen.

La Tour was one of the first French sons of the Canadian wilderness. A born leader, he talked well and fought well. He made friends for life and showed no fear of death. Men died for him. A woman died for him. He was an ally of both "the people of the country" and the Frenchmen with the most splendid dreams for Acadia—except for one: d'Aulnay. Cruel, vainglorious, and sinister though d'Aulnay may have been, he was an effective colonizer, and more important to the future of the Acadian people than the adventurous La Tour.

After Isaac de Razilly died in 1635, his brother Claude had continued to send to Acadia French workers who knew how to harvest salt from marshes, and d'Aulnay started to build up the fertile Port-Royal neighbourhood as the capital of Acadia. The workers "used their expertise to build dikes [and] ... reclaim alluvial land that was flooded twice a day by the strong tides of the Bay of Fundy," Jean Daigle explained in "The Acadians of the Maritimes."[1]

D'Aulnay had three forts built, each equipped with cannons, and kept soldiers at all of them. He fetched immigrants from France, planted them on grasslands he cultivated, organized farms at Port-Royal, and cleared land on the St. John and Penobscot. Every year, he supplied his settlers with three or four cargo ships from France. He ordered the construction of two mills, two seventy-ton ships, and perhaps a dozen sloops and pinnaces. When he died, Acadia boasted more than 400 inhabitants. They included dozens of soldiers and coureurs de bois, and at Port-Royal and the LaHave settlement, there were roughly fifty families. These were the true founders of the Acadian people.

Claude Picard's depiction of Acadians harvesting the
fertile dyked marshlands suggests the communal nature
of labour in living off the land.

CHAPTER 9

ACADIA:
A PUNCHING BAG
FOR NEW ENGLAND

After Robert Sedgwick took Acadia in 1654, its fate remained uncertain for sixteen years, but life among its people changed in only one significant way: they now dealt with the English more than ever before. Meeting increasing numbers of New England fishermen and merchants, some Acadians became bilingual and saw an advantage in getting along as best they could with English authorities.

By the 1670 Treaty of Breda, which followed a conflict between England and the Dutch—during which France declared war on England—France found itself back in possession of Acadia. It had already decided, however, that depopulating the old country to populate the new one would not be prudent, and from then on growth in the number of Acadians would depend on their own fertility. Meanwhile, thousands of English settlers had been flowing into Massachusetts. Fleeing religious persecution, dreaming of land they could call their own, paying their passage without government help, they kept on coming. By 1670, more than 50,000 occupied Massachusetts alone. That was roughly a hundred times the number of Acadians.

French governors had the impossible task of both forcing Acadians to obey French laws and preventing New Englanders from trading and fishing in French territory. The fishermen and merchants of Massachusetts behaved as though they had never heard of the Treaty of Breda. Moreover, Acadians happily traded their grain and furs for Boston's rum, cloth, knives, dishes, and other manufactured goods. "Neither war nor threat of seizure could stop these bold [Acadian traders]," wrote Jean Daigle, and by the 1690s "the colony at the Bay of Fundy seemed more an economic satellite of Boston than of Versailles."[1]

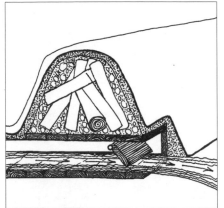

Part of the Acadian dyke system, the "aboiteaux" were devised to drain excess fresh water into the bay.

Small Acadian settlements blossomed as far up the Bay of Fundy as Beaubassin, near what is now Amherst, and through the Annapolis Valley towards Minas Basin. By 1688 there were some thirty families in the Minas area, and they began to dyke marshlands to keep out the salt water and to install "aboiteaux" to drain excess fresh water into the bay.

It was the early Acadians who had brought a form of aboiteau from France. The theory was very simple: a sluice was built into the dyke, with a hinged gate or clapper that opened to let fresh river water flow out and shut against the incoming salt water of the rising tide. The aboiteau itself was at first a small wooden tunnel made from a hollowed-out log, with the hinged door inside the log. All of this was built into the dyke.

The Minas Basin settlers had to build running dykes along the banks of the rivers to confine the inflowing salt water to a narrow channel. Then they built cross-dykes, or dams, across the river to control the flow of water. The toil involved is almost unimaginable today. It was heavy labour, done by a long line of men with spades, oxen, and horses, digging, cutting brush and sod, slithering in the mud with the animals. But by 1755 the Canard River floodplain had been won from the sea. The dykes had to be constantly maintained and repaired, again requiring heavy labour. But in all, the Acadians secured more than 800 hectares of land, which gave superior yields of grain and barley, rich fields for grazing cattle, and, among settlers in both New France and New England, an unjustified reputation as a lazy people.

Most of the Acadians gradually migrated to the Minas Basin region. By 1730 they numbered 2,500, and by 1750 the community had grown to 5,000. They shared Acadia with the Mi'kmaq and the Malecites of the future Maritime Provinces, and the Abenaki of Maine, but the native peoples had already suffered a tragic decline in population.

When the fur trade began, the Mi'kmaq may have been 50,000-strong. They saw themselves as braver, kinder, and richer than the French, and more ingenious, artistic, and honourable. While the French rated themselves as noble representatives of the most civilized nation on earth, the Mi'kmaq often saw them as squabbling, selfish, deceptive, and thievish. Yet Mi'kmaq and

French treated each other as equals, and North American Indians generally had a rapport with the French they enjoyed with no other Europeans. When the French left Port-Royal in 1607, their Mi'kmaq neighbours wept, and when Poutrincourt returned with settlers in 1610, "the people of the country," who had not touched so much as one piece of the abandoned outpost's furniture, greeted them joyfully.

Marc Lescarbot, the poet of Port-Royal, acknowledged, "For [the Mi'kmaq] have courage, fidelity, generosity, and humanity, and their hospitality is so innate and praiseworthy that they receive among them every man who is not an enemy. They are not simpletons like many people [in Europe]; they speak with much judgment and good sense ... If we commonly call them Savages, the word is abusive and unmerited."

The French and native peoples got along well, John Clarence Webster argued in "Acadia at the End of the 17th Century," because "the French never adopted the view, so common among Anglo-Saxon colonists, that the Indians were merely vermin to be removed, and that the best ones were those who were dead."[2] The atrocities natives inflicted on the British were often acts of

Lewis Picard captures the labour-intensive dyke-building by Acadians at Grand Pré. The dykes brought superior crop yields to the marshlands by controlling and confining the flow of salt water.

revenge for equally hideous treatment that the British had inflicted on them.

The French, however, posed no threat. While a few Acadian settlements did pop up, men like La Tour—nomads who knew how to swing paddles and haggle for pelts—had more in common with a Mi'kmaq hunter than with a farmer who craved land to clear and expected his family to work it for generations. Native peoples believed no one had the right to own land, and the last thing a "coureur de bois" wanted was the life of a farmer.

As New Englanders gobbled territory, as hordes of English-speaking farmers stood ready with muskets to defend their "private property," both the would-be builders of Acadia and native leaders watched with horror. "For the temperament, the religious beliefs, and the larger economic interests of the expanding commonwealth impelled the English to ride roughshod over those tribes that stood in their way," wrote Alfred G. Bailey in "The Conflict of European and Eastern Algonkian Cultures."[3] An alliance between the French and the native peoples was therefore natural, but the influence of the missionaries and gifts from the French government strengthened it. For France knew how useful the natives could be. It largely ignored them (and the Acadians, too) in peacetime, but recognized them as masters of guerrilla warfare.

Intermarriage also helped glue the alliance. By the late 1600s, most Acadian families probably had Indian blood in their veins. Jean-Vincent d'Abbadie de Saint-Castin took command of the fort at Pentagouet (now Castine, Maine) on the Penobscot River in 1670 and married the daughter of an Abenaki chief. This gave him such authority that, with his Indian allies, he "made it possible [for a while] to put a stop to English expansion in the region."

In 1687, France named Louis-Alexandre Des Friches de Meneval governor of Acadia, and ordered him to claim for France everything down to the Kennebec River in Maine; to prevent all foreigners from either fishing in Acadian waters or trading with native peoples; and to make Port-Royal stronger than ever. Responding to these threats, a party of New Englanders, led by Governor Edmund Andros, pillaged Baron Saint-Castin's headquarters at Pentagouet. He retaliated at once. Gangs of his Abenaki comrades terrorized English settlements, and Andros recruited a bigger force to attack the Abenakis. Thus began a whole series of bloody skirmishes between the troops and settlers of New England on one side and the French and their native allies on the other.

By 1700, the two centuries that had passed since John Cabot had found Mi'kmaq needles on Cape Breton Island had not been kind to the native peoples of Acadia. Owing largely to contact with the French, the Mi'kmaq population had shrunk by as much as 90 per cent. While European diseases killed thousands of Mi'kmaq, other influences from across the ocean gnawed at their health, independence, and pride.

Iron changed them. Metal arrowheads, spearheads, axes, tomahawks, knives, awls, needles, and kettles replaced the weapons and utensils they had

A nineteenth-century painting of the Mi'kmaq. The introduction of muzzle-loading rifles dramatically altered their lives. For instance, the quantity of game they could hunt increased, making nearby wildlife more and more scarce.

made from stone, bone, wood, bark, and antlers. Muzzle-loading guns made bows and arrows obsolete. Iron and steel not only enabled a band to slaughter more poorly armed enemies, it also made hunting easier. "With an arrow they killed only one Wild Goose; but with the shot of a gun they kill five or six ..." In places, the new deadliness shrank the amount of nearby game. Native peoples increasingly traded pelts not only for metal goods, but also for European food, which may have unbalanced their diets and spread disease.

Metal weapons and tools freed native peoples from much drudgery, enabling them to go further than ever before to get the furs the French wanted. The travel, however, may have watered down the very qualities that made them distinctive and caused instability in their communities. Some historians believe that Christianity, too, subtly weakened the ancient character of the native peoples of eastern North America: "The softening influence of Christianity broke down the fighting spirit of the Indians," wrote Alfred G. Bailey, "and the same religion ... tended to obliterate the primitive motive for warfare on behalf of deceased relatives, and hastened the dissolution of the solidarity of the bands."[4]

The widening race for furs revived tribal warfare, which guns made bloodier than ever. The race was so competitive because the native peoples had a seemingly insatiable appetite for European products. The Mi'kmaq took to wearing European hats, caps, shirts, and cloaks, and slept under European blankets. They forgot how to make spears. Indeed, they lost skills that had once enabled them to live proudly off the sea and the wilderness. Now, they simply could not survive without the trading posts, and French traders used liquor to enslave them further.

Describing what he saw as "the principal cause of all these deaths and disease" among native North Americans, Jesuit missionary Father Pierre wrote in 1616, "Summer time, when our ships come, they never stop gorging themselves excessively ... with various kinds of food not suitable to the inactivity in their lives; they get drunk, not only on wine but on brandy; so it is no wonder that they are obliged to endure some gripes of the stomach in the following Autumn ... " What this failed to acknowledge was European complicity in making native peoples addicted to alcohol. The French saw liquor as a bargaining weapon; the more the natives wanted it, the bigger the flow into French hands of dirt-cheap pelts.

"The Sun King," Louis XIV of France, reigned 1754–93. Under his rule France was regarded as a greedy bully.

If iron, unsuitable food, brandy, and even Christianity were European imports that weakened the native peoples of Acadia, so were rats. "The savages had no knowledge of these animals before our coming," Lescarbot wrote. "But in our time they have been beset by them, since from our fort they went even to their lodges, a distance of over 400 paces, to eat or suck their fish oils."

The rats destroyed food supplies and spread European diseases, which the native peoples had never before faced. Of all the pernicious influences from France, disease was the most devastating. As Bruce Trigger wrote in "The Indians and the Heroic Age of New France," "The greatest impact that the Europeans had on the Indians [before 1665] were the epidemics they introduced, which destroyed fifty percent or more of the native population of eastern North America."[5] By 1700, the number of Mi'kmaq had dwindled to only a few thousand.

The Acadians were victims of deals and wars they had no hand in initiating and no power to influence. Old England and old France, the nations that took turns owning Acadia, ignored it most of the time, but, after European wars, treated it as a bargaining token. Acadia would owe its loyalty to France on one day, only to discover the next morning that France had given the colony to England.

The harbour at Boston was the site from which English attacks were waged on Acadia as England and France vied for Acadian allegiance.

Warfare imposed on Acadia insults of a more violent kind. Its location in "the no man's land between the two enemies" meant it could not escape becoming a battleground. On the one hand, it was an economic outpost of Massachusetts, but on the other, it was a barrier to protect New France. The War of the Grand Alliance (1688–97) offered a prime example of what could happen to Acadia whenever European strife spread to North America. It saw several powers, including England, gang up on France because, under "The Sun King," Louis XIV, the most powerful nation in Europe had become a greedy bully.

As the conflict got under way, Iroquois warriors—armed with English muskets, hatchets, and scalping knives, and encouraged by English officials in Albany, NY—so terrorized settlements in New France that Governor General

Frontenac authorized raids on Schenectady, NY, and two settlements in Maine. Accordingly, the French Canadians and their Indian allies slipped into Schenectady at night, hacked to death men, women, and children stumbling out of bed, burned down houses with people in them, torched every building, left sixty corpses behind, and carried away loot on fifty stolen horses. The Maine settlements endured similar horrors at the hands of French-Indian forces.

Vowing to wipe out the French menace, the northern English colonies agreed to combine forces for a major assault on New France. The raids had aroused not only patriotism among New Englanders but lust for revenge, and Massachusetts chose Acadia as its first target. In 1690 the New England-born adventurer Sir William Phips led a fleet of seven vessels carrying sixty-four guns and 450 militiamen into the Annapolis Basin and demanded that Governor Meneval hand over Port-Royal. Meneval's fortifications were feeble, and he had failed to mount guns. He had only seventy soldiers and no officers. He surrendered.

In 1690 Sir William Phips headed one of the many English attacks on and conquests of Port-Royal.

The New Englanders celebrated their conquest by confiscating livestock and wrecking Port-Royal. "We cut down the cross, rifled the Church, pulled down the High-Altar," said a journal of Phips' proceedings, "breaking their images." The English "kept gathering plunder both by land and water, and also under ground in their Gardens." Phips forced as many terrified Acadians as he could find to swear allegiance to the Protestant King William and Queen Mary of England. Then he entrusted the administration of Port-Royal to a council of Acadians, and returned to Boston with his prisoners: Meneval, two priests, and thirty soldiers.

"Once again," wrote Acadian historian Jean Daigle, "Acadia was conquered as a reprisal against decisions that had been made elsewhere."[6] The conquest of 1690, however, did not amount to much. The English monarchs William and Mary recognized Phips' achievement by declaring, "The territory called Acadia or Nova Scotia is united to and incorporated in the Province of The Massachusetts Bay," but the English never tried to occupy it. Indeed, they pretty well forgot about Acadia—except when it suited them to pummel it.

The small population of the Acadians continued to leave them vulnerable to retaliation for the crimes of others. In 1696, after the French raided English settlements in Maine—and with 240 Abenaki warriors captured Fort William Henry, also in Maine—Massachusetts-born Benjamin Church led a force that vengefully burned and plundered the helpless village of Beaubassin at the head of the Bay of Fundy. Acadia was becoming New England's punching bag.

The 1697 Treaty of Ryswick, which wrapped up the War of the Grand Alliance, was a setback for Louis XIV in Europe, but not in North America. For it gave Acadia back to France. By 1700, Port-Royal was once again Acadia's capital, New England fishermen were once again trespassing in Acadian waters, Acadians were once again trading with Bostonians, and Europe was once again preparing for a major war. This one would see French power banished forever from most of Acadia.

King William and Queen Mary of England did not effectively support Phips' capture of Acadia for England in 1690, although they declared it English land.

The reconstructed governor's residence, also known as the King's Bastion, at Louisbourg. Below the original residence bomb-proof vaults were built for storage and last-resort shelter.

Below: "A Prospect of the City of Louisbourg" after the siege of 1745.

CHAPTER 10

FORTRESS LOUISBOURG: MAGNIFICENT FOLLY

The future of the Acadians lay in decisions made in London, Boston, Versailles, or Quebec. Between 1690 and 1710, the raids they endured, and the way England and France took turns demanding their allegiance, taught them to accommodate whichever nation happened to have power over them. Rather than resist, they prayed for better days to come.

By 1710, they numbered close to 2,000. They had cattle, sheep, hogs, fish, grain, vegetables, fruit trees, maple sugar, and plenty of wood. Spruce beer protected them from scurvy. Hunting provided meat and hides for both clothing and trade. After generations in Acadia, these people were less interested in France than in how their own big family was faring in their own beloved homeland. They were no longer French, they were Acadians.

Just about everyone in an Acadian village was related to everyone else and had kin in other settlements as well. Blood ties created a network of support; the more fortunate rescued the victims of natural disaster or warfare. No one recognized Acadia as a nation, yet it had a kind of national solidarity, and its system of family organization helped it cling to a countryside that great powers coveted for well over a century.

From 1701 to 1713, however, the War of the Spanish Succession badly shook Acadia's confidence. The conflict began because Louis XIV again threatened the balance of power in Europe, and it involved a score of nations. In Massachusetts, the return of Acadia to France in 1697 had angered many colonists. They saw this new war as a chance to make the French colony British forever. Between 1704 and 1710, the British repeatedly attacked Port-Royal.

These assaults, the looting by New Englanders of other Acadian settlements, an economic blockade by Massachusetts, and the British navy's ability to prevent goods from France reaching Acadia caused a decline in both the living conditions and the morale of the Acadians. While privateers from the French West Indies—who seized thirty-five British ships and took more than 400 prisoners in 1709 alone—kept sailing into Port-Royal with loot from Massachusetts vessels, the Acadians knew such derring-do would only intensify New England's thirst for revenge.

Having failed to capture Port-Royal after three attacks in six years, the British, on October 5, 1710, sailed into the Annapolis Basin with an armada big enough to show they at last meant business. Under General Francis Nicholson, the fleet boasted thirty-six vessels and a landing force of 2,000. While most were New England militiamen, Britian provided a regiment of regulars and five of the seven big warships.

France had not been so helpful to Governor Daniel d'Auger de Subercase. Sieges had impoverished Port-Royal, but the war in Europe was costing France so much money that the Sun King had nothing to spare for Acadia. Foreseeing the assault of 1710, Subercase begged for help, only to be told that Louis XIV would abandon the colony if it continued to be such a burden. After earlier sieges, Subercase had given his own linen to the sick and had sold his silverware to finance repairs to the fort. Port-Royal muskets often exploded in soldiers' hands. Many recruits were teenagers, and Subercase saw his officers as dishonest, negligent, or crazy. It did not improve morale that he ran out of money to pay them and the soldiers. He now faced Nicholson's army with fewer than 300 frightened and disgruntled boys and men, many in ill health.

Samuel Vetch took command of Port-Royal in 1710 and served as governor of Nova Scotia 1710-12. The British takeover led to the name change from Port-Royal to Annapolis Royal.

Port-Royal nevertheless held out for a week. Only after nightly bombardments had terrified the settlers, and dozens of Acadian militia had fled, did Subercase capitulate. The garrison marched out with flags flying and drums beating. "Honour was saved, but the sight of these starving soldiers in rags and tatters, many of whom were no more than adolescents, saddened even the victors," wrote René Baudry in Volume II of "The Dictionary of Canadian Biography."[1]

Edinburgh-born Samuel Vetch took command of the fort, with 200 marines and 250 New England volunteers. Before the French sailed for their homeland, Subercase jauntily told Nicholson he hoped to pay Port-Royal a visit in the spring of 1711, but he never came back. Nor did the name Port-Royal. The British called the place Annapolis Royal, and that is what it has been called for nearly three centuries.

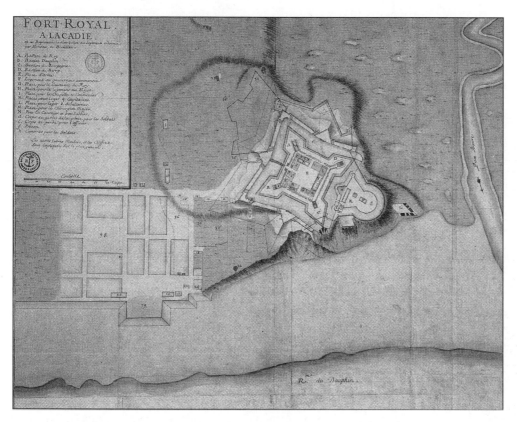

An early-eighteenth-century plan of the fort at Port-Royal prior to the British takeover in 1710.

After the longest reign in European history, Louis XIV died in 1715, four days before his seventy-seventh birthday. He had been the hard-working, autocratic, and vain king of France since 1658, and he had kept his nation embroiled in wars for almost half a century. During the War of the Spanish Succession (1701–13), he had exhibited "a wonderful tenacity of purpose ... and sometimes a nobler and more national spirit than during the years of his triumph."[2] The war, however, had left his nation in terrible shape. France had lost prestige and had gained enormous debt. Historians would later see the peace agreement, the Treaty of Utrecht (1713), as both the death of France's era of expansion and the birth of the British Empire.

Remembering Britain's habit of giving away colonial possessions during peace talks, the New Englanders who had helped take Port-Royal in 1710 insisted that, this time, Acadia not be handed back to the French. When the treaty left France with little more of Acadia than Cape Breton Island (Île Royale) and Prince Edward Island (Île St. Jean), the New Englanders felt these, too, would soon be ripe for conquest.

France, however, had an astonishing scheme for its shrunken Acadia. It saw its North American losses as a mere setback in its battle for supremacy over an empire that stretched from the St. Lawrence to the Gulf of Mexico. "The balance of power was moving, tilting," Donald Creighton wrote in "The Dominion of the North," "but had it tilted irrevocably against [the French]? They could not believe it."[3]

The ink was barely dry on the Treaty of Utrecht when French officials arrived on Cape Breton Island with plans to turn it overnight into a stronger colony than Acadia had ever been. Decades before, Nicholas Denys had cleared fields at St. Peters and St. Anns, but trees had reconquered the land, and now, on the entire island, the French reconnaissance team found only one Frenchman and perhaps thirty Mi'kmaq families. France, however, was determined not only to people Cape Breton with thousands of French settlers, but also to install on the island a fortified capital that would outshine anything New Englanders had even dreamed of building. It would serve as headquarters for the lucrative cod fishery; promote trade with the West Indies, New England, and Quebec; guard the entrance to the St. Lawrence; and show the world that the greatest nation in Europe could still flex muscles in North America.

By 1716, Cape Breton already boasted some 2,000 French pioneers who had come from France and Newfoundland. Under the Treaty of Utrecht the French had lost to England all the territory they had previously gained in Newfoundland. The Bay of Fundy Acadians, however, did not like Cape Breton. After scouting it, some of them went home with reports of heavy fog and rocky soil. Moreover, the British feared that a flow of Acadians to Cape Breton would increase French power there, and they soon refused to let them either sell their property or build boats. Believing Acadians would rise up against the British during any war of conquest, France, too, wanted to leave them where they were.

It was the Acadians themselves, however, who settled the matter. They knew they were better off where they were, and they loved their land beside the Bay of Fundy more than they loved France—or hated England. They yearned to be left alone.

For at least two centuries, European fishermen had known English Harbour on the southeast coast of Cape Breton, and it was there that the French, in 1720, began to erect a magnificent failure: Fortress Louisbourg. Constructed under the direction of military engineers Jean-François de Verville and, later, Étienne Verrier, Louisbourg owed its design to the theories of Louis XIV's master of siege warfare, Le Prestre de Vauban. It was not only a reassertion of French power in North America, but Louis XV's monument to his great-grandfather, the Sun King. For its setting, it was as grandiose as Louis XIV had been egocentric, and as a tribute to a monarch who had left France groaning under horrendous debt, it was appropriately expensive.

It sat on a narrow triangle of land that jutted eastward into the ocean. English Harbour lay to the north and Gabarus Bay to the south. In the west, the French built earthworks and erected a stone wall that faced a marsh. Since the wall ran for a full kilometre from harbour to bay, it seemingly protected the fortress from any enemies who dared to come overland. Ten metres high and four thick, surrounded by a ditch twenty-five metres wide, the wall boasted emplacements for 148 cannons and connected three formidable bastions. The middle one, the King's Bastion, contained the governor's apartments, officers' quarters, barracks, chapel, and down below, bomb-proof vaults for storage and last-resort shelter.

A 1731 view of the busy port of Louisbourg and the ice-free harbour.

Smaller ramparts and gun emplacements encircled the fortress on its seaward sides, and from two major batteries the defenders of Louisbourg could bombard any invasion fleet that approached the harbour. The Treaty of Utrecht had required France to demolish its famous fortifications at Dunkirk on the North Sea, but Louisbourg's apparent impregnability soon earned it a reputation as "the Dunkirk of America." Historians have called it "the first scientifically walled city on the western continent," and "France's Gibraltar in America." While the "Paris of America" seems harder to understand, Louisbourg did have a certain grey elegance and, when trading vessels brought money into town, some "joie de vivre."

With four storeys and a graceful tower, the governor's slate-roofed residence "proclaimed the political grandeur of France." Louisbourg was not merely a fortress; it was a busy port. The walls enclosed twenty-three hectares. Along straight streets with royal French names sat stone and wooden houses. "Shops, homes, inns and chapels never exceed two storeys, so summer air can circulate and blow away the stink of drying codfish," said the "Chronicle of Canada." The townsfolk had vegetable gardens, chicken coops, and goats.

Louisbourg swarmed not only with soldiers in blue uniforms and white greatcoats, but also with merchants wearing gold-trimmed, black tricorne hats, Basque fishermen with leather aprons, bewigged royal officials, and hard-drinking sailors off vessels from Boston, Quebec, France, and Martinique. The population included carpenters, stonemasons, tailors, housewives, nuns, a dancing master, and black slaves. Mi'kmaq came to town with pelts to trade, and Acadians with farm produce to sell.

The town boasted inns, taverns, a theatre, an ice-house, a hospital, two chapels, a clock that chimed to call worshippers to mass, and a convent school for upper-class girls. By 1740, after more than a quarter-century of peace between France and England, Louisbourg was home to 2,000 men, women, and children.

King Louis XV of France commissioned the building of Fortress Louisbourg in honour of his great-grandfather, the Sun King.

Medal with the head of Louis XV, commemorating the founding of Louisbourg in 1720.

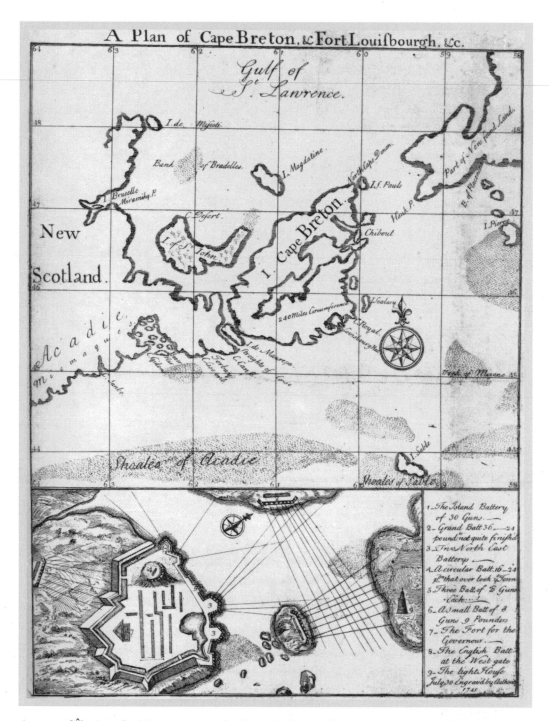

A map of Île Royale (Cape Breton Island), including a plan of Louisbourg and its extensive fortifications, published in New England, 1745. The settlement at Louisbourg was enclosed by a wall that was highest on the landward side and lowest on the water side.

It was a busy outpost of French civilization.

For France's treasury, however, it was a sinkhole. Officials embezzled money earmarked for its construction. The need to bring labour, animals, and building materials all the way from France made costs sky-rocket. Winter frosts and thaws caused huge and unexpected problems. Overworked,

Detailed drawings of the Dauphin Demi-Bastion and Dauphin Gate.

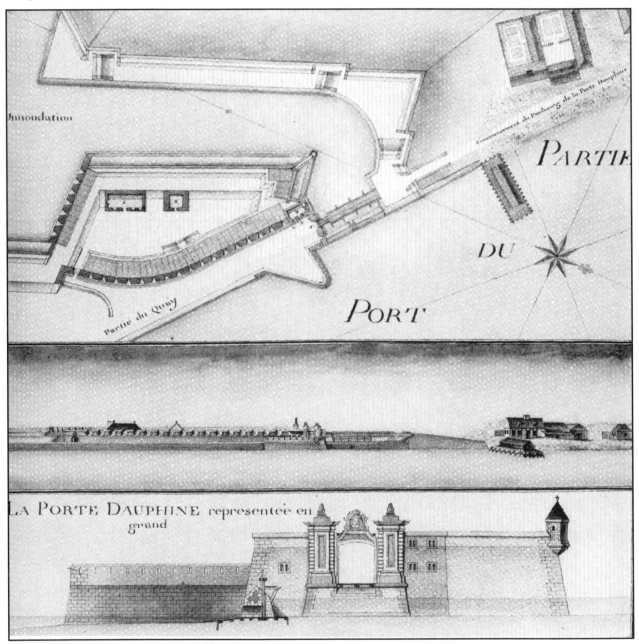

unskilled soldiers did much of the actual building, and the place fell into disrepair so quickly the work never really stopped. Fortress and town cost tens of millions of livres.

"Are the streets being paved with gold over there?" Louis XV is said to have complained. "I fully expect to awake one morning in Versailles to see the walls of the fortress rising above the horizon."

One Frenchman recognized the stupendous wastefulness of Louisbourg from its very beginnings. Joseph de Montebon de Brouillan, the outspoken governor of Île Royale, argued that Louisbourg needed only modest fortifications to protect it from surprise attacks and insisted, "We should not be looked at in the same way as a town in Europe."

French military authorities, however, ignored the opinions of both the governor and the late Sebastian Le Prestre de Vauban. While Vauban's principles of fortress building dominated the whole design of Louisbourg, he had himself warned that it was "wrong to believe that with all the secrets of the art and all the advantages of nature you could make a place impregnable; they can all be taken by an enemy who combines strength and resolution."

Sebastian Le Prestre de Vauban, Louis XV's chief military engineer.

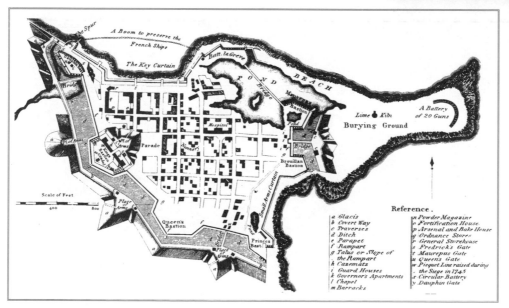

A detailed plan of the fortified town of Louisbourg, New France's stronghold until 1758, when it was captured for the last time by the British.

William Pepperell volunteered his service as commander-in-chief of the New England forces at the first siege of Louisbourg in 1745. Pepperell lent £5,000 towards the enterprise and was later knighted by King George II. He was the only New Englander to have received the distinction.

Pepperell at the first siege of Louisbourg in 1745, the first of two successful captures of the fortress by the British.

CHAPTER 11

AN ARMY OF
AMATEURS
CONQUERS THE
UNCONQUERABLE

After 1713, most of the French-speaking people of Nova Scotia enjoyed more than thirty years of peace and experienced "phenomenal demographic growth." By 1750, the Acadian population amounted to roughly 8,000. While this was not much compared to the 1.2 million English-speaking colonists in New England and further south, nor even the 55,000 French in New France, it was enough to alarm the British who supposedly ruled the colony. In 1730, Governor Richard Philipps called the Acadians "a formidable body, and, like Noah's progeny, spreading themselves over the face of the province."

From Chignecto (Amherst), the Acadians expanded to the banks of the Petitcodiac, Memramcook, and Shepody Rivers. The British wanted this neighbourhood for their own immigrants, but the Treaty of Utrecht had not set clear boundaries. Both France and Britain claimed what is now southeastern New Brunswick. The Isthmus of Chignecto, peopled by some 3,000 Acadians, became a strategic zone between hostile nations.

Many Acadians seemed to live outside British authority. Their highly educated priests helped them run their own systems of justice and government. Some looked with contempt on Port-Royal's feeble successor, Annapolis Royal. For his part, Governor Philipps saw the Acadians as "a pest and an encumbrance." With insufficient troops in a crumbling fort, no provincial revenues, and no British fortifications at major Acadian settlements, how could he govern all the French-speaking Catholics scattered up and down the Bay of Fundy? How could he even get them to swear allegiance to the king of England?

They insisted on remaining neutral, and "the astounded British discovered they did not know what to do with a few hundred obstinate and incomprehensible farmers."[1] If the Acadians had learned anything from their tempestuous history, it was the foolishness of swearing unconditional loyalty to any European monarch. They knew, too, that the Mi'kmaq might kill anyone who fought against France.

In 1730, Philipps did get Acadians to swear they would be "utterly faithful" to King George II and would "truly obey" him. They acknowledged him as "the sovereign Lord of Nova Scotia." Philipps boasted that he had achieved "the entire submission of all those so long obstinate People," but in reporting his triumph in England, he failed to reveal the concession some Acadians had extracted from him. He apparently gave the most obstinate Acadians, the ones at Minas and Chignecto, a verbal exemption from the British subject's normal duty to bear arms, and by not telling his superiors about it, "he told a spectacular and portentous lie."[2]

Richard Philipps, Governor of Nova Scotia 1719–49, imposed the Oath of Allegiance on Acadians.

Artist Claude Picard conveys the dismay of Acadians at taking the oath. In 1730, Acadians signed the qualified Oath of Allegiance, which released them from bearing arms in the struggle between Britain and France, thereby affirming their neutrality.

Shortly after the Acadians signed the oath, two of their priests, Father Charles de La Goudalie and Father Noël Alexandre de Noinville, wrote for the record that, while the people had indeed promised not to take up arms against the British, they had also wrested from Philipps the right never to have to go into battle against either Frenchmen or natives. The Acadians now had a new label: "French Neutrals."

King George II of Great Britain reigned 1727–60 during which time overseas expansion was encouraged.

All through the peace, the makings of warfare simmered. The Treaty of Utrecht failed to state whether Canso, at the eastern tip of mainland Nova Scotia, belonged to Britain or France, and Massachusetts coveted the superb Canso fishery. In 1718, Captain Thomas Smart and his crew sailed a frigate into Canso, wrecked the French installations, banished the French fishermen, and, before returning to Boston, confiscated several vessels.

Smart also arrested some French officers from Île Royale, and it is probable that, once they regained their freedom, they sought revenge by inciting natives to raid New Englanders. In 1720 Mi'kmaq warriors attacked the Massachusetts fishermen at Canso, killed three or four, and stripped the others of everything they owned. While the Mi'kmaq were seizing merchandise, the French moved in to confiscate the New Englanders' fish. Governor Philipps despatched troops to Canso and moved there himself. When gifts failed to persuade the Mi'kmaq to stop harassing fishermen and raiding local shipping, he organized the New Englanders of Canso and his own troops and then scattered or killed the marauders.

From 1722 to 1725, as warfare raged between New England and native peoples, atrocities spread along the coasts of Nova Scotia. New Englanders believed that behind the Mi'kmaq and Abenaki attacks lurked priests whom the king of France paid to promote bloodshed. The crown funnelled the money through Quebec and, as a nineteenth-century Nova Scotian historian saw the situation, "If any of [the priests] proved remiss in ... fanning the fire of hatred to English rule among the Indians, and promoting attachment to French ascendancy among the peasant inhabitants—such refractory priest might look for dismissal at the hands of the Quebec government."[3]

By the late 1730s, New England had still other reasons for wanting to oust the French from North America. As its trade spread across the ocean, Massachusetts saw Nova Scotia as an outpost of its own fishing and commercial organization, and Île Royale as a potentially dangerous and hateful competitor. While Boston dreamed of destroying Louisbourg, Louisbourg dreamed of reconquering Nova Scotia. As early as 1735, Captain François Du Pont Duvivier plotted to capture Canso and thereby wrest its fabulous fishery from the English.

Far from Nova Scotia, Captain Robert Jenkins was sailing home to England from the West Indies when Spaniards captured his vessel and cut off his right ear. That is what he told Members of Parliament, at any rate, and the public outrage helped inspire Britain to declare war on Spain. "The War of

Jenkins' Ear" soon merged with the enormously complicated War of the Austrian Succession, which in the spring of 1744 led to what the leaders of both New France and New England itched to join: yet another major conflict between their mother countries.

Louisbourg heard about the declaration of war before Canso, only a day's sail away, and Duvivier immediately led a surprise attack on New England's favourite fishing station. When Canso offered no resistance, the French carried booty and prisoners back to Louisbourg.

Heartened by this easy victory, the commander of Île Royale, Jean-Baptiste-Louis Le Prévost Duquesnel, put Duvivier in charge of a French campaign, bolstered by native warriors, to capture Annapolis Royal. While leading his troops through Acadian districts, Duvivier, born in Port-Royal, cast himself as a liberator back among his own people. The pose failed. He alienated more Acadians than he impressed and "detached no more than a dozen men from the strict neutrality which by this time had become the practical expedient of government and governed in Nova Scotia."[4]

Governor William Shirley of Massachusetts recognized the weaknesses in the not so impregnable Fortress Louisbourg.

The failure of the expected French warships to show up in the Annapolis Basin, the courage of Annapolis Royal's commander, Paul Mascarene, and the indecisiveness of Duvivier all contributed to the collapse of the siege. As he retreated toward Louisbourg, the Acadians refused even to supply food for his troops.

The French victory at Canso and the assault on Annapolis Royal convinced Governor William Shirley of Massachusetts that the safety of New England required the conquest of Louisbourg. Moreover, he now suspected that the Dunkirk of America might not really be unconquerable.

Sir Peter Warren's fleet blockaded Louisbourg in 1745.

While Bostonians had often visited Louisbourg in peacetime, the New Englanders that Duvivier had captured at Canso lived there as prisoners. They knew that only the last-minute arrival of food from Quebec had recently saved Louisbourg from starvation. They noticed that many gun emplacements had no guns, and that, in this cold, foggy outpost of French civilization, the morale of the soldiers, many of them Swiss mercenaries, was appallingly low. The troops lived in cramped quarters under corrupt officers and ate rotten vegetables. Soldiers had tattered uniforms, no boots, and, for month after month, no pay. In December 1744, army mutineers forced their superiors to give them back pay and better food. Louisbourg was heading toward anarchy.

Released because they added to the mouths Louisbourg was feeding, the prisoners went home with news of the despair within the walled town and details of the fortifications.

Nova Scotia Governor Paul Mascarene defended Annapolis Royal in 1744.

In May 1745, 4,000 men of the New England militia, commanded by the popular owner of a shipping line, William Pepperell, arrived off Louisbourg in ninety vessels, scrambled up the steep beaches of Gabarus Bay, crossed a swamp, and set up artillery west of the fortress. Most were not professional soldiers, but amateurs who preferred rum to drill. They were the clerks, fishermen, and farm boys of New England. They were also hymn-singers who believed that when they killed French Catholics they were not only protecting New England trade, but obliging God. The assault on the Dunkirk of America perfectly illustrated "the peculiar New England talent for finding good religious reasons to endorse what was sound business policy."[5]

Blockading Louisbourg was a fleet of British warships under Sir Peter Warren, who had married a New Yorker and was "one of the first Englishmen to have a dim inkling of the fact that colonists could fight."[6] By June 10, after reinforcements had arrived from Britain, Warren had six ships of the line and five frigates, which carried a total of 554 guns and more than 3,500 marines, seamen, and officers. Jammed within the walls of the fortress, under the command of the thumb-twiddling Governor Louis DuPont Duchambon, were some 1,400 demoralized troops and militiamen, along with 2,000 trembling townsfolk. They faced combined English-speaking forces of nearly 8,000 men.

Bungling by both sides later gave the siege a near comic-opera quality, but the participants saw nothing funny in it. In "Louisbourg Portraits," author Christopher Moore presented this sentence by a New Englander who fought at Louisbourg in the summer of 1745: "It is an awful thing to see men wounded and wollowing in their own blud and breething oute their last

An engraving titled "A View of the New England Forces in ye Expedition against Cape Breton—1745."

breaths."[7] With cannonballs scattering rubble as they crashed into homes, inns, warehouses, and the barracks chapel, no corner of Louisbourg escaped the terror. Their fuses sputtering like fireworks, well-timed mortars exploded just before they landed, "showering death and destruction below."[8]

On June 27, after a seven-week bombardment, hand-to-hand skirmishes, sniping by musketeers, and deadly miscalculations by the officers of both armies, the undermanned, undersupplied, underfed bastion of French power in North America capitulated. With flags flying and muskets shouldered, the defeated troops marched out of the "impregnable" fortress, and the ragtag New England militia marched in. William Pepperell, the Boston merchant who had become a general, went home to discover he was a hero.

While capturing Louisbourg, the New Englanders lost fewer than a hundred men, but misery soon swamped the joy of victory. Since Britain did not provide soldiers for Louisbourg till 1746, the New Englanders lingered there for almost a year. They despised the place. With winter came fever and dysentery. Nearly 900 died.

Meanwhile, a stupendous disaster struck the French. Determined to recapture Louisbourg and Annapolis Royal, harass Newfoundland and New England, and protect Canada against English attacks, France sent to Nova Scotia, in June of 1746, the biggest fleet that had ever crossed the Atlantic. The squadron boasted fifty-four vessels, perhaps close to half the entire French navy, and more than 7,000 men.

The commander of the armada was the Duc d'Anville, a charming but inept nobleman of thirty-seven. Supporting him were two rear admirals, the sensitive Constantin-Louis d'Estournel and the seasoned Jacques-Pierre de Taffanel de la Jonquière, a future governor of New France. France had long neglected its navy, and most of d'Anville's officers and crew had done little sailing for years.

Danville planned to rendezvous around September 1 at Chebucto (Halifax) with four men-of-war from the French West Indies, and several hundred French and Indians who, under the command of Jean-Baptiste-Nicolas Roch de Ramezay, would march overland from Quebec. Scheduled to receive d'Anville's armada at Chebucto was French missionary Father Jean-Louis Le Loutre, who knew the signals to identify the ships. Since it was through him that the French controlled the Mi'kmaq, the British saw him as a fiend in priest's clothing.

Father Jean-Louis Le Loutre incited the Mi'kmaq to attack the British and discourage their settling in Acadia.

But storms tore through d'Anville's armada, wrecking some vessels and crippling others; the fleet also sat for days in dead calm, enshrouded in fog. D'Anville did not reach the future Halifax till the ships from the West Indies and Ramezay's force had already arrived, waited, and gone. On many ships men were starving, and typhus raced from victim to victim. At Chebucto, courageous Acadians brought fresh food to the sick soldiers and sailors moaning in makeshift shelters beside the inner harbour, but hundreds expired there. Unaware of the danger, Mi'kmaq took the clothing of the dead Frenchmen, caught the disease, and spread it among other camps of their own people.

On September 27, while walking on his forecastle deck, d'Anville died of what some believed was an attack of apoplexy. It is possible he poisoned himself. Rear Admiral d'Estournel now took command, but promptly tried to kill himself with his sword. He failed, but his wound was deep and agonizing.

La Jonquière now took command. By October 15, disease had killed 587 of his troops and crew, and another 2,274 were sick. (Later estimates of the total killed by storms and disease would rise to 2,400.) With what was left of his fleet, however, and Ramezay's inland army, La Jonquière still hoped to take Annapolis Royal. His flotilla sailed out of Chebucto and bravely turned west, dropping the newly dead overboard day after day. La Jonquière never made it to Annapolis; murderous weather forced the remnants of the armada to crawl home to France.

When news of the expedition's fate reached Boston, it aroused a frenzy of thanksgiving. "The greatest threat ever made against the British colonies in America had been destroyed without the firing of a shot. No wonder the New Englanders looked upon God as their personal property."9

In 1746 Duc d'Anville led the largest armada ever to cross the Atlantic. It was France's hope to recapture Louisbourg and Annapolis Royal then seize Boston. However, the fleet foundered and troops perished from storms, fog, and disease before any attacks were waged.

With the attack on Annapolis Royal out of the question, Ramezay and his little army settled in for the winter at Chignecto (Amherst), but in January 1747, he learned that hundreds of New England troops had garrisoned Grand Pré in the Annapolis Valley. Led by Captain Nicolas-Antoine Coloun de Villiers, 250 Mi'kmaq and French—many of them young nobles from Quebec—spent seventeen days snowshoeing from Chignecto to Grand Pré. During a post-midnight blizzard, they caught the New Englanders off guard and slaughtered many in their beds. Thirty hours later, the corpses of 130 British and fifteen French lay in the trampled snow, and the New Englanders agreed to give the French their military supplies in exchange for permission to retreat.

With the dead of both sides sharing a shallow grave, the New England officers invited the French officers to a dinner party. They all got along splendidly. The guests stayed for supper, too, and drank with their hosts till late at night. The next morning, the English marched out of the stone house, participated with the French in the ceremony of surrender, and trudged through the snow to Annapolis Royal. A few days later, the French (but not the local Acadians) went off through the snow towards Chignecto.

Governor Shirley immediately sent more troops to occupy Grand Pré, and throughout the rest of the war, which ended in 1748 with the Treaty of Aix-la-Chapelle, there were British garrisons not only at Grand Pré, but also at Louisbourg, Canso, Annapolis Royal, and Minas.

To New Englanders that treaty was the mother country's supreme sell-out of their interests. They refused to acknowledge that France's wartime performance had been much better in Europe than in North America, and that Britain's bargaining position was weak. The British asked France to recognize the Protestant Hanovers as their lawful monarchs and to quit supporting the Catholic House of Stuart and the Young Pretender, Bonnie Prince Charlie. And what would France get in return? Without consulting New England, old England offered to return to France Louisbourg, "the people's darling conquest."

The French were delighted. British troops had spent two years repairing all the damage New England's artillery had inflicted on Louisbourg, and now old England was giving the renovated fortress right back to France. It was as though the siege had never occurred. France was so pleased it gave to Britain, as a kind of bonus, a trading post in India.

Although Britain refunded to the near-bankrupt New England the cost of the Louisbourg expedition, it could not pacify Bostonians. "An ungrateful, untrustworthy Britain had swapped Louisbourg for a trumpery factory in Madras."[10] For what reason had so many New Englanders died at Louisbourg? How long would God-fearing farmers and fishermen have to endure the bloody raids of the French and their native allies? With Louisbourg back in the enemy's hands, what chance could there ever be to conquer Quebec and thereby end the French menace for ever?

New England's Louisbourg veterans were proud to have routed an entrenched European enemy. They now knew they could beat trained soldiers. A generation later, this would bolster their confidence during the American Revolution. The return of Louisbourg taught them something else: mother country or not, England felt free to double-cross them. Some of these feelings would lie behind the coming revolution. Thirty years after the siege of Louisbourg saw New England amateurs fighting French and Swiss regulars, the Battle of Bunker Hill, near Boston, saw some of those very same New Englanders fighting British regulars. Historians have called Louisbourg "the cradle of the United States."

Prince Charles Edward Stuart, "Bonnie Prince Charlie," attempted to seize the throne of Great Britain from King George II.

Richard Bulkeley arrived in Halifax as aide-de-camp to Governor Cornwallis in 1749. He was a member of Council, Provincial Secretary, first church warden of St. Paul's, newspaper editor, and Brigadier General of Militia. As judge of the Vice-Admiralty Court, he held sessions in his drawing room at Carleton House, his Halifax home. His long and outstanding service to the community earned him the unofficial title "Father of the Province."

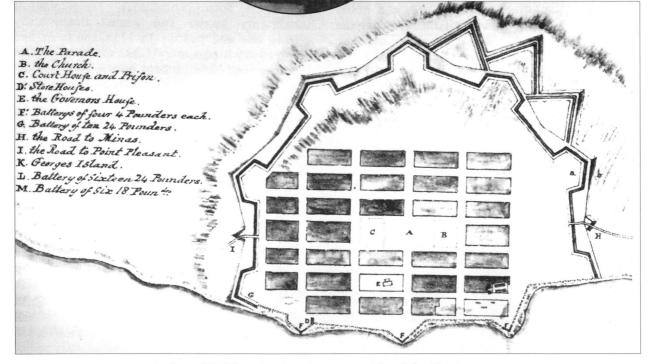

A. The Parade.
B. the Church.
C. Court House and Prison.
D. Store Houses.
E. the Governors House.
F. Batterys of four 4 Pounders each.
G. Battery of ten 24 Pounders.
H. the Road to Minas.
I. the Road to Point Pleasant.
K. Georges Island.
L. Battery of Sixteen 24 Pounders.
M. Battery of Six 18 Poun.ᵈˢ

A plan of Halifax, showing the street grid and fortifications, prepared by engineer John Brewse in 1749.

CHAPTER 12

BRITAIN'S ANSWER TO LOUISBOURG: HALIFAX

For decades, Britain had neglected Nova Scotia, with its thousands of French-speaking Catholics, but even as the mother country returned Louisbourg to France in 1748, it made an unprecedented commitment to the colony. Obeying decades of urgings from its own threatened officers at Annapolis Royal and, more recently, from Governor Shirley of Massachusetts, the British government decided to build a fortified city at Chebucto (Halifax).

Britain's first huge investment in North America, Halifax was founded for strategic reasons, and for two centuries would thrive only during wars or the anticipation of wars. Named after the Earl of Halifax, Lord of Trade and Plantations, Halifax was meant to be headquarters for army and navy forces, a checkmate against Louisbourg, a protector of New England and her trade, and the capital of a colony that would attract a flood of Protestant immigrants to counterbalance the Catholic and supposedly dangerous Acadians. It was to be the new capital of a new Nova Scotia.

Close to the fishing grounds, Chebucto (from the Mi'kmaq for "at the biggest harbour"), was easy to defend and was already known as one of the world's finest havens for vessels. Sieur de Dièrville, writer and surgeon, found remnants of a French cod-drying station there in 1699 and wrote, "This

Harbour is of great extent, and Nature has, herself, formed there a splendid Basin, and around about Green Fir-trees, which afford the eye a pleasant prospect."

Fifty summers later, on June 21, 1749, Nova Scotia's new governor, Lieutenant Colonel Edward Cornwallis, sailing aboard the good ship Sphinx, led more than a dozen vessels up the harbour. "We caught fish every day since we came within forty leagues of the coast," he wrote. "The harbour itself is full of fish of all kinds. All the officers agree the harbour is the finest they have ever seen." The fleet carried nearly 2,600 passengers, perhaps 1,000 of them women and children. They stayed on the ships at first—and some lived on them throughout the following winter—but Cornwallis immediately ordered men to start cutting waterfront trees. Within a month, they had cleared five hectares, and he was pondering where to put his residence.

Lieutenant Colonel Edward Cornwallis, Governor of Nova Scotia 1749-52. He founded Halifax in 1749 as the site for the new capital of Nova Scotia and named it for the Earl of Halifax.

At thirty-six, Cornwallis was a well-connected career soldier. He had fought against the French at Fontenoy (Belgium) and in 1745 had participated in the slaughter of Highland Scots at Culloden. He was brave, handsome, slender, and—unusual among contemporary governors—incorruptible. Cornwallis was also thoroughly aristocratic.

For its founding father, Halifax might have done much worse; for its founding settlers it might have done much better. Most were English, but Irish, Scots, and a few Welsh came, too. Some were London street people. As Thomas H. Raddall described them, "The ragtag and bobtail of London had stepped straight out of Hogarth's prints into the wilds of Chebucto."[1] Few of Halifax's first residents had ever felled towering pines or suffered attacks by black flies and mosquitos. Few had seen a wilderness as formidable as Nova Scotia's or endured any season as punishing as the winters that lashed the colony. The settlers included doctors, clerks, teachers, carpenters, and a handful who claimed to be farmers. But most were war veterans. Lured by the promise of free passage, land, tools, fishing gear, ammunition, guns, protection, and a year's supply of rations, and released from military discipline, too many became loafers, thieves, and drunkards.

By August, however, after ships from Boston had brought shingles and lumber, almost a kilometre of huts, houses, and tents had popped up, and streets were taking shape. Once the settlers had their own makeshift waterfront dwellings, many insisted that, unless Cornwallis paid them, they would lift not a finger to build either the palisade around the town or the fort on Citadel Hill. Colonel Thomas Hopson, who had handed Louisbourg over to the French in July, arrived with the troops that had garrisoned the fortress, and Cornwallis soon had an entire regiment of low-paid redcoats to help build the fortifications.

Cornwallis also hired Acadians to help build the fort on the hill, and by autumn they were looking down on hundreds of buildings. Even before the first snowfall, they saw and heard "streets carved from the forest [echoing] to the mingled sounds of city life; during the day, to the endless bustle of men and women about their tasks; at night to drunken revelries, for there were taverns everywhere and rum was a staple beverage."[2]

A plan of Halifax depicting the harbour shortly after the settlement in 1749, published in the following year in "Gentleman's Magazine," London. It also features illustrations of Nova Scotia fauna and coats of arms of Nova Scotia baronets.

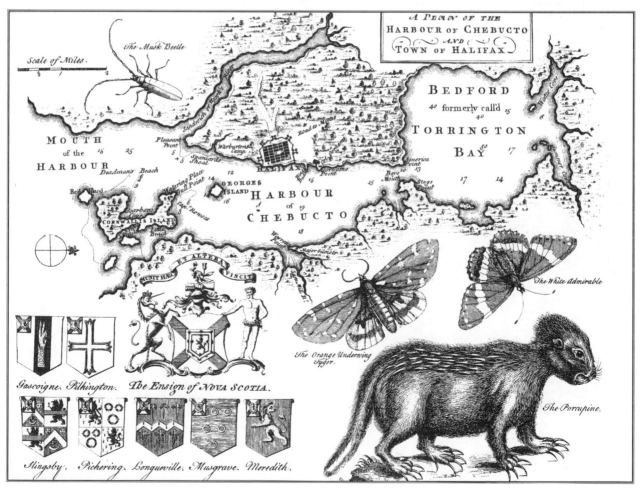

101

Cold, cramped, dirty, and eating little but salt meat and hard tack, hundreds of the first Haligonians died of typhus in the winter of 1749–50. Upon hearing of Mi'kmaq atrocities across the harbour, and discovering that most of Nova Scotia's soil was thin, sour, and boulder-cluttered, hundreds more went back to Britain or skipped off to Boston on Yankee vessels.

But as fast as the British died or fled, pushy New Englanders took their place, and even before Halifax's first winter as many as a thousand may well have arrived. The Board of Trade was spending hundreds of thousands of pounds in founding Halifax, and these aggressive Yankees sensed that the new capital of Nova Scotia was a place to make money. They included fishermen, carpenters, lawyers, traders, merchants, tavern keepers, a newspaper publisher, and the distiller, smuggler, and slave-trader Joshua Mauger.

The British often disapproved of the Yankees. Describing New England men, one wrote, "Of all the people upon earth I never heard any bear so bad a character for Cheating designing people & all under Ye Cloack of religion." The Yankees were outspoken and, to British ears, brash. The British believed in ruling colonies autocratically, but self-made merchants from Massachusetts

Halifax drawn from "ye top of masthead" in 1750. It was meant to be a British fortified city to counter France's Louisbourg.

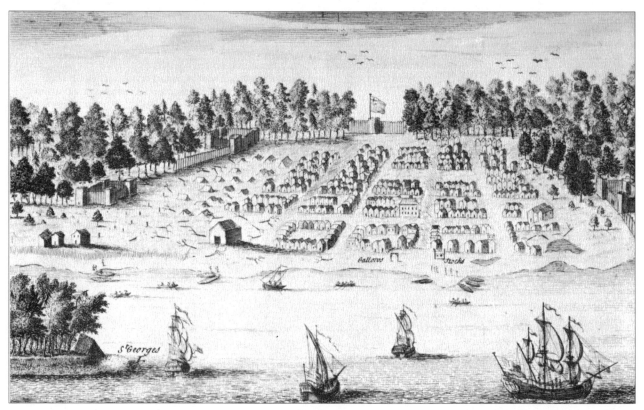

not only resented the bullying style of the redcoats, but believed in the right to govern themselves. In 1758 pressure from New Englanders who had already enjoyed representative government in their homeland forced Governor Charles Lawrence to allow Nova Scotia an elected legislature. By then, the American Revolution was only seventeen years away.

Despite the friction, the old Englanders and New Englanders at first shared the same place of worship. As early as 1750, the spire of the elegant St. Paul's Church stabbed the skyline above the masted harbour. It was the first Protestant church to be built in what is now Canada. When the first Bishop of Nova Scotia, Charles Inglis, arrived in 1787 he consecrated St. Paul's as his cathedral. It was the first Church of England cathedral in Britain's overseas colonies and allowed dissenters to hold prayer meetings there on Sunday afternoons. St. Paul's remains "the mother" of the Anglican communion in Canada.

Among the earliest New Englanders in Nova Scotia were Gorham's Rangers. Under the command of Massachusetts-born John Gorham, these experts in guerrilla-style warfare included some whites, but they were mostly Mohawks. Notorious for being "far more terrible than European soldiers," Gorham's Rangers had helped defend Annapolis Royal against French and Mi'kmaq forces in 1744 and had participated in the capture of Louisbourg in 1745. They never numbered more than a few dozen, but in 1747 and 1748, Gorham had assumed sole responsibility for the defence of Nova Scotia. "These wild men in buckskins, and their canny drawling commander, offended [Cornwallis's] sight,"[3] but the governor needed them to combat the Mi'kmaq.

A 1755 view of Halifax from a French source, showing the town, George's Island, and the fortifications.

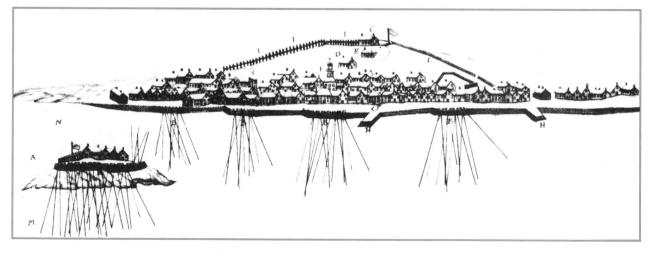

In August of that first Halifax summer, Cornwallis ordered the building of a sawmill on the Dartmouth side of the harbour, but Mi'kmaq ambushed the construction crew. They killed, scalped, and butchered four men. A year later, after 350 settlers had started to build Dartmouth, Mi'kmaq came down the lakes from Shubenacadie, scalped eight people, and vanished with fourteen prisoners. By then, the governor and his council had offered Gorham's Rangers—and, indeed, every other British colonist—ten guineas for each Mi'kmaq, dead or alive. "For years there was a merry trade," Thomas H. Raddall wrote, "the French buying scalps at Louisbourg, the English buying scalps at Halifax, and no one certain, as the money chinked on the table, whether these scraps of withered skin and clotted hair belonged to man, woman, or child, or whether they were English, French, or Indian."[4]

Robert Field's portrait of the first Bishop of Nova Scotia, Charles Inglis, a Loyalist who arrived at Halifax from New York in 1783. Consecrated in 1787, he was the first colonial Bishop.

Behind the Mi'kmaq raids, Cornwallis knew, lurked Jean-Louis Le Loutre, a scheming missionary with headquarters at Pointe-à-Beauséjour (near Sackville, N.B.). On July 29, 1749, shortly before the first Dartmouth scalpings, Le Loutre wrote to his superiors, "As we cannot openly oppose the English venture, I think that we cannot do better than to incite the Indians to continue warring on the English; my plan is to persuade the Indians to send word to the English that they will not permit new settlements to be made in Acadia ... I shall do my best to make it look to the English as if this plan comes from the Indians and that I have no part in it." Cornwallis called Le Loutre "a good for nothing Scoundrel as ever lived."

Le Loutre was a nuisance to the British not only because he had power over the Mi'kmaq, but because he caused turmoil among the 3,000 Acadians living near what became the border between Nova Scotia and New Brunswick. All of what is now New Brunswick remained in dispute, and no sooner had Cornwallis founded Halifax than the acting governor of Canada, the Marquis de La Galissonié, decided to assert French authority. He sent forces to both the St. John River and, under the Canadian-born Louis de La Corne, to the Chignecto neighbourhood.

There, the Missaguash River formed what the French saw as the border between their Acadia and Britain's Nova Scotia, and Le Loutre used bribes and intimidation to induce Acadians to abandon their farms on the enemy's side of the stream and move across to the French side. He promised to get them established, pay them for their losses, and feed them for three years. When some refused to move, he threatened them with Mi'kmaq raids.

In November 1749, Cornwallis sent Major Charles Lawrence and a small force to the Isthmus of Chignecto. They discovered that, to force Acadians to cross the river, Le Loutre had instigated the burning of the entire village of Beaubassin. Confronted by La Corne's troops, Lawrence withdrew, but the following summer he returned with a stronger force and, calm under intense gunfire, routed a war party of Mi'kmaq led by Le Loutre. While La Corne watched from one side of the Missaguash, the British built a fort, which Lawrence named after himself. The French countered with their own new fort. Forts Lawrence and Beauséjour glared at each other from opposite sides of the river. The tension caused hundreds of Acadians to cross the Missaguash, while others fled to Île Saint-Jean (Prince Edward Island).

Back in Halifax, Cornwallis had found that the few Swiss among the original townsfolk were honest, hard-working, and easy to govern. The Board of Trade began to send "Foreign Protestants" who "by their industrious and exemplary dispositions [would] greatly promote and forward the settlement in its infancy."

St. Paul's—the oldest Protestant church in Canada —and the Grand Parade, Halifax 1759.

Charles Lawrence—
Governor 1756–60—
called the first
election and was the
instigator of the
Acadian expulsion.

Broken in health, and frustrated by what he saw as the board's penny-pinching with respect to Nova Scotia, Cornwallis quit his governorship in late 1752, but by the following June more than 2,000 Germans, German-speaking Swiss, and French Protestants were already living in and around Halifax. They were recruited from southwestern Germany and the Montbéliard district on the border between France and Switzerland in an attempt to counter the French and Catholic presence in Nova Scotia. Many had been there for years, and in 1753 Charles Lawrence, now a lieutenant colonel, led some 1,500 to the future Lunenburg. The new settlers found cleared land at Lunenburg, as well as at the other settlement sites, for the Mi'kmaq had been there for years. This was their land.

After living in fetid Halifax huts, the settlers were quarrelsome, and in Lawrence's words, "inconceivably

An illustration of Halifax in 1759 shows the Govenor's House (centre), built under the direction of Charles Lawrence on the present site of Province House, and St. Mather's and St. Paul's churches, all of which appear to be the focal point of the early town.

turbulent." They were eager to start farming, and, since they had never known a Mi'kmaq raid, balked at his insisting they build fortifications before all else. Lawrence gradually made the Lunenburgers realize that "they must 'proceed in another manner, or have their throats cut.' By a mixture of bribery, bullying and verbal persuasion, Lawrence gained their affection—'not only their hats but their hearts,' as he described it—and retained it, to his political advantage, after his return to Halifax in August 1753."

He was now forty-four, a tough, energetic, battle-scarred, six-foot-two-inch veteran of fighting in Europe and Nova Scotia. Popular in the army, he believed in solving problems in the most direct way possible. The future governor of Nova Scotia would soon earn the hatred of generations of Acadians.

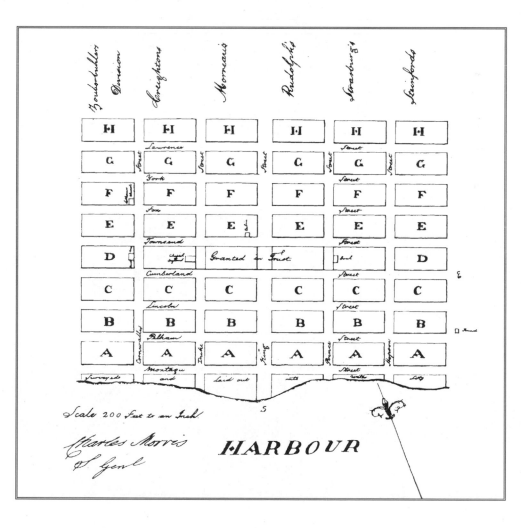

Plan of Lunenburg by surveyor Charles Morris in 1759, made for the foreign Protestant settlers who took over the (partially) cleared land from Mi'kmaq inhabitants.

British Admiral Edward ("Old Dreadnought") Boscawen commanded an impressive fleet during the second siege of Louisbourg in 1758.

A 1758 print titled, "Britain's Glory, or the Reduction of Cape Breton by the Gallant Admiral Boscawen and General Amherst."

CHAPTER 13

ACADIANS BANISHED, LOUISBOURG FALLS—AGAIN

Since the Seven Years' War involved virtually every major power in Europe and ranged from North America to the West Indies to India, historians have called it "the first global war." In North America, however, it was the biggest, bloodiest, most expensive, and last of the French and Indian Wars. To win it, Britain created a mighty military machine: "On the British side particularly there was a great deployment of military power in America which for the first time was Britain's main theatre of operations, C. P. Stacey explained in the "Dictionary of Canadian Biography" "In the crucial year 1759 no fewer than twenty-three British regular infantry battalions were employed in continental North America, as compared with only six in Germany."[1]

While the war officially began in 1756, it was already afoot in North America. As early as 1755 the French and English colonies existed in what a British lord called "a motley state neither peace nor war." At first, the inland conflict went disastrously for the British. Campaigns in 1755 to capture French forts at Niagara, Lake Champlain, and Fort Duquesne on the Ohio River all failed. Of the 1,900 redcoats that General Edward Braddock led into an ambush near Fort Duquesne, the French and Indians killed or wounded more than 1,400, while suffering only twenty-five casualties themselves. Braddock was among the slaughtered.

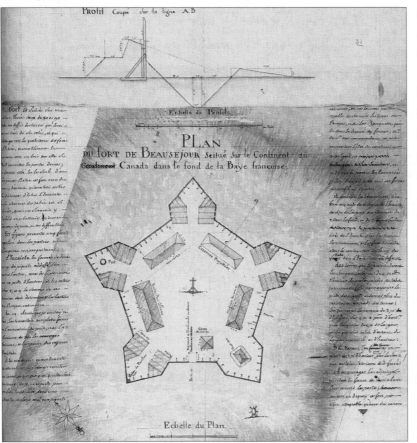

It was only in Nova Scotia that in 1755 British forces achieved an important victory. The Acadians still outnumbered British Nova Scotians by at least three to one, and Governors Lawrence of Nova Scotia and Shirley of Massachusetts saw them as a menace. They seemed particularly threatening on the Isthmus of Chignecto, a potential avenue for invading troops from Quebec, and on June 2 Lieutenant Colonel Robert Monckton landed there with 2,000 New England soldiers. He expected the defenders of Fort Beauséjour, under the bumbling Louis de Vergor, to number 150 regular colonial troops and 1,000 Acadians, but the French had managed to frighten fewer than 300 Acadians into joining the battle.

On June 13, the New Englanders began to bombard the fort from a nearby ridge. Terror spread inside the crowded stronghold. The Acadian militia turned mutinous, and on June 16 Vergor surrendered. Monckton's force now marched smartly across the isthmus to Baie Verte, where the French surrendered Fort Gaspereau. The Acadian boundary dispute was over; the British had won.

Backed by New Englanders in Halifax, and by Governor Shirley, Lawrence now decided to do what previous British governors had never felt strong enough to do. He would give the Acadians an ultimatum: swear unqualified loyalty to the sovereign of England or leave their homelands forever. Ever since the British had captured Port-Royal, forty-five years before, the Acadians had stubbornly refused demands to take such an oath. They still saw themselves as "French Neutrals" and, indeed, British governors had recognized this curious status. The Acadians nevertheless

Lieutenant Colonel Robert Monckton.

Plan of Fort Beauséjour, 1751.

endured threats from both mother countries. British officers threatened to expel them if they did not remain loyal to King George II, and French officers sometimes threatened to kill them if they refused to fight the British.

In the summer of 1755, Lawrence's decision made increasing sense to him. The threat of Louisbourg loomed. Acadians had fought against the British in the Isthmus of Chignecto, and one of them, Joseph Brossard (known as Beausoleil), had led sixty Acadians and Mi'kmaq in an attack on Monckton's camp on the very day Fort Beauséjour fell. Lawrence now feared a counterattack on the isthmus, and Halifax buzzed with reports that the cargo of two French ships that Admiral Edward Boscawen's fleet had captured off Newfoundland included 10,000 scalping knives for Acadians and Mi'kmaq. Moreover, Boscawen had failed to prevent a major squadron of French ships from taking war supplies to Canada. Even more alarming was Braddock's recent defeat. "For if a rabble of French and Indians could cut up a disciplined British force [near Fort Duquesne], they could do it anywhere," Raddall wrote in his history of Halifax.[2]

With the war going so badly, Lawrence and the other five members of his governing council—three of them Halifax New Englanders—saw the Acadians as a potentially over-whelming enemy in their own back-yard. Jealousy and greed coloured the military fears. If the Acadians were British subjects, surely they must accept their duties as British subjects.

A drawing of Annapolis Royal in the 1750s by Captain John Hamilton.

Otherwise, by what right did they occupy the juiciest farmland in a British colony? It was territory many a New Englander coveted.

Some historians argue that Lawrence ordered the deportation of the Acadians without the approval of the British government. He knew, however, that previous governors, while careful not to drive the Acadians into the French camp, had the authority to force them—whenever the time seemed ripe—to take an oath that included a promise to bear arms for the king of England. After Monckton drove the French military from Nova Scotia, the time at last seemed ripe. Lawrence vowed "to bring the Inhabitants to a Compliance, or rid the province of such perfidious subjects."

Colonel Thomas Hopson, who had succeeded Cornwallis as captain-general of Nova Scotia, tried to persuade Lawrence that pressure to make the Acadians swear allegiance should be relaxed. He knew how important the Acadians were to Halifax as a source of food: "How useful and necessary these people are to us, how impossible it is to do without them or to replace them even if we had other settlers to put in their places."

Lawrence was unmoved; he thought that most Acadians, faced with the threat of deportation, would sign the oath. He was wrong. The "French Neutrals" believed that, once again, they would get away without signing it. They, too, were wrong. When they refused their last chance to take the unqualified oath, "he collected the astounded and bewildered people and shipped them off to the other English possessions."[3]

Claude Picard's portrayal of Acadians awaiting British vessels to carry them into exile in the British colonies to the south captures the emotional turmoil of such a despotic upheaval.

The deportation strategy involved both trickery and force. At Grand Pré, for instance, Lieutenant Colonel John Winslow, a New Englander who had helped capture Fort Beau-séjour, summoned more than 400 men and boys to the church in which he had set up his headquarters, and, while his soldiers guarded the doors and windows, he gave them the grim news. They were prisoners. British ships would soon dump them and their big families on unknown shores. They could take their money, clothes, and some furniture, but their cattle, houses, and the land they had farmed for generations now belonged to the king of England. "Winslow termed the business 'Very Disagreable to my natural make & Temper,' but he carried out his orders with care, military precision, and as much compassion as circumstances allowed."[4] By November, he had sent more than 1,500 Acadians to English colonies far to the south. The last thing the British wanted was to see the Acadians flock to Cape Breton, where they would drastically increase the enemy's population.

The troops compelled to do the dirty work during "le grand dérangement" were mostly blue-coated American soldiers like Winslow. New England Protestants were at last expelling Acadian Catholics. At the time of the expulsion there was a small English garrison at Fort Anne [Annapolis Royal]. Most of the redcoats stationed there were married to Acadian wives, and to them fell a most painful duty.

Up and down the Annapolis Valley, in the Cobequid country, the Isthmus of Chignecto, and along the rivers of southeastern New Brunswick, New England soldiers kept rounding up Acadians, herding them aboard British

Claude Picard's rendition of British and New England soldiers who burned the Acadians' houses, barns, and other buildings in order to discourage them from returning to Nova Scotia.

vessels, burning their houses, barns, and crops, and hunting down farmers and their families who had fled into the woods. By December, winter was forcing Acadians who had hidden in forests to surrender.

Colonel John Winslow's own words describe the tragedy, the confusion, and the use of bayonets. In his journal entry for October 8, 1755, at Grand Pré, he wrote, "Began to Embarke the Inhabitants who went off very Solentarily and unwillingly, the Women in Great Distress Carrying off Their Children In their arms. Others carrying their Decript Parents in their Carts and all their Goods Moving in great Confusion & appeared a Sceen of Woe & Distress ... the Kings Command was to me absolute & Should be absolutely obeyed & that I Did not Love to use Harsh Means but that the time Did not admit of Parlies and Delays and Then ordered the whole Troops to fix their Bayonets & advance Towards the French."

Some Anglo historians say the British, as they herded Acadians aboard vessels, tried to keep families together, but Acadians disagree. More than two centuries after the event Father Anselme Chiasson of Chéticamp wrote, "This was the Expulsion: they forced everyone at bayonet point to embark on boats in the midst of confusion, without any concern as to whether they put on the same boat members of the same family ... The boats left, filled with dismembered families, death and despair in the soul, carrying away an entire people that [the British] had sworn to get rid of forever. These human cargoes were dispersed, here and there along the Atlantic coast from Boston to Georgia, with the hope that they would be lost forever in the Anglo-Saxon colonies to the south."[5]

Lieutenant Colonel John Winslow delivered the grim news of the Deportation to Acadians he called together at Grand Pré.

As 1756 began, the British had shipped more than 6,000 Acadians to the Carolinas, Georgia, Maryland, Virginia, Pennsylvania, New York, Massachusetts, Connecticut, and other places where French-speaking Catholics were less than welcome. In the words of the American poet Henry Wadsworth Longfellow, author of the narrative poem "Evangeline: A Tale of Acadia," these Acadians endured "exile without end and a shame without equal in history. Thrown on distant shores, separated from each other, we saw them wander from town-to-town, without friends, without homes, without human hope, resigned, and only asking of the land, a tomb."

Hundreds fled to Prince Edward Island, or hid in northern New Brunswick, where Charles Deschamps de Boishébert, a Canadian, organized backwoods warfare against the British. Joseph Brossard, the swashbuckling "Beausoleil," commanded a privateer that captured British prizes in the Bay of Fundy. With his four sons and Acadians who had taken refuge near the Petitcodiac River, he also harassed British forces on land. Today, in Acadian memory, Beausoleil remains a hero, and Lawrence an arch-fiend.

It was in Grand Pré that, ninety-two years later, Longfellow set the homeland of the seventeen-year-old heroine Evangeline. In this doleful poem, the deportation separates her from Gabriel, the boy she loves, and during her futile search for him, many a nineteenth-century reader shed tears of sorrow. The poem became a kind of 'Gone With The Wind' of the great age of narrative verse, and long after the poet's death in 1882, its influence survived in Nova Scotia's promotion of the joys that awaited tourists in "the far-famed Land of Evangeline."

In May 1758, when Halifax was only nine years old, British brass gathered in the Great Pontac Hotel for an historic military banquet. The host was James Wolfe, commander of the British forces that would take Quebec the following year, and his guests included forty-six army and navy officers, mostly from Britain but also from New England. Some would one day find themselves fighting on opposite sides in the American Revolution, but for now they were all boozing and gorging together before attempting the second conquest of Fortress Louisbourg. Wolfe's bill for the night listed twenty-five bottles of brandy, fifty of claret, and seventy of Madeira, but the carousers had three days to recover before setting sail on the mission that would smash French power in what was once Acadia.

By previous standard of warfare in North America, the assault force was gigantic. Admiral Edward ("Old Dreadnought") Boscawen commanded 157 warships, transports, and smaller vessels, as well as 14,000 sailors, gunners, sappers, and to dig entrenchments, almost 200 miners. General Jeffrey Amherst was in charge of 13,000 soldiers, and his army and Boscawen's fleet boasted more than 2,000 pieces of artillery. The second siege of Louisbourg would feature a rare degree of cooperation between British forces on land and sea.

One of Amherst's brigade commanders was Wolfe. A prickly, red-headed officer, often in poor health, Wolfe at thirty-one was a hardened veteran of European campaigns. No genius as a military strategist and sometimes indecisive, he was a fearless and charismatic leader under fire. As the second great attack on Louisbourg began, the men in his landing boats faced roaring surf, a rocky shore, and heavy French fire. But a few light infantry reached a cove the French could not see, and Wolfe, brandishing his cane among the whistling bullets, sloshed through the crashing waves to join them. The famous 78th Fraser's Highlanders, joined by crack grenadiers, poured onto the beachhead. The British routed the French musketeers, and, within hours, the invaders drove the defenders inside the fortress and began to bring their big guns ashore.

Louisbourg was in better shape than ever before. The garrison boasted high morale, capable officers, ample food, and good guns. The population had grown to 8,000. Yet the French governor, Chevalier de Drucour, commanded

American poet, Henry Wadsworth Longfellow, author of "Evangeline," immortalized Acadia as the Land of Evangeline.

A portrayal of Evangeline in one of numerous editions of the classic poem.

James Wolfe was one of General Amherst's brigade commanders in the second siege of Louisbourg and the leader of British troops in the battle of the Plains of Abraham that vanquished Quebec for Britain.

only 3,500 soldiers, bolstered by militia, 3,500 sailors, and eleven vessels. As the British bombardment thundered through June and into July, his wife went out every morning to boost French morale by firing off three guns herself, but the Drucours knew Louisbourg would fall. With his valiant defence, which lasted almost two months, the French governor did what he hoped to do: tie up British forces for so long that they would have to postpone their invasion of Quebec.

By midsummer, 1758, the British had sunk or burned all the French ships. They had blown a dozen gaping holes through the walls of the fortress. "The French cannon had been silenced so effectively that to Drucour they seemed more like the minute guns at a funeral than a defence."[6] On July 26, with British brass assembled on the parade ground at Louisbourg, Drucour marched up to Admiral Boscawen, saluted, and gave him his sword. By the terms of his surrender, the British got not only Cape Breton, but also Prince Edward Island. Within days, the people of Halifax and Boston were singing and dancing in the streets.

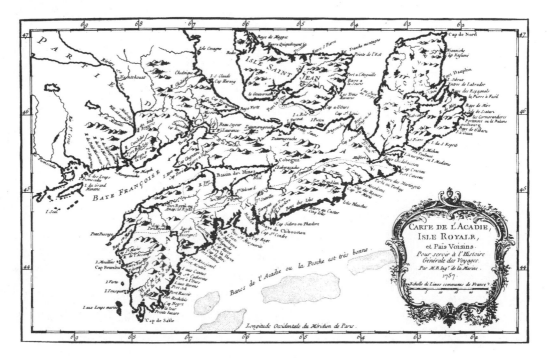

A French map of Acadia and Île Royale in 1757.

Left: The burning of the ship Prudent, one of the last two French ships to be captured by the British in Louisbourg Harbour, 1758.

British General Jeffery Amherst led the 1758 siege of Louisbourg.

A view of Louisbourg from the lighthouse prior to its defeat by the British in 1758.

Simeon Perkins was a prominent merchant in Liverpool.

Perkins House, Liverpool, constructed in 1766, is now part of the Nova Scotia Museum.

An 1813 painting of Elizabeth Headly Perkins, the second wife of Simeon Perkins.

CHAPTER 14

"HALIFAX HAD CEASED TO BE NOVA SCOTIA"

In consecutive springs, Nova Scotian ports—first, Halifax, and then Louisbourg—served as launching spots for the century's greatest British victories over the French in North America. It was from Louisbourg that the British sailed for the St. Lawrence River on May 4, 1759, to win the battle of the Plains of Abraham and capture Quebec. With the fall of Montreal in 1760, French power in Canada vanished. France had spent so much money and blood on Canada that some French actually celebrated Britain's triumph.

The British guaranteed Louisbourg would never again harbour French troops. They shipped its cut stone, quarried in Normandy decades before, to Halifax, where the wealthy used it to build mansions. Soldiers and sailors then spent months blowing up the rest of the fortifications.

In 1760, the British were still rounding up Acadians for deportation. Father Anselme Chiasson wrote, "This manhunt extended to all the coasts and forests of the three provinces of the Gulf. It lasted ... interminable years, bloody, indescribable, where the inoffensive Acadians, tracked like wild animals, slaughtered like dogs or deported without mercy to areas where the people were fanatically hostile, wandered like ghosts in a nightmare of tears and blood ... "[1]

From Prince Edward Island alone the British shipped roughly 3,500 Acadians to France. Of nine vessels in one deportation fleet, Henri Blanchard wrote in his "Histoire des Acadiens de l'Île du Prince Édouard," "One stayed three months outside Plymouth [England] with its 173 passengers with hardly any food and dying of thirst; another, storm-ridden, landed at Boulogne with 179 survivors; two others sank, taking 700 victims to their deaths beneath the waves."[2]

After the fall of Louisbourg and Quebec, the deportation would seem both inhumane and unnecessary. Lawrence, however, was not cruel by nature, and "the chief elements in the affair were confusion, misunderstanding, and fear ... At no time did those who had the power also have the information to decide aright." When Lawrence died on October 19, 1760, it shocked his friends "that this enormous, bluff, and competent man could have been struck down so quickly after catching a chill."[3] As the hero of Halifax, he earned a monument in St. Paul's Church. As the antihero of the Acadians, he earned a deathless reputation as the brute who had sent their forebears on the grim wanderings that became the central epic of their culture.

Barrington Meeting House, built by settlers from Cape Cod, Massachusetts, in 1765, is Canada's oldest standing non-conformist house of worship.

By 1763, the British had deported 10,000 Acadians, roughly three-quarters of the entire population. Owing to filth and overcrowding on ships, and ramshackle lodgings in seaports, smallpox killed hundreds before they reached the English colonies to the south. The survivors endured not only the reluctance of the American colonists to feed and house them, but virulent anti-Catholicism and the hatred that the French massacre of Braddock's redcoats eight years before had aroused.

Certain colonies refused to accept Acadians. Thus, many of these exiles, miserable and stateless, began a grim journey that took them as far away as Louisiana, the West Indies, and France. They were searching for a land where they could make a fresh start. Those who returned to Nova Scotia found New Englanders on what had been their land. Once France was finished in North America, the Mi'kmaq, who now depended for their survival on European products, made peace with the British, and more and more fugitive Acadians surrendered.

By the Treaty of Paris (1763), France kept St. Pierre and Miquelon, tiny islands off southern Newfoundland, as shelters for its fishermen, but recognized British ownership of everything else it had once claimed in northern North America. In the south, it retained Louisiana, west of the Mississippi, but the British-American Empire now stretched, without a break, from Labrador to Florida. English-speaking people enjoyed unchallenged domination of all that was once Acadia, and the British felt confident enough to allow Acadians willing to sign the oath of allegiance to trickle back to Nova Scotia. Some returned from the American colonies, Quebec, and France, while others emerged from New Brunswick forests where they had been hiding for years.

Claude Picard's depiction of the Acadian migrations is somber. Once France's claim in North America was renounced by the British, with broken spirits those Acadians who trickled back took the Oath of Allegiance.

With New Englanders working what had once been their farms, and the British wanting them scattered in small groups, they settled on remote and mostly inferior land: in Nova Scotia, on the west coast, and at Chéticamp and Isle Madame in Cape Breton; in Prince Edward Island, around Malpeque Bay; and in New Brunswick, in the north, northeast, and along the St. John River. (Loyalists would later oust Acadians from around Fredericton, and push them north.) All these districts still belonged to the single colony of Nova Scotia.

Peace plunged Halifax into economic torpor. Without the strategic purpose warfare gave the colony, the British began to regard Nova Scotia as the writer-statesman Edmund Burke did in 1782: "Good God! What sum the nursing of that ill-thriven, hard-visaged, and ill-favoured brat, has cost to this wittol nation ... "

British statesman Edmund Burke wrote some early Nova Scotia imprints.

Long before that outburst, Britain was slashing funds for Nova Scotia. Between 1758 and 1763, the annual grant to the colony dropped from £50,000 to £5,000. Nova Scotia and particularly its capital were not used to such neglect. As the flow of money from the British treasury dwindled, Halifax grew lazier, gloomier, and more venal. Its population peaked at 6,000 in 1752, but by 1763 thousands had left, soldiers and sailors had ripped apart abandoned dwellings for firewood, and only about 1,300 people still stuck it out in their unpainted, weatherbeaten houses on sour soil. Most Haligonians were discouraged, and many officials corrupt.

But over in the Annapolis Valley, up in the Chignecto neighbourhood, and in "out-settlements" along the South Shore, the birth of a more self-sufficient Nova Scotia was under way. Even before the conquest of Louisbourg, Governor Lawrence decided that if Nova Scotia had kept 10,000 Acadians in comfort, then it could do the same for British Americans. As it happened, a bulge of migration was already moving north in New England.

Johnathan Belcher, first Chief Justice of Nova Scotia and lieutenant-governor 1760–63.

After generations of British American colonists had taken the best lands between the mountains and the sea, it was only on the frontiers that newcomers and younger sons could satisfy their lust for spreads of their own. With the French defeated, the safest frontiers lay to the north. In American history, the romance of "the way west" has overshadowed the earlier way north. From Pennsylvania northward, American pioneers in the eighteenth century mostly moved to Maine, Vermont, New Hampshire, central Canada, and in the 1760s Nova Scotia.

In 1758, and again in 1759, Governor Lawrence of Nova Scotia had announced in the "Boston Gazette" that new townships were being established in this province on lands the Acadians had vacated. These lands looked even more attractive when Britain forbade American colonists from settling on Indian hunting grounds west of the Appalachians. This policy, and the disbanding of armies, heightened New England's hunger for land. Lawrence lived just long enough "to know that Nova Scotia would certainly be populated, that firstcomers had attached themselves to nearly all the new townships, and that only a catastrophe could hold off the rest."[4]

The first significant batch of the new settlers, the Planters, arrived in June 1760, in a flotilla of twenty-two ships chartered by the government of Nova Scotia and escorted by a brig of war. Two new townships had been created: Cornwallis and Horton. Halifax required the appointment of commissioners for all townships with dyke systems. They would have to approve and administer major dyke projects and be responsible for repairs, maintenance, or construction of dykes.

All this went nicely with the Planters' understanding of local government. These New Englanders were sturdy, resourceful descendants of North American pioneers. They were used to running their own affairs, and their political outlook would prove to be more democratic than the English governors of Nova Scotia would like. They had brought with them a tradition that included the election of local officials for agrarian, legal, and political duties, and they simply added the dyking responsibilities to the other duties of township officials.

The new arrivals faced an overwhelming task that must have shaken the optimism of even the most fervent Planter. They had almost everything to learn about dyking, which requires not only skill, but understanding of the great natural rhythms working between the tides and the marsh. The marsh had been untended for the five years since the Acadian Deportation, and salt

The proclamation for the first general election in 1758 by Governor Lawrence established the composition of the Nova Scotia Legislative Assembly, the constituencies, and the qualifications required of candidates and voters.

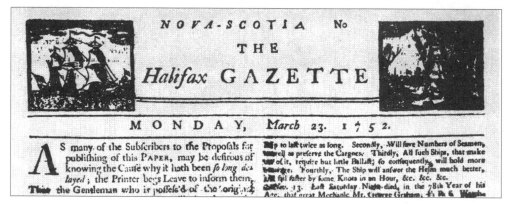

The "Halifax Gazette" published by John Bushell in 1752 was the first newspaper published in what is now Canada.

water had saturated it. The dykes were broken, and a wild storm in 1759 had flooded much of the dykeland.

Clearly the Planters needed the labour and dyking skills of the Acadians. Over the next few years they petitioned the Halifax authorities for permission to use the Acadians for restoring the dykelands. There were 2,000 prisoners in British hands, and other Acadians were coming out of the woods and surrendering. Work on the dykes proceeded.

By 1768, some 8,000 New Englanders were established in Nova Scotia, the largest component in the province's population of 13,000. To Liverpool and other South Shore spots came fishermen and boat-builders from Nantucket and Cape Cod. To the Annapolis Valley came farmers from Massachusetts, Rhode Island, and Connecticut. Arriving when the colony was all but deserted, they "left an enduring impression on its customs and institutions. While not the largest single migration to enter the province, it is unquestionably the most important."[5]

Other parts of the province were also attracting settlers. To the townships of Truro and Onslow, in the formerly Acadian neighbourhood of Cobequid, came Ulstermen and their families. These were Scotch-Irish Presbyterians from northern Ireland. Fleeing both the mercantile policy of England, which was destroying their industries in Ulster, and religious persecution, some journeyed to Nova Scotia directly from northern Ireland, but most came from

View of the Cobequid Mountains known in the 1770s as the Lady Mountains. Areas such as Onslow and Truro, south of this range in present-day Colchester County, were settled by the Planters and Ulster-Scots and Irish from New England in the years following the Acadian Deportation.

settlements in New Hampshire. The promoter who persuaded the New Hampshire crowd to move to Nova Scotia was one of their own, Colonel Alexander McNutt. In "The Neutral Yankees of Nova Scotia," John Bartlet Brebner called him "a highly persuasive, distinctly untrustworthy Ulster immigrant to North America ... a fertile liar."[6]

Speculator-hustlers like McNutt, land-grabbers close to the governor, and upstart development companies in distant cities all sabotaged fairness in the redistribution of land among newcomers. In Philadelphia, however, a leading group of citizens formed a company that, unlike many others, met its obligation to install settlers on its grant. In 1765 they had obtained a grant of 80 000 hectares along the north shore of what is now Pictou County, with the usual provisos regarding settling the land within a certain time.

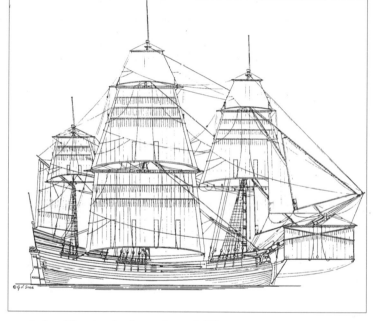

Drawing of the ship Hector by Shea. The brig carried almost 200 Scots across the Atlantic to settle Pictou in northern Nova Scotia

In the spring of 1767, the Philadelphia Company sent a small brigantine, the Betsey (sometimes called the Hope), carrying six families from Pennsylvania and Maryland, to the shores of Pictou County. The forest that confronted them was so dark, towering, and interminable, the Rev. George Patterson said in his history of the county, "Their hearts sank as they contemplated the idea of wresting a subsistence from soil so encumbered."[7]

Wrest a subsistence they did, however; by 1770, after other British Americans had arrived, Pictou boasted 176 settlers. The land of one of the leaders of the community, Pennsylvania-born John Harris, had produced fifty bushels of wheat and oats the previous year. Harris already had six servants or labourers and owned eleven head of livestock.

For at least a century, Scots had been leaving their homeland for the West Indies and America, but few had yet ventured to Nova Scotia. Then, in 1745, the Jacobite Rebellion broke out. The clans fought for the ascendancy to the throne of Prince Charles Stuart—Bonnie Prince Charlie, the Young Pretender—but in 1746 the English defeated them in the grisly battle of Culloden Moor. Now the collapse of the traditional clan system accelerated, and economic pressure forced a change in the near-feudal relationship between Highland chiefs and their clansmen. The chiefs had become landlords, and their clansmen tenant farmers. Moreover, the victorious English forced the chiefs who had backed the prince to pay heavy forfeits, and the

Arrival of the Scots at Mabou in the 1800s.

lairds found themselves having to charge high rents for land that had once been held in common. Many farmers would leave the Highlands because they could not afford the rent for their farms.

Other Scots came to Nova Scotia because their landlords, choosing to graze animals on the land, evicted tenant farmers. As Bluenose novelist Charles Bruce once put it, "Some got pitched off the land when the lairds began to see more money in sheep than in people."8 But the deeper and more lasting reason for the tide of emigration lay in Scotland's having become seriously over-populated. Only when it became brutally clear that the country could not provide enough work or food did the Scots cross the Atlantic. They had no choice. Leaving forever was better than endless poverty, and possibly starvation. Finally, by moving to Nova Scotia they could fulfil a dream: they could own their own farms.

By 1772, the Philadelphia Company had not found its required quota of settlers, and the deadline for peopling its land grant was approaching. Company member John Pagan, a merchant trading between Glasgow and

North America, owned an old vessel, the Hector. In a Scottish newspaper he described Pictou as an emigrant's dream, and in the spring of 1773 the Hector sailed north to Loch Brom on the west coast. It lay there for weeks while the news of its coming voyage to Nova Scotia travelled around the Highlands. On July 1, the vessel sailed for Pictou with about 200 passengers, most of whom spoke only Gaelic.

None of the passengers had ever crossed the Atlantic before, and they now endured a nightmarish eleven-week voyage. Smallpox and dysentery wiped out eighteen people. The Scots ran so low on food they ended up eating the mouldy oatcakes they had thrown out as garbage, thriftily salvaged by one Hugh McLeod. Gales attacked the Hector. It was an old Dutch ship, so rotten the Scots could pluck wood from its sides. On September 15, 1773, however, it limped into Pictou Harbour with thirty-three Scottish families and twenty-five single men, the first immigrant ship from Scotland to Nova Scotia.

A few Scottish settlers had already reached Prince Edward Island, but historians have long seen the arrival of the Hector as not only the start of a flow of Scots to Nova Scotia that would swell to tens of thousands, but also the beginning of the Scottish-Canadian community of the entire nation.

Lieutenant-Governor Michael Francklin 1766–76.

The Scots, however, were not the only significant group of British immigrants to arrive in Nova Scotia just before the American Revolution. By 1770, the lieutenant-governor of the colony, the mercurial land-speculator and merchant Michael Francklin found himself "land poor." While he owned thousands of hectares of Nova Scotia, his failure to fulfil settlement conditions, unpaid quit-rents, and shortage of cash had plunged him into financial hell. To escape, he looked to far-off Yorkshire where, like the Scots, tenant farmers faced spiralling rents. From 1772 to 1775, Francklin lured more than 1,000 Yorkshire people to Nova Scotia. They settled on the Isthmus of Chignecto, south of it around Oxford and Maccan, and north of it in the future New Brunswick.

They were as fine a crowd of settlers as the colony's English masters could possibly have wanted. Some were "men of substance" who bought farms from New Englanders. Since a wave of improvements in agricultural techniques had swept England, these Yorkshiremen were better farmers than their New England-born neighbours. Moreover, they were solid citizens and loyal Britishers. They knew little or nothing about the cauldron of American grievances against mother England that would soon boil over in an astounding rebellion.

Left: King George III.

Right: Richard John Uniacke, charged with treason for his part in the Cumberland siege, later became attorney-general of Nova Scotia.

His Majesty's brig Observer engaging the American privateer Jack off Halifax Harbour, 1782.

CHAPTER 15

NOVA SCOTIA SAYS "NO THANKS" TO REVOLUTION

After a century and a half of building industries and trade, and developing their own political philosophy and styles of local government, the Thirteen Colonies in New England began to buck Britain's efforts to enrich itself at their expense. Britain believed in mercantilism, an economic policy in which the mother country defined colonies as estates to be worked purely for its own advantage. Out of mercantilism came the Navigation Acts. Their purpose was to expand England's carrying trade, get from the colonies materials it could not produce itself, and establish colonial markets for its manufactured goods. A common New England response was smuggling.

The colonies did derive some benefits from the Navigation Acts. England granted certain colonial products—American tobacco, for instance—a monopoly of the home market and preferential tariffs. On the other hand, the mother country's mercantilism destroyed the thriving industries of the Scotch-Irish in northern Ireland. It later hounded Ulster settlers in Nova Scotia right into their houses, where they endured official rebukes for owning spinning wheels to avoid buying English linen. While throughout the American colonies mercantilism discouraged manufacturing, it was long tolerated because England enforced it so loosely.

In 1763, however, the new ministry of George Grenville tried to tighten Britain's control over its colonies, make them earn more revenue for England, and not unreasonably, force them to pay for their own defence. "The tax levied on molasses and sugar in 1764 caused some consternation among New England merchants and makers of rum; the tax itself was smaller than the one already on the books, but the promise of stringent enforcement was novel and ominous."[1]

Then came the Stamp Act of 1765. The first direct tax the British Parliament levied on American colonies, it decreed that virtually any printed paper that any publisher distributed would have to bear an official British stamp. Parliament earmarked the revenue from the stamp sales for colonial defence. In New York and New England, influential businessmen furiously attacked this odious new tax. American merchants even boycotted English goods. The Stamp Act inspired the organization of secret gangs called the Sons of Liberty. They forced stamp distributors to resign and incited both the destruction of stamped paper and violence against British officials.

In Nova Scotia, Governor Montague Wilmot reported that, with respect to the Stamp Act, "the Sentiments of a decent and dutifull Acquiescence ... prevail here." Harvard-trained lawyer John Adams, a future president of the United States, sneered that Nova Scotians were merely "a set of fugitives and vagabonds ... kept in fear by a fleet and an army."

In the fall of 1765, however, Anthony Henry, who operated the "Gazette" in Halifax, and his employee Isaiah Thomas, a printer's apprentice from Boston, launched a spirited campaign against the Stamp Act. The "Gazette" reported the resistance movements in Philadelphia, Pittsburg, New York, and Boston; published the stamp upside down, with cartoons painting it as the work of Satan; and depicted coffins to symbolize what the Act had already done to American newspapers. "Finally young Thomas mutilated the "Gazette's" whole supply of the obnoxious stamped paper by cutting out the stamps, and Henry perforce printed several issues on unstamped paper, in direct defiance of the law."[2] The authorities promptly cancelled the "Gazette's" printing contract and banished Thomas from Halifax.

The Stamp Act Congress of October 1765 lured to New York City delegates from nine of the future United States and adopted a Declaration of Rights and Grievances. Its main point was that Britain did not have the constitutional right to tax colonists who had no representation in parliament. Parliament repealed the Stamp Act in 1766, but invited future trouble by declaring Britain's right to tax its colonies.

A sermon (preached in Lunenburg) printed by Halifax printer Anthony Henry in 1770. Henry blatantly opposed Britain's Stamp Act and printed material in defiance of the law.

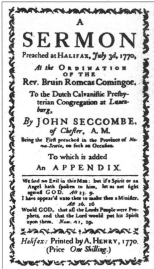

When skirmishes near Boston ignited the American Revolution on April 19, 1775, the population of the Thirteen Colonies stood at about 2.5 million. Nova Scotia's people totalled a mere 20,000, and not even a tenth lived in Halifax. Unlike merchants in the Thirteen Colonies, who had unleashed American radicalism by daring to compete with the British mercantile system, Halifax merchants milked and nurtured their London contacts. Halifax profited from British wars, bought British goods, and lived off grants from the British parliament. "A little group of merchants, war-contractors, and officials, whose business connections lay chiefly in England and whose boss and patron, Joshua Mauger, had retired to London, managed to run the capital and the province pretty much as they liked ... "[3]

As a principal holder of Nova Scotia's debt, Mauger had a high stake in its credit. He knew that whenever the threat of war inspired the British government to feed money to Nova Scotia, the colony could be profitable. The trick was to keep Nova Scotia under his control during its depressed peacetimes, but reap a fortune whenever Britain's defence expenditure increased, and its free-spending forces poured into Halifax. If the more affluent Haligonians stayed loyal to reap the profits of warfare, others were loyal because, after Britain stationed thousands of redcoats there, it was the only safe thing to be.

A well-known icon of the American Revolution.

But what about the rest of the colony? Prince Edward Island had become a colony in its own right in 1769, but Nova Scotia still included the future New Brunswick. In the far-off St. John River Valley, the Isthmus of Chignecto, the Cumberland country, the Cobequid hills, the Annapolis Valley, and the South Shore ports, men openly preached revolution. The Scotch-Irish, whose roots lay in Ulster, had old reasons for detesting English rule, but more important than that, at least two-thirds of all Nova Scotians were New Englanders. New England had included Nova Scotia in its world of trade even when the colony had been French Acadia. New Englanders had conquered the mainland in 1710, taken Louisbourg in 1745, poured into Halifax in the 1750s, urged and carried out the expulsion of the Acadians, and settled on their lands by the thousands. Surely these people were ripe for conversion to rebellion.

Six years before the revolution, resentment against British rule in Nova Scotia's out-settlements was so strong that a nervous governor banned town meetings. But just before the American Revolution began, meetings did occur in Nova Scotia townships, and the Halifax authorities saw the participants as potential rebels. Would the ex-New Englanders not welcome to Nova Scotia an invading army of brethren from the land many still called home?

Perhaps, but they were too poor, weak, vulnerable, scattered, and isolated to raise an army of their own. They knew little about their fellow colonists outside their own villages; Nova Scotia had no sense of colony-wide solidarity. Moreover, it was far from the heart of the revolution and too remote to get caught up in its excitement. Refusing to join it, however, did not mean Nova Scotians wanted to kill revolutionaries. After two American vessels waltzed into Yarmouth, kidnapped its militia officers, and warned the townsfolk not to dare take up arms against them, Yarmouthians told Governor Francis Legge they would rather not put on uniforms and carry muskets to help quell the revolution:

"We were almost all of us born in New England, we have Fathers, Brothers & Sisters in that country, divided betwixt natural affection to our nearest relations, and good Faith and Friendship to our King and Country, we want to know, if we may be permitted at this time to live in a peaceable State, as we look on that to be the only situation in which we with our Wives and Children, can be in any tolerable degree safe."

While the governing council at Halifax rejected this entreaty as "utterly Absurd and Inconsistent with the duty of subjects," most Nova Scotians felt exactly as Yarmouth did. New Englanders had once denounced the neutrality of the Acadians as utterly absurd and inconsistent with the duty of subjects. Now, only twenty years later, the New Englanders in Nova Scotia insisted on neutrality for themselves. "The Neutral Yankees" had replaced "The French Neutrals."

Some Nova Scotia Yankees, however, itched to overthrow British power. They included: John Allan, a Scottish-born farmer living among New Englanders on the Isthmus of Chignecto; Jonathan Eddy, an ex-soldier from Massachusetts who had served at Fort Cumberland (formerly Beauséjour) and later moved back to the Chignecto marshlands; and the Rev. James Lyon, a graduate of Princeton College who had spent years as a poorly paid missionary in the Truro-Cobequid-Pictou area. He had encountered Alexander McNutt and had been tempted by McNutt's flow of words to speculate in land. When his presbytery in New Jersey heard of this, they were not pleased, and in the end Lyon returned to New England and became town minister in Machias, Maine.

Opposite page, top: Drawing of Fort Cumberland, formerly Fort Beauséjour, by Benjamin Grey, 1803.

Opposite page, bottom: "The environs of Fort Cumberland in the Bay of Fundy" as drawn by J. F. W. DesBarres.

Jonathan Eddy was among the Nova Scotia Yankees eager to overthrow British power.

When the revolution broke out, he hoped to use his knowledge of Nova Scotia in the service of the cause. In August of 1755, these three and others urged George Washington to send 1,000 men, four armed vessels, and eight transport ships up the Bay of Fundy to capture Windsor. The rebels planned to use Windsor as headquarters for a general uprising and the destruction of Halifax.

General Washington liked their spirit, but not their plan. Having no navy, he wrote: "As to furnishing Vessels of Force, you, Gentn, will anticipate me, in pointing our Weakness and the Enemy's Strength at Sea. There would be great Danger that, with the best preparation we could make, they would fall an easy prey either to the Men of War on that Station, or some who would be detach'd from Boston ... [Moreover] our Situation as to Ammunition absolutely forbids our sending a single ounce out of the Camp at present."

Without the help of George Washington or Congress, Jonathan Eddy persevered. Encouraged by rumours that Nova Scotians would flock to join an invading army, and urged on by Lyon, who anticipated pillaging Yorkshire Loyalists, Eddy rounded up a few Nova Scotia Yankees, Mi'kmaq, and Acadians and set out in November 1776 to capture Fort Cumberland. His friend John

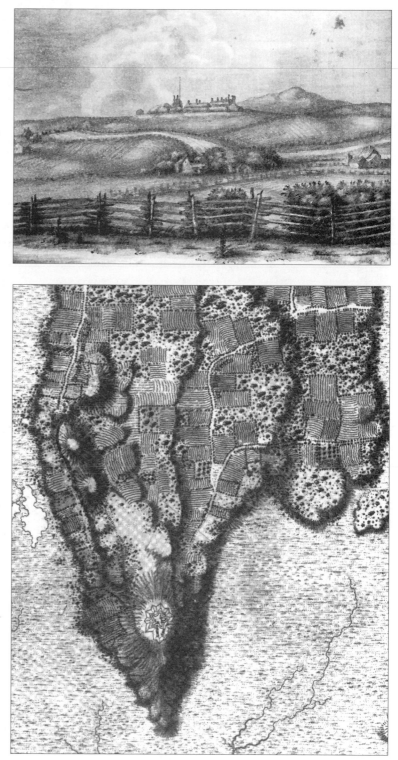

Allan warned him this independent "invasion" would fail, and, sure enough, it was a fiasco.

Eddy's force was so puny and his lack of artillery so obvious that even the most pro-American of the Cumberland farmers found it hard to muster revolutionary fervour. Moreover, the staunch Britishness of the local Yorkshiremen discouraged the pro-American uprising of Eddy's dreams. In the end, he could not assemble more than a hundred attackers at a time, while

American naval hero John Paul Jones led rebel raiders into Canso and was among the privateers sacking coastal villages in Nova Scotia.

snug within the fortifications that doughty Yorkshire carpenters had strengthened, and under the patient command of Colonel Joseph Goreham, sat perhaps twice as many Royal Fencible Americans. Eddy and his harum-scarum force conducted a farcical blockade of the fort for twenty days, but then British marines arrived from Windsor and, with the help of the garrison, chased them back toward Maine. Thus ended the only attempted conquest of Nova Scotia during the American Revolution.

Believing Eddy had intimidated the local farmers who had joined his force, Goreham forgave most of them, but not Richard John Uniacke, a strapping, twenty-six-year-old Irishman. Uniacke stood trial for treason, was released, and later became solicitor general of Nova Scotia, Speaker of the Legislature, attorney-general, a member of the governing council, advocate-general of the Vice-Admiralty Court, owner of the biggest law practice in the colony, and father of twelve children.

While the invasion flopped, the devastation that American privateers inflicted on the coastal villages of Nova Scotia was only beginning. Outside Halifax, scarcely a town in the colony escaped the booty-hungry raiders. Year after year they came. As soon as some ports recovered from an attack, the privateers hit them again. While the attackers sometimes spared the property of relatives and collaborators, and persuaded some to join them in the joys of looting, they left many Loyalists poverty-stricken. The victims often faced starvation.

The privateers were seldom bloodthirsty, but their procedure was "a grim, drab business of systematic intimidation and plunder to the last degree of a helpless little settlement."[4]

When John Paul Jones led rebel raiders into Canso, they burned buildings, looted homes, stole vessels, and destroyed the local fishing industry. Jones later earned immortality for telling a British captain who invited him to surrender his crippled ship, "Sir, I have not yet begun to fight." But at Canso he did not have to fight; the enemy was a huddle of fishermen and their families. In a later century and still angry, Guysborough County historian A. C. Jost compared the thuggery of Jones to that of the German submarines that sank Canso fishing schooners during the First World War.

The behaviour of privateers like Jones stiffened Nova Scotia's loyalty to the Crown, sapped pro-revolution sentiment, and inspired retaliation. Bluenose privateers soon sought revenge and profit. These seagoing adventurers mostly haunted the New England coast, but some cruised all the way from the Caribbean to Newfoundland. They brought scores of Yankee prizes into Nova Scotia ports. In just one year, Nova Scotian privateers showed up at Halifax alone with nearly fifty Yankee vessels.

While the out-settlements endured the rebels' plundering, Halifax swarmed with free-spending British soldiers and sailors, privateersmen with hard cash from the auctioning of their prizes, dockyard workers with money to burn, and hundreds of Loyalist refugees from Boston. "The merchants, the landlords, the brewers ... the bawdy-houses reaped a harvest; but the ordinary townsfolk ... found themselves in open competition with a horde of strangers for a roof above their heads and the very food upon their plates."[5]

The naval battle in Louisbourg Harbour between the British and American vessels, July 21, 1781.

In the spring of 1776 the American War of Independence took a great turn. British General William Howe withdrew to Halifax from Boston along with a huge number of Loyalist troops and civilians. After several months in Halifax—the sole camp for the British forces in North America—he departed to command reinforcements in New York.

The British Army evacuates Boston—thousands of Loyalist refugees depart for Nova Scotia, an event that would change the face of the province forever.

CHAPTER 16

LOYALISTS: THE GREAT DELUGE

If Nova Scotia had joined the American Revolution, Canada might never have come into being. The seacoast colony included all of the future New Brunswick, and from Cape Breton to Gaspé, its ports commanded the gateway to the St. Lawrence. Quebec, conquered only fifteen years before the rebellion began, was French. West of Montreal lay a wilderness shared by native peoples and a few "coureurs de bois." If Nova Scotia had swung over to the revolution, the Union Jack would have vanished from everywhere in English-speaking North America except Newfoundland.

Long before the revolution ended, the first migration of Loyalists reached Halifax; it was the pivotal event in Canadian history. In 1776, British troops evacuated Boston, sailed to Halifax, and brought with them more than 900 loyal refugees who had fled rebel mobs. Shivering, impoverished, huddled in tents, most yearned to escape "Nova Scarcity" forever. In 1783, however, some were still in Halifax to greet further thousands of refugees who had been living under the protection of the British army in New York City. Some Loyalists went to England, the West Indies, Ontario, Quebec, Prince Edward Island, and Newfoundland, but most came to Nova Scotia.

It was a young, promising, royal colony, unlikely ever to succumb to the republicanism that Loyalists had such good reason to loathe. They swallowed reports that "the land was good, the cattle plentiful, the taxes few, the government cheap," and that Nova Scotia, protected from the vile Yankees by a royal government, was in a good position to exploit the fisheries, the British market, and West Indies trade.

Nearly 34,000 newcomers swamped the 20,000 people of Nova Scotia, and a further 6,000 settled in Canada West, the future Ontario. By November 1783, 12,500 had landed in Halifax. Fourteen thousand more sailed to the St. John River. "Here, in a river valley which seemed one dense and unending mass of green," Donald Creighton wrote, "the whole long adventure of their flight—the perils, hardships and dissipation that had filled their days with excitement—ended at last in the terrible reality of pioneering."[1]

Joseph Frederick Wallet DesBarres, Lieutenant Governor of Cape Breton, 1784-87.

Since Halifax was too far away to govern the throngs on the St. John, Britain in 1784 carved out of Nova Scotia the colony of New Brunswick and named Fredericton its capital. Expecting thousands of Loyalists to descend on Cape Breton Island, Britain named it, too, a separate colony with its own governor, Joseph Frederick Wallet DesBarres. Born in either Switzerland or Paris to a Huguenot family, this surveyor, mapmaker, colonizer, army officer, and military engineer was one of the most extraordinary characters in Nova Scotia's history. But a diplomat he was not. As a governor, his prickly, unyielding personality and knack for making enemies hampered Cape Breton's development. Loyalist

South Entrance of Grand Passage.

DesBarres' cartographic skills and his published drawings in "Atlantic Neptune" won him international acclaim. The Grand Passage (Digby County) is one of many drawings of the north Atlantic seaboard DesBarres completed in the years 1773-77.

predominance there soon vanished. Cape Breton endured thirty-six tempestuous years as a colony before Britain put it back under Nova Scotia's jurisdiction. DesBarres died in 1824; he was 102.

By 1791, enough Loyalists had settled in Quebec's west to justify splitting the colony into Upper and Lower Canada, the future provinces of Ontario and Quebec.

Finally, the Loyalists exploded the cultural, linguistic, and religious patterns of British North America. Now, for the first time, the Protestant, English-speaking people outnumbered the Catholic, French-speaking people. This strange invasion by the defeated and bullied Loyalists guaranteed that British North America would become what Lord Durham, in 1839, would call "two nations warring in the bosom of a single state."

For some American Tories, loyalty was like a religious conviction; no matter what, they would live and die under the Union Jack. Other Americans were Loyalists because they had been on Britain's payroll, and 19,000 more had enlisted in British units with names like the King's American Regiment and the King's American Dragoons. Pro-revolution Patriots seized their homes, and later, when the victors proved vengeful and bloodthirsty, the Loyalist soldiers had no choice but to join the civilian exiles. Some native peoples, religious groups, and European minorities became Loyalists because they preferred the tolerance of British rule to the Patriots' mobocracy. Many Blacks joined the British military in return for freedom from their American masters, while others arrived in Nova Scotia still enslaved to Loyalist masters.

The house of Sydney Loyalists Rev. Ranna Cossit and his wife, Thankful. It was built in 1787-88, after their move to Cape Breton from New Hampshire.

In all, more than 3,000 black Loyalists came to the colony. Still other Americans were Loyalists because that was what their neighbours were, or because they lived near camps of British troops.

Some had ignoble motives. General Benedict Arnold was a traitor to the revolution. And, since the British government offered Loyalists not only compensation for their losses, but also free transportation, land, rations, building supplies, tools, and farm animals, assorted drifters and opportunists also joined the exiles.

Many Loyalists had been middle-class fence-sitters of the revolution. Many agreed with the Patriots about the desperate need to reform the British Empire and revitalize colonial institutions, but they wanted to achieve the improvements without bloodshed. What often pushed moderates into loyalism was the Patriots' extremism. Most American states insisted their residents undergo a patriotic test, and those who refused were constantly spied upon or, worse, fell victim to mob violence.

An illustration depicting the evacuation of New York by the British military and Loyalist civilians destined for Nova Scotia.

The Sons of Liberty crushed liberty. It was the Loyalists who had urged freedom of speech and the right to dissent from the mob's opinion. It was the Loyalists who had objected to the enforcement of ideological conformity and opposed the new totalitarianism. They lost. They had to leave.

The brutality that mobs inflicted on Loyalists aroused an anti-Americanism that lingered in Canada for generations. In the last essay New Brunswick historian W. S. MacNutt wrote before he died in 1976—exactly two centuries after the Declaration of Independence—he described the rebels in terms that would have enraged many Americans:

"Gangs of vigilantes, mouthing slogans of liberty ... moved through the countryside to force compliance on all and sundry ... Plunder became commonplace ... Unprotected women and children were stripped of their belongings and driven from their homes. The observation of a Georgian lady that 'the scum rose to the top' was applicable everywhere ... .Seldom has this systematic terror of the American Revolution been presented in popular accounts ... Admittedly there was no guillotine, but there is opportunity to speculate on the relative merits of tarring and feathering as against the compulsory and liberal doses of castor oil administered by Mussolini's squadrone in Italy."[2]

John Wentworth and his wife and cousin, Frances, became the most illustrious Loyalists in Halifax. A graduate of Harvard, Wentworth was the scion of a wealthy New England family and popular on both sides of the Atlantic. He was the first surveyor-general of the King's Woods in Maine and New

Hampshire, and then governor of New Hampshire, with an estate that boasted fifty servants and a mansion thirty metres wide. When rebel gangs came for him, he and Frances fled with their infant son, while a mob descended on his mansion to strip it of its furniture and wallpaper. In Halifax, Frances shone as the most beautiful woman in society. In his biography of Wentworth, "The Loyalist Governor," Brian Cuthbertson described Frances: "She stood first in fashion and dressed herself in quite magnificent clothes, favouring the wearing of splendidly coloured feathers in her hair."[3]

For generations, Canadians have thought of Loyalists as John Wentworths—as Harvard men, Conservatives, Anglicans, and luminaries of New England's aristocracy and governing classes. A few did fit the picture. They brought to Nova Scotia their Hepplewhite and Chippendale chairs, their mahogany tables, silver wine strainers, pewter candlesticks, tortoise-shell combs, and as many of their other valuables as they could cram aboard the refugee ships leaving New York. In Halifax, Loyalist gentlemen wore velvet coats with silver buttons, Loyalist ladies powdered their hair and dressed in silk, and together they played cards, enjoyed a busy round of concerts and feasts, and danced minuets at the governor's balls.

They were, however, but a tiny minority. And there were few opportunities for men with Harvard degrees. After the creation of New Brunswick in 1784, Nova Scotia's 20,000 pre-Loyalists suddenly found

This 1789 drawing shows the short-lived boom town of Shelburne that arose with the Loyalist influx after the American Revolution.

themselves sharing a smaller colony with 20,000 newcomers, and these were mostly farmers, soldiers, fishermen, sailors, and practitioners of trades ranging from baking, butchering, and barrel-making to tanning, tailoring, and tavern-keeping. Coming from New York, New Jersey, Pennsylvania, New England, and North and South Carolina, the Loyalists were a cross-section of American society.

Ross Thompson House in Shelburne, built in 1783-84 by Loyalists George and Robert Ross, served as both a house and a store. Today it is part of the Nova Scotia Museum Complex.

While the elite ate sumptuously at banquets, got government jobs, and finagled land grants that cheated other Loyalists, lesser folk trembled under the twin threats of starvation and freezing to death. "I cannot better describe the wretched situation of these people," Governor John Parr wrote to London in January 1784, "than by enclosing a list of those who have just arrived in the Clinton [from the American South], chiefly women and children, scarcely clothed, utterly destitute, still on board the transport, crowded like a sheep pen, as I am totally unable to find a place for them and we cannot move them by reason of ice and snow." Thousands tried to keep warm in Halifax churches, warehouses, sheds, and stables. They haunted bread lines, and barely survived on government rations of molasses, corn, and codfish. The diet, cold, and filth spawned diseases that killed hundreds.

In 1783–84, 10,000 Loyalists settled at Shelburne, far down the South Shore. It blossomed overnight as one of the most cosmopolitan spots in British North America. Shelburne Loyalists built handsome mansions, a flourishing lumber trade, shipyards, and other industries. The town buzzed with news from three local journals. The Shelburne neighbourhood, at its peak, may well have welcomed 16,000 Loyalists, including 2,700 Blacks. It owed its flash of prosperity, however, mostly to the one-shot investments that richer Loyalists made to set themselves up in style and to subsidies from the British government. When the subsidies died out, so did the town. As early as 1800, Shelburne was almost deserted, its handsome houses empty, and its streets overgrown with weeds. It was Canada's first boom town to become a ghost town.

Loyalists shared an attitude that said to the settled Nova Scotians, "More loyal than thou, and therefore more deserving." They saw themselves as a Chosen People, and their Promised Land as a betrayal. "Most Loyalists … would not have questioned the reference to 'Nova Scarcity,' " Neil MacKinnon wrote in "This Unfriendly Soil." " 'All our golden promises have vanished,' one of them ruefully observed. 'We were taught to believe this place was not barren and foggy … but find it ten times worse … It is the most inhospitable climate that ever mortal set foot on. The winter is of insupportable length and coldness, only a few spots fit to cultivate, and the land is covered with a cold, spongy moss, instead of grass, and the entire country is wrapt in the gloom of perpetual fog.' "[4]

Many Loyalists felt cheated, abandoned, and shabbily repaid for everything their loyalty had cost them. Some denounced Nova Scotians both as shiftless wretches who gouged unfortunate strangers with exorbitant prices and as near-traitors who had paid lip-service to loyalty while celebrating rebellion in their hearts. There was method in this meanness. The more convincingly the Loyalists depicted the "oldcomers" as slackers and turncoats, and themselves as heroic victims of republicanism, the better their chances of beating the locals in races for government appointments, good land, and political power. "Some of the most prominent had as many as four grants of land," MacKinnon continued. "They expected to be given jobs, even at the expense of pre-Loyalist office-holders, and deluged the governor and the secretaries of state with their applications and demands."

Not surprisingly, the oldcomers, whose ports had been unprotected by the British during Yankee privateers' raids, bitterly resented the Loyalists' insults. MacKinnon quotes one oldcomer: "They had a numerous British army to protect them. We had to combat the sons of darkness alone … We had much less than they to hope for by unshaken loyalty, and considerably more to fear."

Since Governor Parr and the Halifax establishment failed to speedily obey the more influential Loyalists' barrage of demands, the newcomers denounced Halifax as a nest of republicanism. The Loyalist elite dreamed of seeing their own royal red representatives dominate both the Executive Council and the Assembly. John Wentworth, who had been appointed surveyor-general of the king's woods in North America, schemed to have Parr ousted and to become Nova Scotia's first Loyalist governor.

Loyalists often behaved as viciously towards one another as towards oldcomers. They fought over property lines and shamelessly stole land. The

John Parr served as governor of Nova Scotia 1782–86 and as lieutenant-governor 1786–91. During his time of office, the Loyalist migration took place.

elite sneered at the preening of those who could only pretend to be elite and called them the dregs of mankind. In their own desperate scramble for position, as MacKinnon said, they "wrapped their exclusiveness about them like a mantle. With their sense of class, status and privilege, and their contempt for the lower classes, these Loyalists were far closer to the oligarchy in Halifax than to the common refugee."

St. George's Church, Sydney, (1785) was built a year after Cape Breton became a separate colony.

"Plan of the Town of Sydney," 1788.

The Halifax oligarchy, however, while enduring accusations of republicanism, sniffed that same republicanism in their pushy, disrespectful accusers. Governor Parr said certain Loyalists had inherited "a deal of that Liver, which disunited the Colonies from the mother country." With their constant backbiting, unfair criticism, underhanded attacks on officials, and their fraudulence, deceit, and whining, Loyalists changed Parr's governorship from a comfy sinecure to a daily hell.

He was a fat, Irish-born army officer—hard-drinking, quick-tempered, tormented by gout and piles, and furious at the way Loyalists generated work for him. While New Brunswick was still part of Nova Scotia, he said Saint John was already infested with "many turbulent Spirits, who are full of groundless complaints, lies and false representations, and their Agents replete

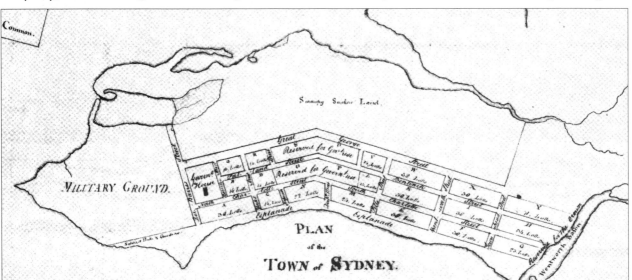

with gross partialities." He complained that Loyalists were such trouble-makers that even if the governor of Nova Scotia were an angel, they would have made "malignant representations" against him. Loyalists were "a cursed set of dogs," and the ones in Shelburne were "the Dregs and Banditti" of New York, Boston, and other ports. Others shared Parr's revulsion for Loyalists. Surveyor-general Charles Morris described the Loyalist sea captains of Shelburne as "Ungreatful Rascals" and blamed Loyalists for turning his job into "Egyptian Slavery."

The doubling of Nova Scotia's population in the mid-1780s caused turmoil, bitterness, hardship, heartbreak, disease, and death. After anti-Loyalist bigotry cooled off in the United States, thousands forsook their status as Loyalists and fled "Nova Scarcity" for their homelands. More stayed than went, however, and for those who put down roots, Nova Scotia offered a life in which they felt free of intolerance, free to speak out, and free to help shape the future of a colony that still proudly flew the Union Jack.

An illustration by C. W. Jefferys of "Loyalists drawing lots for their lands, 1784."

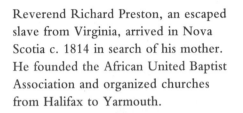

Reverend Richard Preston, an escaped slave from Virginia, arrived in Nova Scotia c. 1814 in search of his mother. He founded the African United Baptist Association and organized churches from Halifax to Yarmouth.

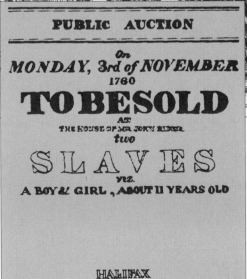

PUBLIC AUCTION

MONDAY, 3rd of NOVEMBER
1760
TO BE SOLD
AT
THE HOUSE OF MR. JOHN RIDER
two
SLAVES
viz.
A BOY & GIRL, ABOUT 11 YEARS OLD

HALIFAX

Black refugees await British ships on the shore of Chesapeake Bay, Maryland. In the years 1813–14 many Blacks from that area sought freedom in Nova Scotia.

A Halifax slave auction poster.

CHAPTER 17

ABUSED BLACKS FLEE, POOR SCOTS ARRIVE

To the floundering economy of Nova Scotia, the Loyalists brought a major injection of British money. Britain provided money and land for immediate resettlement, and by paying compensation and military pensions, it also pumped funds into Nova Scotia long into the future. Since the elite Loyalists benefited more from both flows of money than the common folk, the payments helped keep them dominant. That suited Britain, ever fearful of republicanism.

Acadians, Mi'kmaq, and Blacks did not fare as well.

Little more than a quarter-century had passed since New Englanders had helped expel the Acadians, but now, in the 1780s, Acadians who had painfully made their way back to Nova Scotia endured more injustices. Loyalists elbowed Acadians off their farms in Chezzetcook on the Eastern Shore and squatted on cleared Acadian lands in Yarmouth County.

But if the Loyalists hurt some Acadians in the short run, they hurt all native people in the long run. The wilderness had been big enough, and the white settlers few enough, to allow everyone to survive without much friction, but the Loyalists changed all that. "With the arrival of hordes of new settlers, [the Mi'kmaq] traditional sources of food practically disappeared," Mi'kmaq leader Daniel Paul wrote in 1993. "Their former allies the Acadians were in almost as bad shape, and could offer little assistance."[1]

The question of land continued to disturb the interludes of wary peace between the Mi'kmaq and the British. From time to time war threatened, or actually broke out; afterwards hatchets would be buried, gifts made, treaties ratified and confirmed. Historian Leslie F. S. Upton gives a detailed description of Mi'kmaq attitudes in his "Micmacs and Colonists." "This second generation of Micmacs to face the British," he wrote, "had learned something about the value of land from their elders. The very importance that the British placed on land ownership was a lesson in itself ... And whether or not the Micmacs had any idea of land ownership before the whites came, they certainly had acquired it by 1750."[2]

After the arrival of the Loyalists, the Mi'kmaq began to lose land rapidly. Not only did many of newcomers get land grants, but worse, others simply squatted where they pleased on Crown lands Year by year the Loyalists were turning the Mi'kmaq hunting grounds into farmland. Each winter brought a new crisis for the native peoples, with new petitions for food, clothing, and money. Many lived, often starving, on miserly government subsidies.

Certain colonial administrators realized the grievances were real, but the authorities had no coherent policy with respect to the Mi'kmaq. While some believed the best thing to do with the Mi'kmaq was to turn them into farmers, the land the government reserved for native use was never even surveyed.

"Lieutenant-Governor Lord Dalhousie made the first full-scale attempt to face the government's responsibilities to the native peoples," Upton wrote. "Despairing of any initiative from the assembly, he took the matter up in council and proposed the establishment of a reserve in each county, not to exceed one thousand acres, to be held in trust for those Indians who were disposed to settle." Desperate to have at least some land, the Mi'kmaq agreed to live on reserves, although this subjected them to control from Halifax. Moreover, their reserves were tiny. "By 1821 the acreage set aside for the Micmac in the entire colony had reached a 'princely' sum of 21,765," Dan Paul wrote. "This great estate of swamps, bogs, clay pits, mountains and rock piles represented a tiny fraction of one per cent of Nova Scotia's land base."[3]

The Mi'kmaq were not without leaders. "One such man," Upton wrote, "was Andrew Meuse, who...became the chief of the Bear River settlement, from which position he lobbied both the colonial government and London philanthropists for support."[4] Meuse also organized a petition calling for the prohibition of the sale of liquor, and Chief Charles Clower presented it to the House of Assembly. A law was enacted in this case, but with respect to the plight of the Mi'kmaq, the usual legislative inertia and indifference soon returned.

Among the Loyalists, it was the Blacks who endured the most abuse.

Between 10 and 20 per cent of all the Loyalists who descended on Nova Scotia were black; more black than white Loyalists had served in the British army and navy. Britain had promised the Blacks the same benefits as white refugees, but on Nova Scotia's stony shores they got the dirty end of every stick. Their rations of food were less nourishing than the whites'. For unloading ships and building houses, they received either lower wages than the going rate, or no pay at all. "Their land claims were met even more slowly than those of whites," Walter Stewart wrote. "They almost never received the full allotments promised, and they were fobbed off on the worst town lots and the scrubbiest, rockiest farmland."[5]

The biggest of the instant black settlements was Birchtown, near Shelburne, where the newcomers suffered winters fiercer than any they had ever known. To get food, some sold their blankets and clothing. Weakened by hunger, cold, disease and despair, many died during their first months in the Promised Land. Walter Stewart offered the horrifying memories of a survivor: "Some killed and ate their dogs and cats, and poverty and distress prevailed on every side."

Several black tradesmen lived not in Birchtown but right in Shelburne, and in July 1784, a mob of disbanded white soldiers, furious because the blacks were working for such low wages, drove them out of town and wrecked their houses. These blacks were an excuse for whites to explode. Shelburne boiled with land disputes, anger over the incompetence and corruption of officials, and growing fears about the way reality was already shattering dreams. The Blacks were scapegoats. The assault on them gave the

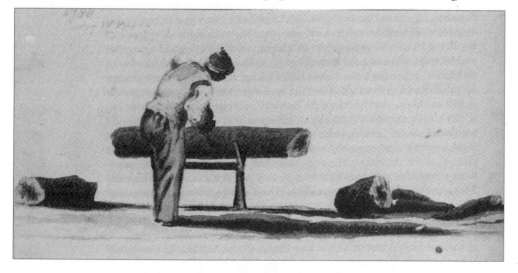

A drawing of a Birchtown workman, rendered shortly after the arrival of the Black Loyalists in Shelburne.

attackers a taste for violence that erupted in riots all summer long. "Thus part of the character of Shelburne," Neil MacKinnon said, "was this undertone of conflict, violence, and the threat of anarchy."[6]

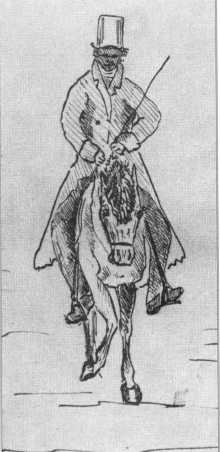

Dr. Gilpin's drawing of Rev. Richard Preston. As a black preacher in Nova Scotia who had been a slave, he took part in the abolition of slavery debates in Britain, Canada, and the United States.

White Loyalists drew food rations for their slaves, but when hunger loomed, often kept the food for themselves, turning their Blacks out to fight starvation on their own. Some owners of slaves shackled and whipped them, rented them to other masters, sold them, or left them to relatives in wills. Free Blacks were not much better off. If starvation drove them to theft, they risked court sentences that included dozens of lashes, and even hanging; white thieves escaped with fines. Britain had promised that free Blacks would be able to live off their own land, but many ended up as sharecroppers for wealthy whites. Blacks had neither the right of trial by jury, nor the right to vote. When trade slumped, crops failed, and famine struck, whites blamed them. Blacks were attacked for working, for not working, for simply being alive. Shelburne outlawed "Negro dances and Negro Frolicks in this Town," and threatened to charge the frolicsome with "riotous behaviour."

Eight years after arriving in Nova Scotia, hundreds of black Loyalists found themselves in desperate poverty. One of their number, the freed slave Thomas Peters of Annapolis Royal, made his way to London, where he met the British humanitarians William Wilberforce and Thomas Clarkson. These men were part of a group that had formed the Sierra Leone Company to assist liberated slaves. Nova Scotia Blacks were told that they could get passage to the experimental colony, and, once there, would receive free land and enjoy racial equality. They signed up in numbers that startled the governor and angered the whites who wanted to continue exploiting them as cheap labour. Despite efforts to halt the migration, 1,196 black Loyalists, roughly one in three of all those who had come to Nova Scotia with such high hopes, joyfully boarded British ships on January 15, 1792 and sailed away to help found the future nation of Sierra Leone.

They had some exceptional leaders. Among them were David George, founder of the Black Baptist Church in Nova Scotia, and in Sierra Leone a member of the Legislative Council; and Boston King, who won the respect of the Company directors, was sent to England to study, and returned as a schoolmaster.

The exodus was expensive, and John Wentworth, who had just succeeded the dead John Parr as governor of Nova Scotia, told King George III he thought it odd "for government to spend so much to remove laborious people and will spend nothing to help those who remain."

Even more white Loyalists than black bailed out of Nova Scotia, and many who stayed denounced the white deserters as lazy, ungrateful drifters and criminals. In 1785, Governor Parr said, "I wish more of their Gentry would follow them whose Loyalty might be comprehended in a Nuttshell."

As fast as they left, however, Scots arrived. In the thirty years following the Hector's arrival in Pictou in 1773, at least ten shiploads of immigrants from the Scottish Highlands reached Nova Scotian ports. The American Revolution had halted the flow of Scots to British North America, but in 1790 a group of Highland settlers landed at Prince Edward Island, and, from then on, vessels full of Highlanders arrived at both Pictou, Nova Scotia, and Prince Edward Island."

The Scottish civilians who settled in Pictou County and spread to Antigonish County and Cape Breton Island in the 1790s, and the Scots from disbanded British regiments who both preceded and joined them as pioneers in the same neighbourhoods, were harbingers of enormous waves of Catholic and Protestant Highlanders and Lowlanders that soon swept all across the eastern end of the colony.

In 1803 Nova Scotia, including Cape Breton, boasted some 10,000 Scots. Cape Breton alone jumped from 6,000 in 1815 to 35,420 in 1838, thanks mostly to Highland immigration. And still they came. In the next dozen years, 14,000 people from Britain, a hefty proportion of them Scots, moved to Nova Scotia. By then, the Scots had long been Nova Scotia's biggest ethnic group, and even in 1871, after the more adventurous had left for other lands, every third Nova Scotian was of Scottish descent.

Half a century before then, eastern Nova Scotia, including Cape Breton, already had a decidedly Scottish flavour. The earliest arrivals had plunged into the religious, educational, cultural, and political affairs of the colony. As generations passed, Scottish immigrants helped make education and religion "the cement of society" in Nova Scotia.

Back in the 1790s, colonial authorities had seen the Highlanders as godsends. Surveyor-General Charles Morris, who had endured such mental torture from the Loyalists, called the Scots, "the only People who are calculated for well directed and laborious Husbandry." There was no duty "more pleasing and grateful for us to Discharge than the accommodation of [these] Valuable People."

The Scots were truly loyal. Within a single generation of the slaughter of Highlanders by English forces at Culloden Moor in 1745, Scots transferred to the crown their ancient and near-fanatical loyalty to clan chieftains. Thus, it

had been the British Army that North American Scots joined during the revolution, not the rebels. Moreover, Highland Scots had no background of local self-government, and unlike the troublesome Loyalists, no tradition of either questioning authorities or demanding services from them.

Finally, the Scots saw the colony not as wretched compensation for the superior things they had lost in their true homeland, but as their first real chance, in a better country than they had ever known, to own their own land. To the tenant farmers of the

Stone buildings in Pictou reflect the architectural style of old Scotland.

mountainous Highlands of Scotland, even the meagre soil of rocky Cape Breton looked inviting. As one historian noted in 1869, "None had reason to regret the change from the wretched abodes they left to the comfortable homes they now occupy. Even the long hut, in the depths of the forest, is a palace compared to some of the turf cabins of Sutherland or the Hebrides."

Many Nova Scotia Scots had to learn a dozen skills they had never before known: how to handle an axe, build a cabin, pull roots, move stones, make barrels, repair nets, patch sails, control a balky horse. They also had to learn that keeping their families from starving or freezing to death was forever a matter of making do with whatever lay to hand. These immigrants would raise able and venturesome emigrants; as early as the 1830s, younger Nova Scotian Scots were finding it either necessary or exciting to travel to New England in search of work.

But many more stayed, and in the early 1940s, American writer Dorothy Duncan described certain descendants of Cape Breton's Highland settlers: "These men are all broad-shouldered creatures with pale-blue opaque eyes, high complexions, gnarled hands, and features so inelegant as to seem handsome. The girls are pretty, and the mature women are fair to look upon at any age. All of them, including their polite children, speak with a lilt in their voices that clings to one's memory like the odour of lavender or the sound of the sea. Locally they are said to 'have the Gaelic' because most of them are still bilingual."[7] The forebears of some of these very Cape Breton Islanders had crossed the Atlantic in the 1790s. That was when Governor John Wentworth had just started to give Nova Scotians both a sense of themselves as Nova Scotians, and a loyalty to their homeland that, in the words of Bluenose historian Brian Cuthbertson, "has remained their most distinguishing characteristic."[8]

Lone Sheiling near Pleasant Bay, Cape Breton, is a replica of a crofters stone hut used while tending sheep; a reminder of old Scotland.

American Loyalist refugee John Wentworth became Lieutenant-Governor of Nova Scotia 1792–1808.

Government House at Halifax was constructed under the direction of Lieutenant-Governor John Wentworth at a cost of £20,000. The cornerstone was laid in 1800.

CHAPTER 18

THE AGE OF JOHNNY WENTWORTH

No resident governor of Nova Scotia held office longer than John Wentworth, who received the job in 1792 and in 1808, when he was a sixty-eight-year-old physical wreck, heard from a gloating enemy that he had been pushed out in favour of a soldier twenty-seven years his junior. Wentworth and his audacious, cigar-smoking wife Frances spent so much money on entertainment that some historians overlooked his accomplishments. He may have loved a party, but, in many respects, he was as able an administrator as ever sat in the governor's chair. Skilled at entrenching his power in Halifax, he also knew the people of the backwoods and out-settlements better than anyone else.

In 1792, the colony was reeling under stupendous debt. Hordes of disillusioned Loyalists were trooping back to the United States, and feuding between pre-Loyalists and Loyalists had paralysed government. Yet Wentworth inspired in oldcomer and newcomer alike a love of Nova Scotia that made the turbulent past pale beside visions of a splendid future. A war-driven surge in the economy bolstered his efforts to make Nova Scotians proud to be Nova Scotians, and by 1797 he had managed to get his appointed executive council and the elected assembly to work together long enough to wipe out the colony's debt.

Wentworth, said his biographer Brian Cuthbertson, helped turn Nova Scotia into "a thriving and awakened society." It was British gold flowing into the colony during warfare with France that created the prosperity, not him, but his spirited leadership gave Nova Scotians "the confidence to seize the opportunities that the new wealth gave them."[1] His supporters called him "The Father of Nova Scotia," and the first decade of his governorship would long be remembered as a Golden Age.

Frances Wentworth, along with her husband John, lived extravagantly at Halifax amid such friends as the Duke of Kent.

He came to office as a newcomer neither to governing nor to Nova Scotia. Wentworths had run New Hampshire for generations and, through the export of pine masts and lumber, had become notoriously rich. John earned an M.A. at Harvard, became the most staunch of all Wentworth Anglicans, moved to England to oversee his family's interests there, ingratiated himself with nobles, and in 1767, at age thirty, sailed home to become the third Wentworth governor of New Hampshire. He brought with him connections to British aristocrats, as well as English servants and horses. "Johnny," as New Hampshire people called him, was the most popular governor in North America.

No Loyalist's charm, however, could withstand the rebellion. In 1775, when he and his wife and infant son fled New Hampshire forever, he was thirty-eight. He went first to Boston, next to Halifax, and then to New York City. He organized a corps of New England Loyalists and a network of New Hampshire agents who recruited more soldiers for the Crown. New Hampshire therefore forbade his return and confiscated his property. The Continental Congress declared him an outlaw.

The Wentworths spent from 1778 to 1783 in England, which the society-loving Frances adored. John then showed up in Nova Scotia as surveyor-general of forests throughout British North America. While Frances stayed in Halifax, he vanished among the untracked hills of Nova Scotia, Cape Breton, New Brunswick, and Quebec. Wentworth was forty-six in 1783, yet he roamed wildernesses for the next seven years. Chewing salt pork, swallowing rum, travelling by coastal boat, canoe, and on foot, he reserved the towering pines that gave the Royal Navy the masts it required to defeat Napoleon. "He could truthfully declare that his journeys were so physically demanding he could never find any man who could stay with him through a whole trip."[2]

Like many British aristocrats, John and Frances indulged in extramarital affairs. After delighting in upper-class England, Frances beheld the dowdy women of Halifax society with contempt and scandalized them by bedding Halifax's first royal visitor, Prince William Henry. At forty-one, she was still a beauty. At twenty-one, Coconut Head, as the prince was known in the Royal Navy, was a boozing, whoring, red-faced scapegrace. He was also the most illustrious of the officers with whom Frances relieved her boredom while John exhausted himself in distant forests.

On May 13, 1792, Wentworth became the first civilian governor of Nova Scotia, and Halifax celebrated his appointment with fireworks. If any eighteenth-century governor was "the people's choice," it was he. Nova Scotians expected him to end the colony's political feuding and lead them to prosperity. He solved the feuding by helping the newcomers conquer the oldcomers. As early as 1793, Loyalists drove from public office the eloquent Richard Uniacke, a giant among pre-Loyalists. Owing to the agony New Hampshire rebels had inflicted on Wentworth, he was blind to the worth of anyone not utterly loyal to him. He packed his bureaucracy and executive council with Loyalist comrades and, since Nova Scotians elected other Loyalists to the assembly, managed to preside over seven years of rare governmental harmony. With "his masterly distribution of patronage," he "laid the foundations of a predominantly Loyalist oligarchy which governed Nova Scotia ... through the terms of five succeeding governors."[3]

After getting the assembly to raise taxes to whip Nova Scotia's finances into shape, Wentworth promoted road construction, farming, the fisheries, and commerce. In the spring of 1793, republican France declared war against Britain, at precisely the right time to arouse local patriotism. Wentworth promptly founded the Royal Nova Scotia Regiment and used the danger of privateers' raids not only to persuade the British to arm Lunenburg, Liverpool, Shelburne, and Annapolis Royal, but to revitalize Nova Scotia's militia. He also created the Nova Scotia Legion, a team of infantry, cavalry, and artillery, trained to speed to any port the enemy attacked.

Wentworth gave Nova Scotians both pride in their homeland, and confidence they could defend it. In Cuthbertson's assessment, he exploited the menace of "revolutionary, atheistic and republican France to inspire in Nova Scotians a love of country and loyalty to Britain and her monarchical constitution."[4] He pursued this policy even among the Acadians and the Mi'kmaq. The Acadians declared their loyalty and denounced "democratical French practices." Four hundred joined the militia.

In May 1794, Prince Edward, the future Duke of Kent, arrived in Halifax as commander of British troops in Nova Scotia and New Brunswick, and with him came his French mistress. Born Thérèse-Bernardine Mongenet, she was known as Julie de Saint-Laurent. The prince was twenty-seven, and she thirty-four. She had accompanied him as he took command of the British garrison in Quebec City, thus "beginning a twenty-seven-year liaison of great mutual happiness."[5] It was not until 1817, when the prince submitted to pressure to provide an heir, that he sorrowfully broke the relationship and married a widowed princess from Germany. They had one child: the future Queen Victoria.

In just six years, Prince Edward, Duke of Kent rebuilt a dilapidated Halifax into the strongest fortress outside Europe.

The time Edward and Julie spent in Nova Scotia may have been the happiest of their lives. The Wentworths liked them and relished the royal aura that Edward's goodwill bestowed on the governorship. For more than a year, the prince and his mistress lived with the Wentworths at Government House. George III heartily disliked his fourth son, but in John Wentworth, Edward found a surrogate father: "Thrilled at the friendship offered by a prince, Wentworth acted as a fatherly guardian (he was twice the prince's age) assiduously ensuring that no disrespect was shown and surrounding Prince Edward with an impenetrable protectiveness."[6] The attentiveness paid off; in 1795 Wentworth became a baronet. He was now the most revered governor of Nova Scotia since Edward Cornwallis had founded Halifax.

It was probably Frances Wentworth who exposed the younger couple to as many balls and banquets as they could bear. While they lived at Government House, 2,437 guests came to dinner. Perhaps to escape this social whirl, Edward ordered construction of "the Prince's Lodge." North of town, it overlooked Bedford Basin on an eighty-hectare tract owned by Wentworth. Edward continued to use an apartment in Government House as an office, but late in 1795 he and Julie moved to their suburban love nest. Athletic and more than six feet tall, the prince was also ambitious and temperate. Since Haligonians feared offending him, sales of wine and liquor plummeted. A fanatical disciplinarian, he discouraged heavy drinking among his soldiers by making them parade before him at five o'clock every morning. He was notorious for the number of soldiers he ordered flogged and hanged.

Edward's three years at Quebec City had convinced him France planned to send a monstrous force across the Atlantic and, using Halifax as a base, reconquer Canada. Beginning in 1795, when he drew on the treasury for £100,000, the prince sucked from Britain enormous lumps of money to fortify the city. As French armies mauled Europe and England needed all its resources to repel an invasion that appeared imminent, Edward extracted from the mother country troops, munitions, and gold for Nova Scotia.

The Halifax that Edward inspected in 1794 was a ramshackle, wooden town, with rickety fortifications that had been deteriorating since the American Revolution. The Halifax that he left forever, just six years later, was the strongest fortress outside Europe. Powerful batteries surrounded it, and all the fortifications were in the latest and most expensive European style. An amateur architect, obsessed by punctuality, Prince Edward paid for the installation, at the foot of Citadel Hill, of the Town Clock that remains the most charming symbol of the city. Just before he left Halifax, late in 1800, Haligonians witnessed the ceremonial laying of the cornerstones for the new Government House and for the beautiful St. George's, the "round church."

Julie de Saint-Laurent had a twenty-two-year relationship with Prince Edward. The heart-shaped pond at Hemlock Ravine Park and the rotunda are what remain of the love nest the duke built for himself and Julie.

Embryos of Nova Scotia's first political parties were stirring. Halifax merchants and other backers of the governor held power as members of the "Court Party" and in 1799 made sure the assembly voted £10,500 for construction of the stone mansion the Wentworths felt they deserved. As the couple added luxurious touches, the bill rose to a stupendous £30,000. Opposing the Court Party were assorted malcontents and men from Pictou and Colchester Counties who wanted public monies invested not in Halifax mansions but in country roads. They belonged to the "Country Party," and their craftiest champion was William Cottnam Tonge, the pre-Loyalist assemblyman for Hants County. Wentworth had tried and failed to have Tonge fired from his job as provincial naval officer. They loathed one another.

Behind their feud lay a constitutional struggle. Rural assemblymen reacted to the sky-rocketing bills for Government House, and to their constituents' demands for new roads, by fighting to wrest from the executive more control over revenue and money bills. In the minds of both politicians and their constituents the issues of road funding and constitutional rights became inseparable.

Despite the opposition, Government House arose. Once reviled as an outrageous extravagance, it now stands as a Georgian monument to Wentworth's taste. No other governor in the history of Canada has left such an architectural treasure. As its construction began in 1800, just above the masted harbour, Nova Scotia was in better shape than ever before. It owed its flash of prosperity to the governor, the prince, the war, and the weather. Harvests were bountiful during much of the 1790s, and prices for farm produce high. The clamouring for roads never stopped, and Wentworth did oversee their extension into newly prosperous agricultural districts. Nova Scotians could now ride carriages all the way from Halifax to Annapolis Royal.

Constructed in 1794, the rotunda, once part of Prince's Lodge, still overlooks the Bedford Basin.

The war inflicted French privateers on Nova Scotia's fisheries and seagoing trade, but it brought more rewards than penalties. Imports and provincial revenues surged. A new class of merchant-traders pocketed fast gains. Halifax found money to yank the last of the stumps and rocks from its streets and to pave certain avenues. Indeed, this small, dismal, grubby and dispirited seaside burg grew, in only one decade, into a bustling, cosmopolitan port with 10,000 residents, three newspapers, crowded theatres, a taste for balls, banquets, fireworks, and parades, and a reputation as the home of beautiful, bejewelled, and fashionably dressed women.

By 1794, the Halifax Grammar School was on solid financial footing, and within a few more years hundreds of boys had studied at King's College, Windsor. "The literary and educational achievements of the 1790s were of Loyalist inspiration and gave the Loyalist ascendancy an intellectual character unrivalled in any other British North American colony."[7]

In 1765 a group of Maroons were exiled from Jamaica to Nova Scotia for waging guerilla war on British slave owners in the eighteenth century. Discontented, they soon emigrated to Sierra Leone to escape the harsh climate and living conditions in Nova Scotia.

For that supreme Loyalist John Wentworth, however, the Golden Age, at the turn of the century, was already losing its glow. His health, popularity, grip on the levers of power, and influence in London were all weakening. As he waned, his enemies waxed.

Rheumatism tortured Wentworth, and what were probably neuralgia attacks shot such agonizing spasms of pain through his hands, chest, neck, and face that sometimes he could not write, nor even see nor hear. He spent his later life on the brink of financial ruin and incurred heavy personal debts with a pig-headed scheme to convert hundreds of Maroons—exiled warriors from the mountains of Jamaica—into gentle, Christian farmers and labourers in Nova Scotia. The

King's College opened at Windsor in 1788. The college moved to Halifax in 1920 after a fire destroyed the main building.

disgruntled Maroons soon followed the earlier flight of Black Loyalists to Sierra Leone.

The older Wentworth got, the more insistent he grew about the Crown's power over Nova Scotians. To assert his dwindling authority he picked fights with the assembly and lost; the lower house gained complete control over money bills. His most eloquent enemies in the assembly, where his network of patronage now had little influence, were two pre-Loyalists, Tonge and Uniacke.

St. George's Church, Halifax, built in 1800, was constructed through a public subscription campaign and a grant of £200 from King George III.

Loyalists had once driven Uniacke from public life, but by the turn of the century this formidable politician, the possessor of the biggest law practice in the colony, was not only back in the assembly but back in the speaker's chair. Tonge was a descendant of men who had arrived in Nova Scotia even before the founding of Halifax. A skilled orator and canny parliamentary tactician, he was the assembly's natural leader during fights with Wentworth's hand-picked council.

After the election of 1806, Wentworth tried to cut the assembly down to size. Thomas Walker, son-in-law of one of his Loyalist friends, gained the most votes in Annapolis Township, but the assembly, after finding him guilty of bribery, declared the seat vacant. The speaker asked Wentworth for a new election writ but, in line with British precedents, refused to explain why Walker's election had been nullified. Giving the governor reasons would have amounted to an admission that he had the right to decide the validity of the assembly's requests.

Wentworth not only refused to issue the writ, he referred the whole matter to the British government. If Britain backed him, Cuthbertson explained, the case would "establish his prerogative rights and curtail the assembly's constitutional ambitions."[8] Making the case for the assembly, however, was no less a lawyer than Uniacke. He argued that a governor's use of royal instructions to limit the rights of an elected assembly was illegal; it was only the law and constitution of the British Parliament that governed those rights; Parliament had enjoyed the exclusive privilege of determining disputed elections for more than two centuries; and the assembly of Nova Scotia had precisely the same right.

The British authorities agreed with Uniacke, handing Wentworth a supremely humiliating defeat. Nova Scotia was no longer a mere colony whose fate depended on a monarch's orders. Now, it shared the rights and liberties of Britain. Now, it was a partner in a great empire.

Wentworth finally and vengefully fired Tonge as provincial naval officer in 1807, but a year later Tonge was among the first Nova Scotians to learn of the unexpected arrival of Wentworth's successor at Government House, General George Prevost. Wentworth was out at Prince's Lodge with Frances, who was recovering from a grave illness. Tonge saddled a horse and galloped north so he could enjoy being the first to tell the old governor he had lost his job.

The Wentworths retreated to England, where Frances died in 1813. By then, John, having fled his creditors, was back in Halifax. Shortly after hearing of the death in 1820 of his old friend the Duke of Kent, Wentworth also expired and was buried beneath St. Paul's Church in Halifax. Despite his grudges and reactionary constitutional stand, he was "a well-beloved governor, a kind, charming, earthy little man, devoted to the service of his monarch and hospitable to citizen and stranger alike."[9]

Completed in 1803, the Old Town Clock was a gift to the town of Halifax from Edward, Duke of Kent.

A portrait of Provo Wallis by Robert Field captures the confident air of this young man who would have a stellar military career.

Artist Reuterdal vividly depicted of the quarterdeck battle scene which resulted in the capture of the Chesapeake by the Shannon off Boston Harbour in 1813.

The commanding officer of the Chesapeake, Captain James Lawrence, died during the battle with the Shannon. His body was buried in the Old Burying Ground (St. Paul's) in Halifax, but was later disinterred and returned to the United States.

CHAPTER 19

THE WAR OF 1812: WASTEFUL, BLOODY, LUDICROUS

Uniacke so disliked Wentworth he refused to join the executive council until Sir George Prevost took over the governorship in 1808, but even before then the big Irishman was becoming the most influential figure in Nova Scotia. During the Napoleonic Wars, the War of 1812, and all the vicissitudes of his political career, he remained advocate general of the Vice Admiralty Court. His fees from this work earned him wealth, much of which he spent on the education of his dozen children. He had married their mother, Martha Maria Delesdernier, when he was twenty-two and she was twelve. Long after her death in 1803, Haligonians marvelled at the sight of Uniacke and his six strapping sons ambling through town.

He mastered Britain's enormously complicated laws of navigation and trade and campaigned tirelessly to free Nova Scotians from restrictions that seemed like perverse punishment for their loyalty. The Americans, with their rebellion, had shucked off the burdens of British mercantilism.

To take just one example of how the navigation laws worked, they harshly penalized Bluenose fish merchants. Having traded fish in the Mediterranean for salt (to cure more fish), they could not supplement their homeward-bound cargoes with wine, oranges, and other goods without stopping in Britain to pay duties. Free of such restrictions, Americans grabbed the lion's share of the Mediterranean fish business. Uniacke repeatedly urged Britain to change the commercial system to give Nova Scotians a fair chance to compete for this vital trade. At last, in 1806, Britain complied, and its decision "marked the turning point in Nova Scotia's commercial fortunes."[1]

Uniacke saw Nova Scotia as just one part of a British North America destined to be huge and prosperous. He was both a conservative and a visionary. More than forty years before Canada's birth in 1867, he wrote his "Observations on the British colonies in North America with a proposal for the confederation of the whole under one government." As a conservative, however, he believed his united British America would have but one purpose: to counterbalance the forces of atheism, revolution, and vile democracy that swept through the barbaric United States.

As advocate general of the court that decided the fate of prize ships captured by privateers, Uniacke was at the heart of Nova Scotia's most adventurous industry. With guns, swords, and flames, privateers did legally what pirates did illegally. They seized ships and cargoes at sea, plundered small ports, and sometimes killed those who fought back. They were instruments not just of greed, however, but of war. Indeed, as John Leefe wrote in "The Atlantic Privateers," they "were to the Atlantic Provinces what the militia was to Canada."[2] This was a militia that used sloops, schooners, and brigantines to scud from Newfoundland to the Spanish Main.

Uniacke House at Mount Uniacke, former home of Richard John Uniacke, is now a Nova Scotia Museum Historic Site. Sketch by A. W. Wallace.

The blossoming of Nova Scotia privateering occurred not long after the founding of Halifax: "The Seven Years' War, the American Revolution, the French Revolutionary and Napoleonic Wars, and the War of 1812 saw thousands of [Nova Scotian] seamen and hundreds of vessels embark on cruises designed to sting the enemy and enrich the privateers."[3]

For even the most successful, however, windfalls were rarely sure things. The court might rule that, since the owner of a captured vessel was not a citizen of a hostile nation, the ship was not a prize of war. Or perhaps the ship belonged to an enemy, but not its cargo. Once the court did rule a capture was legal, the prize went by auction to the highest bidder. Out of the proceeds came money to cover court costs, officials' fees, and wharfage bills. The deductions often left little for those who had done the dirty work at sea. Speculating in captured prizes soon proved not only less dangerous, but also more profitable. By the 1790s, merchants were hoarding cash so they would be ready to snap up the goods and vessels that privateers brought into port.

If privateering was legalized piracy, the Royal Navy's practice of sending ashore cudgel-swinging bands of sailors, the notorious press gangs, to

Province House at Halifax was completed in 1819. It was designed by a local contractor and construction was overseen by a stonemason.

"impress" males into seagoing service was legalized kidnapping. When an admiral ran short of crew, the governor persuaded his council to issue him a press warrant, ostensibly to rid Halifax of vagabonds. The victims, however, were usually apprentices, fishermen, visiting farmers, or youthful townsmen out for a night of pub-crawling. As Thomas H. Raddall put it, "For two generations of almost incessant war young Nova Scotians vanished into the lower decks of His Majesty's ships, to die in distant battles, or of the scurvy, the typhus, or the yellow fever which in those days scourged the British service."[4]

Impressment also occurred at sea. British warships routinely stopped homeward-bound merchantmen and strong-armed crew into custody. They needed every sailor they could nab. Except for a lull in 1802–03, Britain, by 1812, had been at war with France and its allies for nineteen years. The Royal Navy had grown to 621 vessels, with 145,000 officers, seamen and marines. As Rear Admiral H. F. Pullen wrote in "The Shannon and the Chesapeake," "Those far-distant, storm-beaten ships upon which the Grand Army [of Napoleon] never looked, stood between it and the dominion of the world."[5] Fighting for Britain's very life, the Royal Navy took to halting vessels from the United States, searching them for British deserters, and imprisoning American sailors for service on British warships.

Since Britain believed that "once a subject, always a subject," it claimed the Americans it grabbed were not really Americans. The United States insisted that those who had chosen to become naturalized Americans owed their allegiance only to their new nation. As the Royal Navy pressed more and more Americans into service—and the number may eventually have totalled more than 5,000—outrage spread throughout the United States.

In his history of Halifax, Raddall describes "an act of supreme folly when [in June 1807] HMS Leopard actually fired upon the United States warship Chesapeake and seized a number of her men."[6] The captain of the Leopard believed the Chesapeake's crew included deserters from the Royal Navy and opened fire after the American skipper refused to let the British search his ship. The gunfire killed three men and wounded eighteen. The British now boarded the American frigate, arrested four "deserters," and sent them to Halifax for trial by court martial. The incident so enraged Americans that, if their government had not been impotent, it might well have ignited the War of 1812 five years early.

Vice Admiral George Berkeley of the Royal Navy pardoned three of the four crewmen believed to be "deserters" from the HMS Leopard to the American Chesapeake. The other crew member was hanged.

The Royal Navy hanged one of the unfortunate four from the yardarm of HMS Halifax. The court sentenced the others to five hundred lashes with a cat-o'-nine-tails, but Vice Admiral George Berkeley pardoned them. On June 11, 1812, two of them found themselves back aboard the Chesapeake. Seven days later, the United States declared war on Britain.

The impressment of American sailors was only one cause of the War of 1812. After Americans exploited the Napoleonic Wars by grabbing much of the lucrative carrying trade between Europe and the West Indies, Britain began to harass American vessels and ports. It declared a 1300-kilometre blockade of the European coasts Napoleon dominated. While Napoleon also sabotaged American shipping, the United States found the high-handedness of Britain more infuriating.

In frontier states, Americans believed the British were encouraging natives to oppose the westward surge of white settlers. Many wanted to drive the redcoats out of North America forever and thought that while a big war kept the British military busy in Europe, the United States could conquer Canada in a walkover.

Seven months before the war began, Enos Collins, a thirty-seven-year-old merchant, financier, and shipowner from Liverpool, N.S., paid £440 at a Halifax auction for a skinny two-master. Only sixteen metres long, and "cut away at stem and stern and sides until she was nothing but a wedge, held upright by her pig-iron ballast,"[7] the schooner had little cargo space, a freakishly long bowsprit, and masts that tilted aft so sharply they looked ready to crash on the stern. The craft was almost comically rakish. Having served as a tender to a Spanish slave ship, it smelled so rank that Collins and his partners had it fumigated with vinegar, tar, and brimstone.

The new owners called the vessel the Liverpool Packet, but Halifax knew it as the Black Joke. It would prove no joke to New England shipping. The war had hardly begun when it started its career as the most successful privateer in the history of British North America, with Joseph Barss her famous captain. "On the last day of August [1812], the Liverpool Packet hoisted the Red Jack and put to sea as a privateer, victualled for sixty days, with 200 rounds of canister and 300 of round shot in her magazine, four hundred-weight of gunpowder ... and twenty-five muskets and forty cutlasses for her forty-five men. She had five guns, one 6-pounder, two 4-pounders, and two 12-pounders."[8]

Its black hull nearly invisible against dark shores, the Liverpool Packet would lie in wait, then crowd on sail, charge out to sea, and run down its victim. It sailed both fast and close to the wind. Its rig was so simple that when most of its crew were busy sailing prizes home, a mere half-dozen could handle the Packet. It was small enough that, when American warships threatened to capture it during a dead calm, the crew hauled out spruce oars and rowed to safety. The Packet found rich pickings off New England and in only two years brought home prizes worth more than a quarter-million dollars.

On New Year's Day, 1813, the "Boston Messenger" bitterly complained, "That an insignificant fishing schooner ... should be suffered to approach the

Harbour of the Metropolis of Massachusetts, capture and carry home in triumph eight or nine vessels of sail valued at from seventy to ninety thousand dollars and owned almost exclusively by merchants in Boston, in the short space of twenty days ... would seem utterly incredible were the fact not placed beyond any doubt."

The American privateer Thomas captured the Liverpool Packet in June 1813 and towed her into Portsmouth, New Hampshire, where the Nova Scotian sailors soon found themselves in jail. Captain Joseph Barss lay in fetters. An indication of American hatred for him and his men was the confession by an officer of the Thomas that he felt "great sorrow" that he had not killed them all. HMS Fantome soon recaptured the schooner, and one year after Enos Collins and friends first purchased it, he and Joseph Allison bought it again. By war's end in 1814, the Packet had brought fifty vessels to the prize court and had probably captured and released as many more.

A painting of Rear Admiral Philip Bowes Vere Broke. Earlier in his naval career he commanded the Shannon which overtook the American Chesapeake in about fifteen minutes.

The war began with five brutal shocks for everyone who believed the Royal Navy invincible. Between mid-August 1812 and the following February, the USS Constitution demolished both HMS Guerrière and HMS Java; the USS Wasp captured HMS Frolic; the USS United States captured HMS Macedonian; and the USS Hornet took all of fourteen minutes to conquer HMS Peacock. In each bloody engagement, the American ships and crews were bigger than the British and boasted heavier guns and better gunners.

These humiliations shattered the morale of the Royal Navy in Halifax.

Captain Philip Bowes Vere Broke, a future rear admiral from an old Suffolk family, wrote to his wife, "We must catch one of those great American ships and send her home for a show." Broke had joined the navy as a boy, and by 1811, when he sailed to Halifax as commander of the frigate Shannon, he was a seasoned captain of thirty-four. He drilled his men daily in the use of muskets, cutlasses, and boarding pikes and in the firing of "great guns."

On June 1, 1813, the Shannon hove to at a spot off Boston. Broke could see the Chesapeake, the vessel that HMS Leopard had treated with such contempt in 1807, lying at anchor. It was slightly bigger and heavier than the Shannon, and its 387 officers, seamen, and marines outnumbered the British. They were, however, far from being the well-oiled machine the Shannon's crew had become.

To the American vessel's captain, the gallant James Lawrence, Broke sent an invitation that began, "As the Chesapeake appears now ready for sea, I request you will do me the favour to meet the Shannon with her, ship to ship, to try the fortune of our respective flags ... "

Lawrence never received the letter. The British frigate was cheekily awaiting him off Boston, and that was all the challenge he needed. As the Chesapeake tore past Boston Lighthouse under full sail, a flotilla of yachts bobbed in its wake. The parade suggested naval warfare was a spectator sport, like public hangings. Meanwhile, Broke told his men that, after years of training, their moment of glory had arrived: "You will let them know today that there are Englishmen in the Shannon who still know how to fight ... Fire into her quarters; maindeck into maindeck; quarterdeck into quarterdeck. Kill the men and the ship is yours. Don't hit them about the head, for they have steel caps on, but give it them through the body ... Remember, you have the blood of hundreds of your countrymen to avenge."

At 5:50 P.M., the Shannon opened fire on the approaching Chesapeake. After moments of chaos, screams, and slaughter, after ear-splitting roars from the big guns of both ships, Broke saw his chance. Sword in hand, he leapt aboard the crippled American warship. Some seventy men followed him.

In 1877 Provo Wallis attained the navy's highest rank—Admiral of the Fleet. During the War of 1812 he was given command of the Shannon by the wounded Captain Broke. He and the ship's crew made a triumphant return to Halifax with the Chesapeake as their prize.

British and American sailors now fought a short, nose-to-nose battle. An American sabre gashed Broke's head and may have fractured his skull. The wound would torment him for the rest of his life.

Struck by a musketball, the dying Lawrence uttered the command that would echo in the ears of generations of United States naval officers: "Don't give up the ship!" But his leaderless crew did give it up, and very soon. "Eleven minutes elapsed between the first gun and the boarding of the Chesapeake, and in four more minutes she surrendered ... "9

Covered by the United States flag, the body of Captain Lawrence lay on the Chesapeake's deck as the Shannon led the defeated vessel up Halifax Harbour, captained by the twenty-two-year-old Provo Wallis, who had taken

The HMCS Shannon leading and the captured American frigate Chesapeake entering Halifax Harbour on June 6, 1813.

command of the ship when Captain Broke was so badly wounded. "The garrison bands marched down to the waterfront to greet them with brass and drums. The troops and people cheered. One venerable Halifax merchant was seen at the end of his wharf playing 'Rule Britannia' on a vast cello, and capering as he played. Handkerchiefs waved. Ships in the anchorage manned their yards."10

The battle killed sixty-two of the Chesapeake's officers and men and thirty-four of the Shannon's. The wounded from both ships totalled 128. The "Pall Mall Gazette" later reported, "Nor has anything like such slaughter been common in our sea-fights since the bloody Dutch wars of the seventeenth century."

Thomas Haliburton, a future judge and renowned humorist, was seventeen on that historic June 6 and, remembering the Chesapeake half a century later, wrote, "The coils and folds of rope were steeped in gore, as if in a slaughterhouse. Pieces of skin, with pendant hair, were adhering to the sides of the ship; and in one place I noticed portions of fingers protruding, as if thrust through the outer wall of the frigate."

Opposing the American war effort, New Englanders refused to surrender their militia to national service, and some even contemplated secession from the union. A vigorous trade continued between New England and its "enemies" in Nova Scotia. Smuggling, rising demand for timber, and big spending by the British commissariat all helped to stimulate briefly the Nova Scotia economy.

Following the Shannon's victory, the Royal Navy bottled up the American east coast. Then, in the spring of 1814, after a generation of Nova Scotians had grown up knowing only a time of war, the thrilling news of Napoleon's defeat reached them. Now, wrote Robert Collins in "The Formative Years," "Britain shook itself like a weary mastiff and turned around to properly deal with the pesky Americans."[11]

Sir John Coape Sherbrooke successfully defended Nova Scotia during the War of 1812. In 1814 he commanded the British troops from Halifax to overtake the port of Castine in eastern Maine.

Twenty-two British ships sailed into Chesapeake Bay in August 1814 and landed thousands of battle-hardened redcoats in Maryland. After routing an American force—ineptly led by President James Madison and Secretary of War James Monroe—the British strolled into Washington. While many Americans cursed it as the "Capital of Miserable Huts" and "A Mudhole Almost Equal to the Great Serbonian Bog," they were nevertheless enraged when the enemy set fire to the Capitol, the White House, and other public buildings.

The British then sailed up the Patapsaco River to bombard Baltimore, but defenders at Fort McHenry halted them. It was while watching this battle, with its "rocket's red glare" and "bombs bursting in air," from an internment vessel flying the Union Jack, that Francis Scott Key, a Washington lawyer whom the British had arrested, felt inspired to write "The Star Spangled Banner." The British troop commander, General Robert Ross, who had led his men into Washington, died during the failed attempt to capture Baltimore. While an American folk legend claims his body went to England preserved in a barrel of rum, he was buried with full military honours in downtown Halifax.

Shortly after that, Sir John Coape Sherbrooke, lieutenant-governor of Nova Scotia and commander of British forces in the Atlantic Provinces, led troops from the Halifax garrison during the conquest of eastern Maine. His occupation of the port of Castine yielded customs revenues sufficient to enable the governor, Lord Dalhousie, to found Dalhousie College. Planned on the principles of Edinburgh University, it was (unlike King's College at Windsor) non-sectarian and open to all. Lord Dalhousie saw the college as a necessity for the colony. It was destined to become the biggest university in Atlantic Canada.

The wasteful, bloody, and often ludicrous War of 1812 officially ended on Christmas Eve, 1814. One of its results was that the Americans lost their right to fish and cure their catch on the coasts of Nova Scotia, but the wording of

Admiralty House was built between 1814 and 1818 in Halifax as a residence for British admirals. The Georgian structure stood empty between 1906 and 1914. The Naval Hospital made use of the large rooms in 1914. The building is now a National Historic Site and serves as the Maritime Command Museum.

this fisheries arrangement was so vague it would cause international friction for almost a century to come.

The peace treaty failed even to mention the war's causes and, despite Britain's victories in Maine, reinstated the pre-war boundaries. Still, the war was not a total waste: "Never again did the Americans actually take arms against Canada. And the Canadian spirit was intact; was, in fact, for the first time a strong identifiable thing. By holding fast in the War of 1812 Canada took a long step toward nationhood."[12] What the war did for Nova Scotians, aside from enriching some, was confirm their ties to the British Empire, their distrust of Americans, and their pride in their homeland as a cockpit of seagoing history.

George Ramsay, 9th Earl of Dalhousie, was lieutenant-governor of Nova Scotia 1816–20. His administration established many advancements in both agriculture and education.

Dalhousie College, originally located on the Grand Parade, Halifax, was established in 1820.

A contemporary engraving of Joseph Howe, who was the founder of the "Novascotian." He became the first giant of Canadian journalism and was devoted to political reform in Nova Scotia, advocating responsible government.

CHAPTER 20

IT WAS JOE HOWE
BY DAY AND
BY NIGHT

During the summer that Washington burned, nine-year-old Joseph Howe, son of king's printer John Howe, spent his evenings reading and his days romping in the seaside forest surrounding his family's small house south of Halifax. For generations, Liberals would remember Joe Howe as the greatest Nova Scotian who ever lived.

Defender of a free press, champion of responsible government, master of stump oratory, and folk hero, Howe was so beloved that one Lorenzo Sabine wrote in 1864, "It was 'Jo Howe' by day and by night ... Ships and babies were named 'Jo Howe.' The topers of the shops and taverns swore great oaths about 'Jo Howe.' The young men and women flirted and courted in 'Jo Howe' badges, and played and sang 'Jo Howe' glees. It was 'Jo Howe' everywhere."

Howe owed to his father—"my only instructor, my play-fellow, almost my daily companion"—many of the qualities that made him politically attractive. A friend of Wentworth's, the Boston-born John Howe was the only member of his family to side with Britain during the American Revolution. He was a widower with six children when he married Mary Edes, who gave birth to Joe, his last and favourite child, on December 13, 1804. Mary was the daughter of a British sea captain. John worshipped all things bright and British, and Joe would one day vow, "I am a clear lover of Old England, and to save her would blow Nova Scotia into the air."

John was handsome, modest, calm, learned, charitable, and religious. As non-partisan as any Tory could be, he scrupulously avoided controversy. He had a fine library, which young Joe ploughed through. "From the old man," he remembered, "between whose knees I was trained ... I learned to prize knowledge for its own sake ... and to prefer peace on honourable terms to fruitless and aggressive war."

John Howe, a Loyalist from Boston, learned his trade at the "Boston News Letter" prior to coming to Halifax in 1781.

A member of the Sandemanian Christian (primitive Presbyterian) sect, John passed down to Joe not only moral courage, but also what historian J. Murray Beck called "his preference for simple, non-ritualistic, religious practices; his willingness to perform public services without thought of financial gain; and his compassion for society's unfortunates."[1] John, sixty when Joe was born, gave him such a grounding in the Bible and Shakespeare that, throughout his life Joe could enrich his speeches with off-the-cuff quotations from both.

Joe also inherited a taste for journalism. Of the three Halifax newspapers of the day, John Howe's "Journal" was the best. Indeed, it set the standard for newspaper printing throughout North America. At thirteen, Joe was already

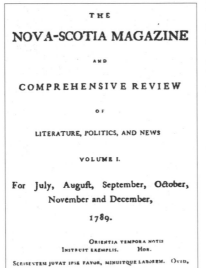

THE
NOVA-SCOTIA MAGAZINE
AND
COMPREHENSIVE REVIEW
OF
LITERATURE, POLITICS, AND NEWS

VOLUME I.

For July, Auguft, September, October, November and December, 1789.

ORIENTIA TEMPORA NOTIS
INSTRUIT EXEMPLIS.   HOR.
SCRIBENTEM JUVAT IPSE FAVOR, MINUITQUE LABOREM.   OVID.

As well as the "Halifax Journal," John Howe's other publication "Nova-Scotia Magazine" appeared in 1789. It was in the "Journal's" print shop that Joseph Howe apprenticed.

helping John perform as postmaster general and king's printer, but since one of his half-brothers would inherit these offices, he would have to build his own career. He became the first giant of Canadian journalism.

By December 1827, when he turned twenty-three, he was physically strong, widely read, and cocky. He bought the "Novascotian" from George Renny Young for £1,050, to be paid over five years. The price was reasonable, but Howe was already paying for another newspaper, and his purchase of the "Novascotian" introduced him to the kind of financial problem he had to struggle with for the rest of his life. He drove himself furiously to make the "Novascotian" the best paper in British North America. Having discovered the "maiden loveliness" of Susan Ann McNab, a captain's daughter who lived on McNab's Island ("yon fairy isle") in Halifax Harbour, he married her in February 1828, but when spring arrived, not even she could keep him from tramping all over the colony to write his "Rambles" for the "Novascotian." In his often protracted absences, Susan Ann ran the business and put out the paper. She must have been the first woman editor in Canada, though perhaps she never had the title.

Howe was not only the newspaper's backwoods travel writer, but its publisher, circulation manager, editor, literary critic, theatre reviewer, poet, business reporter, foreign affairs editor, and most significantly, legislative reporter. From the press gallery, he reported up to 200 columns of debate during each session of the elected assembly. In 1834, at twenty-nine, he boasted he had written as much manuscript as he could carry, and that if he had not, Nova Scotians would have been "about as incapable of judging their Representatives, as if they had assembled in the moon."

An 1860s Notman photo of Susan Ann McNab Howe, wife of Joseph Howe. She ran the business and put out the "Novascotian" in her husband's absence.

Howe began his career as a mild Tory, but quickly became the most articulate enemy of the Tory power structure. He called it "this miserable system of irresponsibility, folly and corruption." Like the Family Compact in Upper Canada, members of the Council of Twelve met in secret, gave wedges of the patronage pie to relatives and cronies, set government salaries and public policy to suit themselves, and owed their positions not to elections but to a British-born governor. Most were government officials or well-to-do merchants, and adherents of the Church of England. They lived in Halifax and saw the rest of the province as territory to exploit. Nova Scotia's most famous nineteenth-century writer, Thomas Chandler Haliburton, called them twelve old women, one in lawn sleeves (the bishop).

While no one knows precisely why Howe threw his life into political reform, his inspiration probably came from Pictou County. It was typical of the disdain Tory potentates felt for the elected members of the House of Assembly from rural districts like Pictou that an attorney general labelled them "the Caribous." The feeling was mutual. Half a century later, Pictou's contempt for the old Council of Twelve remained fresh. Writing in 1877, the Rev. George Patterson, a local historian, remembered the councillors as "their high mightinesses ... trained in the narrowest school of political sentiment, full of the highest notion of arbitrary power."

As early as 1827, there in the land of Presbyterian Scots, "The Colonial Patriot" was hammering the governing Anglicans in Halifax and applauding "the march of liberal principles." It was the first newspaper to call for responsible government in the British North American colonies. Its editor was Jotham Blanchard, a student of that fighting reformer Thomas McCulloch,

founder of the Pictou Academy. To charges of disloyalty and radicalism, the "Patriot" snapped, "This has been the refuge of all the supporters of existing abuses and new oppressions since the world began." Three years later, Joseph Howe acknowledged, "The Pictou scribblers have converted me from the error of my ways." From 1830 on, the "Novascotian" championed the reform cause with increasing intensity.

Jotham Blanchard edited "The Colonial Patriot," the first newspaper published in Nova Scotia outside Halifax.

Thirty years old and a known enemy of the establishment, Howe in 1835 dared to publish a letter, signed "The People," that accused the magistrates whom the governor had appointed to run Halifax of filching money designated for the poor and extracting from the public thousands of pounds for their private use. The attorney general submitted an indictment for criminal libel to the grand jury of Halifax County, and the jury returned a true bill. The attorney general himself would prosecute Howe. The chief justice, a member of the Council of Twelve, would be on the bench, and the establishment expected the trial to destroy Howe as a threat to their grip on the colony.

Lawyers not only refused to take his case, they told him to prepare his public apology, plead guilty, and pray his jail sentence would be short. "I asked them to lend me their books," Howe later wrote, "threw myself on a sofa and read libel law for a week ... Another week was spent in selecting and arranging the facts and public documents on which I relied. I did not get through before a late hour of the evening before the trial, having only had time to write out and commit to memory the two opening paragraphs of the speech."

On March 3, 1835, when he arose to prove himself innocent of libel, no one knew him as an orator. He was used neither to courtrooms nor to public speaking. He began hesitantly, but soon noticed something he had said had sent a tear rolling down an old juror's cheek. That made Howe feel better. He stormed on for six more hours. His speech was among the most astounding events in Nova Scotia's history. It not only earned him his acquittal, but also, in the words of J. W. Longley, established him as "a heaven-inspired hero ... It is scarcely going too far to say that the whole history of forensic eloquence in British jurisprudence has rarely furnished a more magnificent address to a jury than Mr. Howe's."[2]

If the speech was a landmark in eloquence, the acquittal was a landmark in journalism. It established the right of the British North American press to attack the corruption and failings of colonial administrations. Journalists would no longer fear going to jail for saying hard things about the way governments ran colonies.

People stayed up all night to celebrate Howe's triumph. He was now the hottest political figure in the colonies, and in 1836, running as a Reform candidate in Halifax, he won a seat in the House of Assembly.

On the hustings, Howe would prove to be a fighter, flatterer, joker, needler, teacher, pleader, and preacher—a visionary with mist in his eyes, warm thunder in his voice, and a hundred facts, classical references, and homespun metaphors on his lips. One authority on nineteenth-century oratory ranked him the finest speaker in British North America, better even than the most persuasive of the Fathers of Confederation.

For the next dozen years, while leading Nova Scotia toward responsible government, Howe fought blinkered and hidebound governors and their

Artist R. Hebert sculpted in relief Joseph Howe's landmark trial on the base of a statue erected in Howe's honour at Province House.

allies. He drove two governors from office. His weapons were speeches, editorials, political organization, letters to the Colonial Secretary in London, and, at times, vicious ridicule. During his notorious squabbling with Lieutenant-Governor Falkland, he suggested some colonist might one day "hire a black fellow to horsewhip a lieutenant-governor." In the "Dictionary of Canadian Biography," historian J. Murray Beck, the best of all Howe scholars, said Howe's "lampoons and pasquinades reflecting on [Falkland]—the 'Lord of the Bed-Chamber' was the best known—not only horrified the colonial Tories but also hurt his reputation for moderation in England."[3]

A drawing by C. W. Jefferys of Joseph Howe addressing an open-air meeting. His effect as an orator is captured in the crowd's expression.

On one occasion, Howe so angered the establishment that it might have cost him his life. John C. Halliburton, son of Chief Justice Brenton Halliburton, decided that Howe had insulted the old judge and challenged him to a duel. Howe regarded duelling as a custom for fools, but felt any hint of cowardice on his part would jeopardize the reform cause. The duel occurred one spring morning, not far from his boyhood home. Halliburton fired first and missed. Howe shot at the sky and retreated to his breakfast.

Howe's vision of reform was fuzzy until Lord Durham, having investigated the causes of the rebellions of 1837 in Upper and Lower Canada, wrote his Report on the Affairs of British North America. To break the grip of a corrupt Tory clique in Upper Canada, Durham, whom some called "Radical Jack," recommended responsible government, a system whereby the executive (cabinet) could not remain in office unless it had the confidence of the elected branch of the legislature. The Durham Report appeared in February 1839, and in April, Howe's "Novascotian" declared: "The remedy ... being perfectly simple and eminently British. It is to let the majority and not the minority govern, and compel every Governor to select his advisers from those who enjoy the confidence of the people and can command a majority in the popular branch."

Nova Scotia had still not received this remedy when Charles Dickens visited Halifax in 1842, but the opening of the legislature struck him as familiar: "It was like looking at Westminster through the wrong end of a telescope. The Governor delivered the Speech from the Throne. The military band struck up 'God Save The Queen' with great vigour; the people shouted; the Ins rubbed their hands; the Outs shook their heads; the Government party said there was never such a good speech; the Opposition declared there was never such a bad one; and in short everything went on ... just as it does at home."

But, as James Morris wrote in "Heaven's Command: An Imperial Progress," what Dickens did not know was that "the Halifax Assembly ... had no ultimate responsibility at all. Its arguments were impotent. Its decisions could be vetoed without question by the Governor, who governed with the help of a Council nominated entirely by himself, and was accountable only to London."[4]

The assembly's impotence, however, would soon vanish. Throughout British North America, agitation against England's domination continued to bubble, and, even in London, the arrival of responsible government among the colonies seemed inevitable. In 1846, a new lieutenant-governor, Sir John Harvey, persuaded his executive council to offer memberships to Howe and three other Liberals, but they declined. Howe held out for an election in which a clean-cut, two-party battle would at last force on Nova Scotia a form of government in which the cabinet was truly responsible to the majority in the assembly.

Lieutenant-Governor Sir John Harvey held the title from 1846 to 1852. He was in office when responsible government was won in 1848.

The election came on August 5. Howe's Reform (Liberal) party won by seven seats, and since none of the new assemblymen were "loose fish," the governor's Tory ministers were obliged to step down. Early in 1848, the Reform administration took power, and Nova Scotia became the first British colony to win responsible government.

While the Colonial Secretary, Lord Grey, had conceded the victory and had instructed Lieutenant-Governor Harvey to accept control by the party with the majority in the assembly, the achievement belonged mostly to Howe and his allies. "We owe [the new constitution] to no Colonial Secretary," Howe insisted. "We wrested it, step by step, against the prejudices and apprehensions of various Secretaries from 1837 to 1847." Conveniently forgetting that Nova Scotia could thank earlier rebellions in the Canadas for the historic change, Howe bragged that it had come about without "a blow struck or a pane of glass broken."

The Nova Scotia Industrial
Exhibition 1854 was
accommodated at Province
House and in two tents on
the grounds.

Sir William Young served
as premier of the province
from 1854 to 1860, when
he resigned to accept the
office of chief justice. He
is best remembered for
his philanthropy during his
twenty-one years on the
bench.

CHAPTER 21

1815–1850: THE GREAT AWAKENING

In 1849 Nova Scotia became part of an adventurous pony express designed to establish a fast link between Halifax and New York, with rival riders charging through the excited villages of the Annapolis Valley on foam-flecked horses. The express service lasted less than a year, but it was a landmark in the history of journalism. The New York newspapers that founded it called their partnership the Associated Press (AP), and Daniel Craig, the tough Yankee they sent to Halifax in 1849, was the agency's first foreign correspondent. AP eventually became the greatest news organization in the world, but few among the thousands who served it ever knew about the 230-kilometre horse races of its infancy.

Samuel Cunard of Halifax had revolutionized transatlantic communications by launching a scheduled steamship service between Britain and America. The westbound Cunarders carried not only passengers, but news of European political debates, revolutions, and market conditions.

The vessels dumped the dispatches at Halifax, but telegraph connections from New York came no closer than Saint John. That was why AP founded its pony express. At Halifax, Craig would fetch the packages of news from the incoming steamship and hand them to a horseman. With the dispatches in a shoulder bag, the rider charged out of town. Every nineteen kilometres, another horse awaited him, and as he neared each relay post, he blew his horn to warn the stable ahead. Hopping off his exhausted steed, he leaped aboard a fresh one. At Kentville, another rider took over and carried the news further down the Annapolis Valley.

Meanwhile, a ship that AP had chartered would be waiting at Digby, and as the last pony galloped toward the port, a blast from a cannon upriver warned the skipper to get up steam. The vessel carried the news across the Bay of Fundy to Saint John, where a telegrapher zipped it down to New York by Morse code. The Cunarder, having left Halifax, was still plodding south-

Nova Scotia issued its first postage stamps in 1851. The stamps were printed in London by Messrs. Perkins, Bacon & Petch.

westward toward the States. The system cost AP $1,000 per trip, but it was worth every nickel. It got the news into New York as many as thirty-six hours before the transatlantic steamship reached the city.

As the riders thundered through the Valley, excited inhabitants lined the roadsides to cheer them on. The excitement intensified when AP's rivals founded a competing service. It was Craig, however, who went down in journalistic history. In Halifax, he set up the first AP office outside the United States and arranged for the express to speed to American readers exclusive news of an attempt to kill Queen Victoria. He also persuaded Boston newspapers to subscribe to the service, bringing AP its first big clients outside New York.

By 1850, the telegraph had reached Halifax, and the express was already a memory. Soon, the humming lines would reach the Pacific. Soon, an underwater cable would span the Atlantic. Soon, the Cunarders would have little use for Nova Scotia. Far out at sea, they would steam past on non-stop voyages to New York.

The pony express was a punctuation mark for Nova Scotia's progress at mid-century. After the War of 1812, the British closed the Halifax dockyard. Most of the workers were discharged, and the rest moved to Bermuda. A depression struck, and later changes in Britain's commercial policy also damaged the colony's economic health. Yet Nova Scotians came out of the war with growing patriotism, knowing their home-bred seadogs had acquitted themselves well against the Americans. The colony experienced an upwelling of political feistiness, intellectual ferment, entrepreneurial courage, and seagoing boldness. A sense of pride and unity spread across the colony and stimulated growth and enterprise.

By 1815 the population had grown to about 80,000. Halifax was sixty-six years old. As shiretowns, Amherst, Truro, Windsor, Annapolis Royal and Dorchester (Antigonish) all had courthouses, jails, and lawyers. Arichat, Pictou, Yarmouth, Liverpool, and Lunenburg were beginning to thrive on shipbuilding, the cod fisheries, and international commerce. At first, American and British shipowners controlled the carrying trade, but by the 1820s and 1830s native Nova Scotians such as Samuel Cunard were beginning to dominate the business scene. They built bigger and better vessels, took fish to the West Indies, and brought home flour from New England and tobacco, sugar, and molasses from the Caribbean. Vessels from Yarmouth and Liverpool sailed regularly to the Mediterranean. Shipbuilding blossomed on every coast of Nova Scotia, and Bluenose merchant mariners sailed on all the world's trade routes. Warehouses sprang up in port after port.

Descendants of the German-speaking farmers who had first settled Lunenburg were harvesting fish off Labrador, and already turning the town into a storied fishing village. In westernmost Nova Scotia and Cape Breton Island, the Acadians, the descendants of farmers as well, were proving to be bold and skilful fishermen.

The shipbuilding industry in Nova Scotia peaked in the mid- to late-1800s. The merchant fleet of the Maritime Provinces was world class. Nova Scotia alone owned over 2,800 vessels by 1846.

From Pictou County, it took a hundred vessels to carry a year's cut of local lumber to Britain. Returning to Pictou, the ships brought thousands of Scottish immigrants. By 1815, Scots had been flowing into the county for four decades, while in the Bay of Fundy districts settled by New Englanders and Scotch-Irish, farmers had been succeeding one another for three and even four generations. It was "time for a virile and vigorous people to demonstrate that they had in some measure subdued the wilderness into which they had come."[1]

In 1815, forests seemed almost to smother farm villages, and Nova Scotians outside Halifax knew few people other than their neighbours. The men of a typical backwoods settlement gathered to build barns, and the women to make quilts and string apples for drying. Men and women alike shared in the shrinking and thickening of woollen cloth. To scratch a living from land that was often rocky and sour, every able member of every family endured work that in some seasons was back-breaking. Fishing families were no different. "Wherever fishing was conducted from small boats near the shore," D. A. Muise said in "The Atlantic Provinces in Confederation," "the unit of production was the family, whose head owned or mortgaged both boat and equipment and whose male and female members caught, cured and prepared

The Van Norden Line on Cliff Street in Yarmouth. The stagecoach in the foreground is the same one on display today at Uniacke House.

fish for sale to merchants who would in turn sell it on international markets."

At a crossroads or near a bridge, there slowly arose the structures that made life tolerable and sociable: a store, a blacksmith's shop, a grist mill, a sawmill, and above all, a church. Whether Catholic or Protestant, the church turned a settlement into a community, and the pioneer clergy were mostly strong-minded and intelligent men. According to an old poem, the early Scots of Pictou County "met the saffron morn upon their knees," and throughout Nova Scotia it was the settlers' religious faith, more than anything else, that made their lives bearable. The clergy nurtured this faith, and were usually the first to urge construction of a school.

Few places outside Halifax had schools in 1815, but by 1854 Nova Scotia boasted more than 1,200 schools. Stoves were replacing the big kitchen fireplaces across the province; 11,000 hand-looms were seeing service; the population had soared to almost 300,000; and a mighty surge in road construction had produced more than a 1,600 kilometres of routes suitable for stagecoaches. When Queen Victoria came to the throne in 1837, two-wheeled gigs were a routine sight in Nova Scotia, and wealthier families went to church in four-wheeled carriages. In that same year, Joseph Howe marvelled:

An 1817 drawing by Lieutenant-Governor Dalhousie's personal draughtsman, John E. Woolford, of a wind-powered sawmill and grist mill in Pictou.

"Had any one told them, ten years ago, when Hamilton used to carry the mail on horseback, from Halifax to Annapolis, and sometimes in a little cart, with a solitary passenger beside him, who looked as if he was going to the end of the world, and expected to pay accordingly, that they should have lived to see a Stage Coach, drawn by four horses, running three times a week ... Would they have believed, as they travelled on foot with Stewart, the old Postman from Pictou to Halifax, who used to carry the mail in his Jacket pocket, and a gun to shoot partridges for sale as he went along, that before their heads were cold they would travel the same places in a Coach and four, with a ton of letters and papers strapped on before and behind?"

By 1850, a passenger in robust health could ride stagecoaches from Sydney all the way to Yarmouth, and coaches visited every important part of the province two or three times a week. The roads helped Nova Scotians get to know one another. Newspapers from Halifax gave them common cause and political speeches they could debate among themselves.

Thomas McCulloch, minister and educator.

A Notman photograph of Pictou Academy, c1860.

The campaign for political reform, however, began not in the papers of Halifax, but in Pictou's "Colonial Patriot," where as early as the 1820s Thomas McCulloch, a Scots Presbyterian missionary, teacher, naturalist, philosopher, and author regularly lambasted the Council of Twelve. "We have

attacked them ... by argument, sarcasm and drollery," he wrote to a friend, "and now I believe they are heartily sorry that they made us their enemies ... Sometimes with sound argument we have proved them an unconstitutional body, and everything that is politically bad, and at other times set the whole province laughing at them."

Thomas McCulloch came from Scotland to Pictou, with his family, in 1803. Wishing to do something about the inadequate education in Pictou, he began a school in his house, but as early as 1805 he dreamed of founding an academy, something like a junior college. His first plan was to train local youths for the ministry, for it was proving difficult to attract young Scotsmen to such a wilderness. But he soon realized that what the colony needed was men trained for the professions. "For a few years in the early 1800s in the little town of Pictou his teaching created a kind of intellectual ferment that had not occurred anywhere else in the country," wrote Marjory Whitelaw. "Had he remained in Scotland he might never have been more than a mildly dissenting minister in some small town near Glasgow. He was fortunate in coming to Pictou when he did ... The time, the place and the man were all right for each other, and McCulloch in consequence had a lasting impact on Nova Scotia, and eventually all of Canada."[2]

For much of his life he was one of the most controversial men in Nova Scotia. He fought many battles: in the press, in his humorous essays published as "The Stepsure Letters," and always for educational enlightenment and the Academy.

Not only McCulloch's writing but his college enraged official Halifax. In 1788, the Anglican Church had founded King's College at Windsor, N.S.,

An engraving of Town of Pictou and its harbour in 1863. Calls for political reform were unwavering in this seemingly quiet town.

expecting it to serve as a bastion of Loyalist principles, both political and religious. King's accepted only Anglican students, and "to the Scots in particular this was a shameful heresy, for in Scotland the universities had by tradition accepted students of all faiths."[3] Against stupendous financial and political odds, McCulloch opened the doors of his Pictou Academy in 1817, and kept it alive for fifteen years.

The centre of his battle for the Academy was the issue of funding comparable to that of King's College, paid regularly. But McCulloch was not always an easy man, and he never got the grant. The Academy continued on a shaky financial footing.

The governor, Lord Dalhousie, also a Scot, disapproved of King's exclusivity and fully supported the idea of another college. But he thought it should be in Halifax. McCulloch fought valiantly for his Pictou Academy, but it was Lord Dalhousie who was able to establish the college in Halifax. McCulloch's great talents were not to be wasted; he became the first principal of Dalhousie College.

The Academy closed when he went to Halifax, where he died in 1843. After his death, a Pictou group, called the Friends of the Pictou Academy, rebuilt the school into an honoured force in Nova Scotian education. And in the Academy's second flowering, during the last half of the nineteenth century, an army of scholars and professional men marched out its doors—ministers, doctors, lawyers, bankers, and others who helped earn Nova Scotia a reputation as the producer of the best brains in Canada.

All through the 1830s and most of the 1840s, the province seethed with debate over political reform. The governor and his twelve-man executive

Enos Collins, born in Liverpool, N.S, was owner of the Collins Bank in Halifax. Upon his death he was reputed to be the wealthiest man in North America.

Collins established his private bank on the Halifax Waterfront in a building that today is part of Historic Properties.

were all Haligonians, and since other Halifax men often sat in the assembly as representatives of outlying districts, so were a disproportionate number of the elected councillors.

Not only politically but financially, Halifax ran the province. By the 1820s, the Halifax Chamber of Commerce was flexing its muscles all over Nova Scotia. In 1825, eight of the city's most powerful merchant-financiers—they included Enos Collins, other members of the Council of Twelve, and a future member, shipping tycoon Samuel Cunard—founded the Halifax Banking Company. The first bank in the Maritime Provinces, it virtually controlled the economic life of Nova Scotia.

The handful of shareholders of the Halifax Banking Company, better known as "Collins' bank," enjoyed a lucrative monopoly for seven years, but partly in response to their autocratic policies, other Halifax businessmen, backed by the young newspaperman Joseph Howe, urged the founding of a public financial institution. The Legislative Assembly therefore incorporated what would one day become an international giant among Canada's chartered banks: the Bank of Nova Scotia. That was in 1832, and it soon opened branches in Windsor, Pictou, Yarmouth, Annapolis Royal, and Liverpool.

Halifax merchants financed much of the shipbuilding and warehouse construction in coastal towns and, through ownership of ocean-going vessels, controlled access to the markets for Nova Scotia staples. By exploiting this

The Bank of Nova Scotia, Canada's second-oldest chartered bank, was organized at a Halifax meeting of the Merchant's Exchange in 1832. The bank issued its own currency.

Queen Victoria and the Royal Family at the opening of the Great Exhibition in London in 1851. This exhibition, as well as others in London and Paris, included products from Nova Scotia. The London event no doubt inspired Nova Scotia's own industrial exhibition at Province House in 1854.

The frontispiece of Thomas C. Haliburton's highly acclaimed book "The Clockmaker," published in 1838.

power, fixing prices, and extending credit, the merchants kept hundreds of farmers, fishermen, and timbermen in constant debt, while amassing wealth for themselves.

No homes in Nova Scotia were as sumptuous or lavishly furnished as those of the Halifax aristocrats who felt at ease beneath the chandeliers of Government House. It is scarcely surprising, then, that during the rancorous debates and name-calling from which responsible government eventually emerged, Joseph Howe drew much of his support from people outside the capital.

Thanks to politics, Halifax was nothing if not lively. James Morris wrote that it was "unexpectedly sophisticated. Political parties slandered each other, newspapers thundered, debates went on all night. Province House, where the Assembly met, was so much the most impressive building in the colony that country people came hundreds of miles to look at it, and inside it the legislators—farmers, merchants, sea captains—honoured all the forms of British parliamentary procedure."[4]

Along with the political uproar, the spread of roads, schools, and libraries, and the growth of fisheries, shipbuilding, and international trade came a revolution in farming. Its leader, a Scot named John Young, arrived in Halifax in 1814, set up a trading business, and, in a series of newspaper letters signed "Agricola," showed he knew more about advanced methods of farming than perhaps anyone in North America. For the farmer who wanted to exploit principles of scientific agriculture that had swept Europe, Young's articles were both bible and textbook. He inspired the formation of dozens of agricultural societies. Under the patronage of Governor Dalhousie, much interested in farming himself, a province-wide body came into being, with headquarters in Halifax and Young as secretary. The societies held county fairs, which led to district exhibitions, and in 1854 to the first Provincial Exhibition. The fairs brought farmers together and enlightened them about selective breeding and raising vegetables, fruit and grain.

Men like Young, McCulloch, Cunard, Howe and the writer Thomas C. Haliburton "were not isolated evidences of genius appearing, as it were, from nowhere," but "leaders in a general awakening."[5] The Nova Scotia created by the awakening would soon find itself rudely shunted into Canada.

The "Father of American humour," Thomas C. Haliburton, coined many popular clichés such as: "the early bird catches the worm," "drank like a fish," "penny wise, pound foolish," "raining cats and dogs," and "honesty is the best policy."

An 1840s Bartlette print of Haliburton's house "Clifton" at Windsor.

Halifax-born Samuel
Cunard founded
Cunard Lines.

SAILINGS of the British and North American Royal Mail Steam-Ships, being at the rate of 20 voyages in 12 months, (beginning 4th September 1841.) from England to America.

Steamer.	Leaves Liverpool.	Leaves Boston.	Leaves Halifax.
Caledonia,......	September 4	October 2	ober 4
Acadia,..........	" 19	" 16	" 18
Columbia,......	October 5	November 1	November 5
Britannia,.......	" 19	" 16	" 18
Caledonia,......	November 4	December 1	December 5
Acadia,..........	" 19	" 16	" 18
Columbia,......	December 4	1842 January 1	1842 January 5
Britannia,.......	January 4 1842	February 1	February 5
Caledonia,.......	February 4	March 1	March 5
Acadia,..........	March 4	April 1	April 5
Columbia,.......	April 5	May 1	May 5
Britannia,.....	" 19	" 16	" 18
Caledonia,.......	May 4	June 1	June 5
Acadia,..........	" 19	" 16	" 18
Columbia,.....	June 4	July 1	July 5
Britannia,.......	" 19	" 17	" 19
Caledonia,.......	July 5	August 1	August 5
Acadia,..........	" 19	" 16	" 18
Columbia,.......	August 4	September 1	September 5
Britannia,.....	" 19	" 16	" 18

GEO. BURNS SYMES.

Quebec, 27th October, 1841.   u s l w

The Cunard steamer the Royal
William leaves Pictou Harbour, 1833.

Top: Schedule of Cunard's sailings,
advertised in the Quebec "Gazette," 1841.

CHAPTER 22

STEAMSHIPS, RAILWAYS, A GOOD WAR FOR NOVA SCOTIA

O n New Year's Day, 1830, the first steamboat built in Canada, the Sir Charles Ogle, slid down its way in Dartmouth and splashed into service as a Halifax–Dartmouth ferry. Joseph Howe marvelled that, while its predecessor, powered by a team of horses, had often taken an hour to traverse the harbour, the Ogle shot across in seven minutes. In 1833, the Royal William, launched in Quebec and built for runs between there and Halifax, made history by steaming from Pictou to Cowes, England.

The Royal William boasted 180-horsepower engines driving side paddlewheels and three masts, which at times during the epic voyage carried sails. It was therefore not, as so many claimed, the first vessel to cross the Atlantic under steam power alone. It was merely "the first Canadian ship to cross the Atlantic almost continuously under steam power."[1]

The Rev. George Patterson, a Pictou County Presbyterian who reviled extravagance, later complained it was "fitted up in a style of elegance that would compare with the floating palaces of the Hudson." Patterson was nevertheless proud to acknowledge that "a Canadian built ship, sailing from Pictou, first proved the practicability of ocean steam navigation, and introduced a new era in the trade of the world." The firm that had ordered construction of the Royal William was the Quebec and Halifax Steam Navigation Company, and among its directors were the Halifax-born brothers, Samuel, Joseph, and Henry Cunard.

Joseph Howe and Thomas Haliburton, bound for Britain aboard the sailing ship Tyrian in 1838, found themselves in a dead calm in mid-Atlantic. The steamer Syrius overtook them, and when it stopped to take on the Tyrian's mail, Howe visited it to grill the captain. Back aboard the becalmed Tyrian, he watched the Syrius vanish over the eastern horizon and promptly became a vigorous advocate of steamship communication between Britain and Nova Scotia.

While many sneered at the notion of "iron tea kettles" plying the high seas, Samuel Cunard, whose firm operated forty sailing ships, believed steamers "might start and arrive at their destination with the punctuality of railway trains." He won a contract from the British Admiralty to use steamboats to carry mail from England to Halifax twice each month, with services to Boston and Quebec as well. Cunard then persuaded Scottish investors to help him found the British and North American Royal Mail Steam Packet Company (the Cunard Line), and on July 17, 1840, with Cunard and his daughter Ann on board, the Britannia completed the firm's first scheduled transatlantic voyage, reaching Halifax thirteen days out of Liverpool. The service did not fulfil joyful predictions that it would turn Halifax into the centre of steam navigation for all North America, but it did make the port the chief distribution point for colonial mail. As soon as a Cunarder reached Halifax, stagecoaches rattled north with the mail for New Brunswick and over to Pictou where a steamer awaited the packages for Canada.

In 1840 the Cunard steamer Britannia completed the Cunard Line's first scheduled transatlantic voyage.

By mid-century, sailing ships still dominated trade routes on the high seas and in registered tonnage of shipping, the Maritime Provinces, small as they were, stood fourth in the world. "In the year 1874, Nova Scotia reached her peak," wrote Dorothy Duncan in "Bluenose: A Portrait of Nova Scotia," "when she had 3,025 craft registered on her books, with a total tonnage of over half a million. This amounted to one and a quarter tons per capita, surpassing any other country in the world."[2] Steamships, however, already threatened the Age of Sail. Ever bigger and faster steamers were helping Nova Scotians get to know—and trade with—New Brunswickers and Prince

Edward Islanders. As early as the 1850s, steamships crossed the Bay of Fundy four times a week from Nova Scotia to Saint John. Pictou had regular steamship connections with Charlottetown, Shediac, and the mouth of the Miramichi River. Writing only a couple of decades later, the Rev. George M. Grant told readers of his "Ocean to Ocean" that sailing by steamer from Pictou to Quebec was "the most charming voyage in America for wretched half-baked mortals, escaping from the fierce heat of summer in inland cities."[3]

As the number and efficiency of ferries and stagecoaches grew, so did talk of the three colonies uniting as one. By mid-century, the idea had been simmering for decades, and as railway fever infected the colonies, union seemed increasingly attractive to many Maritimers.

In 1835, ten years after a railway in England started the world's first steam-powered freight and passenger service, Joseph Howe urged construction of a line between Halifax and Windsor. That same year, Haliburton's most famous character, Sam Slick, described a railway as "river, bridge, road and canal— all one. It saves what we haven't got to spare—men, horses, carts, vessel, barges, and what's all in all— time." In 1839, Nova Scotia got its first railway. Its job was merely to cart coal from Albion Mines to Pictou Harbour, a distance of nine kilometres, but its owners celebrated the opening with free rides, a ball, and a banquet, and "there was not an unemployed bagpipe" in the entire county. By 1840, Britain boasted 2142 kilometres of trackage, and "railway mania" gripped the nation for the next decade. But as the 1850s began, Pictou County's little coal-carrier remained Nova Scotia's only rail line. Howe was still tub-thumping for railways and thought he had inspired the British government to guarantee construction of a line from Halifax to the St. Lawrence. "I believe that many in this room will live to hear the whistle of the steam engine in the passes of the Rocky Mountains," he said in 1851, "and to make the journey from Halifax to the Pacific in five or six days."

The Samson, one of Atlantic Canada's first steam locomotives, went into service in 1839 in Pictou County. The Museum of Industry in Stellarton features the original Samson as a part of its collection.

"To the advocates of legislative union I say, your scheme is impracticable without the railroads," he told a cheering crowd in Quebec City. "To the Federalist my advice is, make the railroads first, and test your theory afterwards. To the people of the Maritime Provinces [I say], make the railroads, that you may behold the fertile and magnificent territory that lies behind you. To the Canadians [I say], make the railroads, that you may come down upon the seaboard and witness its activity, and appreciate the exhaustless treasures it contains."

At forty-seven, Howe was the most prominent figure in British North America. Complications beyond his control dashed his hopes of seeing Britain finance an intercolonial railroad, but by 1858 the young Nova Scotia Railway Company had trains running to Windsor, Truro, and the rich farmland surrounding both towns. One of its locomotives was the Joseph Howe.

Howe was still as true and blue a Briton as his father had been. In 1855, with the Crimean War under way and Britain desperate for troops, he set up secret recruitment machinery along the eastern seaboard of the United States. Since Congress had forbidden foreign powers from recruiting soldiers on American soil, and the United States was both pro-Russia and anti-Britain, his activities were dangerous and illegal. Moreover, by cutting short his preparation for an election back home, they contributed to one of the bitterest defeats of his life. Nova Scotians returned the Liberals to power, but in Cumberland County, Charles Tupper of Amherst—a doctor, a Tory, a stripling of only thirty-four—whipped Howe, the Grand Tribune himself.

At a public meeting during an earlier election, the "Eastern Chronicle" reported, Howe had treated Tupper as "a naturalist would an insect of extraordinary size or colour, sticking a pin through it ... for study at a suitable time." Tupper would become the most forceful proponent of Nova Scotia's joining Canada. Some would remember him as having rammed the province into Confederation (though his nickname, "The Ram of Cumberland County," had more to do with his private life than his political achievements.) He was one of a cadre of younger politicians from a new middle class.

Nova Scotia Railway timetable, 1857.

NOVA SCOTIA RAILWAY.

TARIFF.

PASSENGERS.

Morning and Evening Trains run daily between Halifax and Grand Lake, and a Mid-day Train to and from Bedford.

Miles.	Stations.	1st Train.	2d Train.	3d Train.	Fares. 1st Class. s.	1st Class. d.	2d Class. s.	2d Class. d.
	Up Trains.	A. M.	NOON.	P. M.	s.	d.	s.	d.
	Halifax, depart	7.30	12. 0	3. 0				
3¼	Four Mile House	7.40	12 10	3.10	0	7½	0	5
8	Bedford	8. 0	12 30	3.30	1	8	0	10
10¾	Scott Road	8.10		3.40	1	10	1	3
13¼	Windsor Junction				2	3	1	6
20	Fletcher's	8 40		4.10	3	4	2	3
22½	Grand Lake, arrive	8.50		4.20	3	9	2	6
	Down Trains.	A. M.	P. M.	P. M.	s.	d.	s.	d.
	Grand Lake, depart	9.25		5.10				
2½	Fletcher's	9.35		5.20	0	5	0	4
9¼	Windsor Junction				1	6	1	0
11¾	Scott Road	10.15		5.50	1	11	1	3
14½	Bedford	10.25	1.45	6.	2	6	1	9
19¼	Four Mile House	10.45	2. 5	6.20	3	2	2	8
22½	Halifax, arrive	10.55	2.15	6.30	3	9	2	6

Excursion Tickets—for use same day, up and down—a rate and a half. Tickets for Children under 12 years of age, half price. Passengers not providing themselves with tickets before entering the Cars, will be required to pay 7½d. extra. Special Trains provided on reasonable notice, and Passenger Cars hired to parties or families at diminished rates.

HORSES & CARRIAGES.

	Bedford. s.	Bedford. d.	Grand Lake s.	Grand Lake d.
1 Horse and empty Carriage	1	10½	2	9
1 do. Carriage and load	2	6	3	9
Driver in Horse Car	0	7½	1	0
2 Horses and empty Carriage	3	1½	4	8
2 do. Carriage and load	3	9	5	6
Driver in Horse Car	0	7½	1	0
3 Horses and empty Carriage	4	4½	6	8
3 do. Carriage and load	5	[illegible]	[illegible]	6
Driver in Horse Car	0	7½	1	0
4 Horses and empty Carriage	5	0	7	6
4 do. Carriage and load	6	3	9	6
Driver in Horse Car	0	7½	1	0
Saddle or other Horse	1	6	2	3

MISCELLANEOUS.

Small Parcels and Packages according to size and value.	Bedford. s.	Bedford. d.	Grand Lake s.	Grand Lake d.
Barrels, each	0	4	0	7½
Hhds. and Puns., 80 to 120 galls.	1	3	2	0
Bags of 2 bushels	0	3	0	5
Do. of 3 do.	0	4	0	7½
Bundles, equal in size to a barrel	0	4	0	7½
Heavy Articles, by weight, per ton, per mile	0	3		
Furniture, per ten cubic feet, at	0	5	0	7½
Dry Fish, in bundles of 1 cwt	0	2	0	4
Parcels under 50 lbs. or bulk of half-barrel size	0	3	0	4
Cordwood, per cord	2	6	3	9
Bark	2	6	3	9
Lumber and Scantling, per M.	2	0	3	0
Screwed Hay, per ton	2	6	3	9
Shingles, per 4 bundles	1	0	1	6
Timber, per ton, per mile	0	3		
Do. per M. soft	2	9	4	0
Do. per M. hard	3	3	5	0
Calves and Pigs, each	0	4	0	6
Sheep	0	3	0	4
Neat Cattle, single	0	10	1	3
Do. when more than one	0	8	1	0

The rates between Bedford and Grand Lake are the same as those between Halifax and Bedford. Freight [illegible] in quantity by agreement. Freight to be labelled or marked legibly in all cases—unless so marked, transportation will be at freighter's risk. No responsibility assumed by carriers, unless contents of packages or parcels are distinctly and legibly marked upon them. ☞ No Horses, Carriages, or other freight received within ten minutes before the starting of Trains. In all cases the Cars to be loaded and discharged at expense of freighters—and not loaded above the stancheons.

JOSEPH HOWE, Chairman.

N. S. Railway Office, Feb. 2, 1857.

Earlier leaders and merchants exploited colonial resources to reap profits for themselves and English investors. The most powerful of the older Halifax merchants grew rich on the staples trade and wanted no disruptions of business. They would be vehement enemies of Confederation. But the new breed of politician had the future of Nova Scotia in mind. These men dreamed and preached about the development of a more diversified economy, with factories that Nova Scotians would found, own, and operate; the building of railroads to link industries; and the forging of an intercolonial union that would make the region strong enough to turn these hopes into reality.

By 1860, the Liberals were back in power in Nova Scotia with Joseph Howe, elected in Hants County, serving as premier. He may have grown a bit weary of politics. His government did not distinguish itself. Tupper attacked it mercilessly, and Howe yearned for an imperial posting from the mother country he loved so dearly and had served so passionately. While still premier, he happily accepted a job as fisheries commissioner under the Reciprocity Treaty with the United States. In the election of 1863, however, he foolishly agreed to contest Lunenburg, and this attempt to land a second salary left him vulnerable to Tory ridicule. He lost by 500 votes, and his party, in hopeless disarray, won a mere fourteen out of fifty-five seats.

The premier was now Tupper.

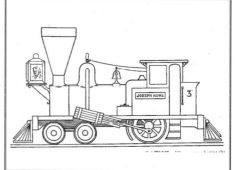

A conceptual drawing of the Nova Scotia Railway locomotive "Joseph Howe" by Robert Brown.

On April 12, 1861, Pierre Gustave Toutant Beauregard, a brigadier-general in the new Confederate army of the South, ordered his men to bombard Fort Sumter at Charleston, South Carolina, and thus opened the Civil War. In thousands of battles across thousands of miles, it raged for four years, causing at least 600,000 casualties, but it was sweet news for Nova Scotia. The colony was already profiting from the Reciprocity Treaty, which Britain and the United States had signed in 1854. The agreement admitted American fishermen to the Atlantic coastal fisheries of British North America, but also established free trade for coal, fish, lumber, and farm products. Nova Scotia's exports to the United States promptly rose.

The Civil War was a magnificent bonus.

Confederate cruisers destroyed much of the North's merchant navy. Indeed, tonnage of American merchantmen plummeted from 2.5 million tons in 1861 to under 1.4 million in 1866, and many of the surviving vessels became troop-carriers. The American fishing fleet shrank from above 200,000 tons to below 100,000. Bluenose shipyards hummed as never before. As wartime prices sky-rocketed in the North, Bluenose merchants grew rich, selling fish, lumber, and Pictou County coal to New England. Fully a third of the ships entering Boston Harbour in 1862 were Nova Scotia sailing vessels, and by 1865 Americans were buying 41 per cent of the colony's exports.

From the South, too, came good news. When the Union blockaded Southern ports, ocean freight rates soared, making shipbuilding even more profitable. At the same time, there descended on Halifax a crowd of Southern blockade-runners, smugglers, adventurers, and agents. They gobbled up everything from boots to bonnets, from saddles to ribbons. In his history of Halifax, Thomas H. Raddall said that one local marvelled, "I have seen a man go into a large wholesale dry goods store ... and ask the proprietor in the most matter-of-fact way what he would take for his whole establishment—spot cash ... Hesslein of the Halifax Hotel could hardly buy champagne fast enough; for the Southerners, with old-fashioned notions of hospitality and with the official classes and the military and navy to win over, put no restraint on their lavishness."[4]

Finally, as Britain prepared for a possible war with the United States, fresh British money flowed into Halifax. Just before the Civil War began, US Secretary of State W. H. Seward had made the bizarre suggestion that the United States unify its people by waging war against European nations, preferably Britain. Then, in November 1861, with the Civil War well under way, an American warship, the Jacinte, halted the Trent, a British merchantman, in the Bahamas Channel and arrested two passengers. They were Confederate emissaries to London and Paris. Britain insisted on reparations for this breach of international law, and the resulting uproar

Confederate and grandson of Zackery Taylor, fourteenth president of the United States, John Taylor Wood took up residence in Halifax following the American Civil War.

The United States Confederate ship Tallahassee, under the command of John Taylor Wood, was trapped in Halifax Harbour while US Union gunboats lay in wait off the entrance to the harbour. The Tallahassee slyly escaped through Eastern Passage in the cover of night.

brought Britain and America to the brink of war. Britain saw Canada as vulnerable. The provinces called out their militia, and Britain sent reinforcements for Montreal of 7,000 men and guns. But London knew little about Lower Canada, especially in winter, and the reinforcements arrived too late to travel up the St. Lawrence River. They landed at Saint John, N.B.

From there the men and guns travelled overland, up the St. John River valley, through the snowy forests of the New Brunswick–Maine border. The officers were in sleighs, under warm buffalo robes, the men on foot. A wave of patriotism was sweeping across British North America, and as the troops made their way through New Brunswick, the villages hailed them with banners strung across the road. "The Illustrated London News" reported that this costly expedition had been a great success. The men had behaved well, and there had been few casualties.

The expedition, however, made the need for a railway through Nova Scotia and New Brunswick more obvious than ever. So a railway was promised. But endless interprovincial disputes delayed the work, and the official opening of the Intercolonial Railway did not occur until 1873. Three more years would pass before it would be up and running.

A modern aerial view of the Halifax Citadel, the fourth fort to be built on the site. In 1862 the British began to rebuild Halifax's extensive defence system.

Back in 1862, the British had begun to rebuild Halifax's entire defence system and strengthen the naval force there. "Now, presto!—the harbor was alive with twenty men-o' war, Britannia's latest, every one a steamship,"[5] Raddall wrote.

Out of the war the Maritimes got a much-needed railroad, and out of the wartime prosperity sprang the Merchants Bank of Halifax, which would eventually become the Royal Bank of Canada and move its head office to Montreal.

The Civil War was good to Nova Scotia, but its conclusion was ominous.

A scene from 'The Merry Wives of Windsor,' featuring caricatures of (from left) George E. Cartier, Sir John Macdonald, Sir Francis Hincks, H. L. Langevin, and Joseph Howe. An allusion is made to Howe's support of annexation.

Sir Charles Tupper, educated as a physician, was premier of Nova Scotia before serving for less than a year in 1894 as prime minister of Canada. He was among the Fathers of Confederation.

CHAPTER 23

THE TEMPESTUOUS CREATION OF A BRAND-NEW NATION

Newspapers and orators had long touted a union of the British North American colonies, but it was not until 1864 that many people took the idea seriously, and even then only in the Province of Canada. In 1841, Britain had turned the English-speaking Upper Canada and the largely French-speaking Lower Canada into one colony with a single legislature. Since British immigration would increase rapidly, representation by population ("rep by pop") would have guaranteed an Anglo-Canadian majority, but the Act of Union provided equal representation in Parliament for each of the two old Canadas. The result, by the 1860s, was a political deadlock and governmental paralysis.

When the government of John A. Macdonald and Étienne Taché was defeated in Ottawa in the House in June 1864, it had lasted less than three months. In two years, Canada had endured two general elections and three administrations. Members now faced dissolution, another futile election, and a continuation of the stalemate. On the day of the defeat, however, a parliamentary committee recommended a federative system for either Canada alone or for all the provinces of British North America.

George Brown—Toronto newspaper editor, towering Grit, and Macdonald's most formidable enemy—promptly agreed to enter a coalition government to help clean up the constitutional mess. Brown's speech was one of the most dramatic in Canadian history. On June 30, Baron Charles Stanley Monck, the governor general of British North America, wrote to the lieutenant-governors of the Maritime Provinces to ask if some Canadians might attend a proposed meeting about Maritime Union.

The Maritimes had been mumbling about a union and considering calling a meeting about it. They had not decided when or where to hold the conference, or who should attend. Yet here were the Canadians, asking themselves in already. Maritime leaders now agreed to meet on September 1, 1864, in Charlottetown, and they agreed that the Canadians could come, too.

The campaign for Confederation was an exercise in hard sell at the backwoods level. The salesmen were Canadian politicians who dearly hoped a federation of all the colonies of British North America would solve their constitutional predicament. The customers, a suspicious bunch, were the politicians of the Maritimes. Only two or three of the Canadians had the slightest first-hand knowledge of Maritimers. Thomas D'Arcy McGee, Macdonald's eloquent, Irish-born colleague, reported that one Canadian earnestly asked him, "What kind of people are they?" as though they were Mongolian tribesmen.

Nova Scotians were almost as ignorant of Canada, and what they did know about it they did not like. Canada was a land of rebellions, shootings, and hangings, the jaded home of railway scandals, high taxes, and incompetent government. The Canadians had a monumental selling job ahead of them.

Meanwhile, and quite by chance, dozens of jolly good fellows from Canada—politicians, newspapermen, and businessmen—made a back-slapping, hand-shaking trip to Saint John and Halifax. Magical weather and good spirit clung to them throughout their trip. They gleefully attended the Halifax Yacht Club's "Hodge-Podge and Chowder Party." Bunting streamed from the yachts, and a good wind drove them up Bedford Basin. The Canadians and their Bluenose hosts disembarked, walked up to the Duke of Kent's old estate, and dug into an outdoor feast. The "Toronto Leader" reported:

"Leap-frog became the order of the day and a lively scene ensued ... Bluenoses sprang over Canadians with a shriek of delight. Canadians bounded over New Brunswickers and tripped over Nova Scotians. Editors and correspondents mingled in the fray and perilled their valuable persons by seeking the bubble reputation."

McGee made a speech, Howe made a speech, bagpipes skirled, and it was not until a full moon rose over Bedford Basin that the party headed back downtown. Two nights later, everyone endured one of those fierce exercises in gluttony which the Victorian gentlemen of British North America regarded as ceremonial dinners. Fisheries Commissioner Joseph Howe invited the visitors aboard HMS Lily for a harbour cruise. "Nature smiled upon us," the "Toronto Leader" reported. "On one side the city of Halifax looking resplendent in the fullness of the noon-day sun, and on the Dartmouth side ... the fields still green and lively with pretty cottages peeping out from charming clusters of trees." Ending shortly before the Charlottetown Conference, the trip served as a lubricant for intercolonial frictions.

The political stand-off in Canada was not the only reason why uniting British North America made sense to supporters of the Union Jack on both sides of the Atlantic. They saw it as the only way to prevent the colonies from falling to the Americans. The North was winning the Civil War, and it was hostile toward Britain, which was so friendly to the South that British shipyards built Confederate raiders. At war's end, would the Grand Army of the Republic invade Canada? By 1864, bellicose Union newspapers were demanding the seizure of British North America.

The last thing Britain wanted to do was send an army across the Atlantic to defend colonies against the world's biggest military force. Shipping reinforcements to Canada during the Trent Affair had cost nearly a million pounds. Maintaining Britain's total defence establishment in North America in one financial year, 1862–63, cost another million, and Canada's refusal to invest in its own defence enraged British MPs.

By October 1864, after the future Fathers of Confederation had met twice, Colonial Secretary Edward Cardwell prayed for the emergence of a new nation—one strong enough to avoid falling into American hands without help from Britain. "And from that time forward," Donald Creighton wrote in "Dominion of the North," "all the influence of the British government was used to push the plan to its conclusion, and all its diplomatic power was employed to protect the reorganization until it was complete."[1]

The future of the Prairies, the far west, and the northwest also concerned Cardwell and many Canadians. Farmers had settled most of the better land in Canada West (Ontario) and Canada East (Quebec). Canadian politicians, and even a few in Nova Scotia, dreamed of a state stretching from the Atlantic to the Pacific. If the colonies failed to become a nation, build a railway to the Pacific, and claim that vast territory, surely they would lose it all to pushy Americans.

Left as they were, the northern colonies might well have withered under new economic pressures. While Nova Scotia had balked at restrictions in the old Navigation Acts, it and other colonies, as children of a mighty empire, had enjoyed certain trade advantages within international commercial systems.

Sir Adams G. Archibald, Father of Confederation, practiced law in Truro and Prince Edward Island and later became Lieutenant-Governor of Manitoba. He succeeded Joseph Howe as leader of the Liberal party after his return to Nova Scotia.

Their job had been to supply staples to distant and preferential markets and import manufactured goods from the mother country. To do that, they needed neither major native industries or substantial trade within British North America.

In the United States, the North promoted big factories, transcontinental railways, westward expansion, self-sufficiency, and economic nationalism. The Reciprocity Treaty was a boon to British North America, but as the curtain fell on the Civil War and the victors became more anti-British and pugnacious, everyone knew the treaty was doomed. The United States abrogated it in 1866. To survive, the colonies would have to rely on one another as never before.

Meanwhile, the Industrial Revolution spread both hopes and threats. Sail was giving way to steam, wood to iron, and, in flour and lumber mills, water power to steam. Railways were replacing canals. By 1866, the Maritimes had 584 km of track, and Canada more 3200 km. New tools and machines were changing the work in farm and forest. They helped the Bluenose coal industry grow and sped the shift from the square timber trade to production of sawn lumber for export. Factories sprouted, especially in Canada.

Where would the colonies sell their manufactured goods, if not to one another? Intercolonial trade could not flourish without an intercolonial railway, and the promise of a line from Halifax to the Canadas—over a route strategically distant from the threatening Americans—was a major inducement to get the Maritimes to join Confederation.

Along the railway that ran from Halifax to Truro and would continue through Tupper country on its way to Quebec, Nova Scotians tended to back Confederation. The vision also won support in Pictou County, which boasted coal and factories, and parts of Cape Breton Island. But among Halifax merchants, the ports of the South Shore, and the farmers and apple-exporters of the Annapolis Valley, Confederation was anathema. Many Nova Scotians reviled it. Most opposed it.

"Over in Nova Scotia," R. M. Lower wrote in "Colony to Nation: A History of Canada," "people were sympathetic with those who had not the good luck to be Nova Scotians, and throughout the peninsula, from North Cape to Cape Sable, whether a man were a Highlander, Englander, German or Acadian by descent, he was first and foremost a Nova Scotian."[2] Proud of their history and culture, many Nova Scotians feared absorption in a bigger nation. Canadians outnumbered them nearly eight to one. Confederation would shrink the significance of the provincial legislature and allow Nova Scotia only the feeblest representation in the federal parliament.

"Our nationality," one journalist warned, "would be merged into that of Canada; we would be made use of by the Canadians, as were the Israelites of old by the Egyptians, to dig their canals."[3] Others wondered why Nova Scotia should sacrifice its own constitution simply because Canada's was not working.

Canada seemed a distant and uncivilized land. Its future lay in the interior, in which most Nova Scotians were supremely uninterested. They still looked outward to the ocean and down to Boston. Having long enjoyed amicable trade relations with New England, they were less inclined than Canadians to see Yankees as fiends.

In Nova Scotia, the loss of the Reciprocity Treaty was not the disaster it seemed to Canada. The seacoast colony still had its fisheries and hoped to see the Americans barred from them. Was there not a danger that a federal government with its capital in Ottawa would allow Americans to exploit Nova Scotia's fisheries? Was there not a danger, too, that the more advanced manufacturing industries of the Canadas would drive Nova Scotia's young factories out of business? Up there, taxes and tariffs were high, and the government debt alarming. Why would Nova Scotians risk being milked for the construction of railways and fortifications that would chiefly benefit Canada?

Despite such misgivings, shared by many New Brunswickers and Prince Edward Islanders, the Charlottetown Conference was a spectacular success for the eight Canadian cabinet ministers who showed up. They had worked out their Confederation pitch in detail. All were highly familiar with the plan. They had a clear idea of what each would say and a powerful recognition of their common purpose. With "the fanaticism of converts," they sold the political reorganization they saw as their salvation.

Their most effective ally among the Maritimers was Premier Charles

Edward Chandler, Father of Confederation, was born in Amherst, Nova Scotia. After his admission to the Bar he moved to New Brunswick and was a delegate for that province at the Confederation conferences. Later he succeeded Sir Leonard Tilley as lieutenant-governor of New Brunswick.

William Alexander Henry, a Father of Confederation, was a Halifax lawyer and represented Antigonish in the legislature.

Amherst lawyer and politican Robert Barry Dickey, also a Father of Confederation, was an outspoken critic at the Quebec conference.

Tupper, head of Nova Scotia's five-man delegation. Tupper was arrogant, ambitious, crafty, and in his crusade for Confederation, unwavering. He had asked his most bitter political enemy to join Nova Scotia's bipartisan team in Charlottetown, but Howe decided he could not escape his duties as fisheries commissioner. While others made history, the most famous Nova Scotian of the nineteenth century was at sea on HMS Lily.

At the conference, the extracurricular activities were convivial or, to hear the critics of Confederation tell it, downright indulgent. On Friday, September 2, the day after the Canadians arrived, the provincial secretary of Prince Edward Island, W. H. Pope, held a buffet lunch at his house and, on Saturday afternoon the Canadians countered with the most significant piece of shipboard hospitality in the history of Canada.

At 4 P.M., aboard the Queen Victoria, the champagne bottles began to pop. The most eloquent Canadians—George Brown, D'Arcy McGee, and Montreal lawyer and railway promoter George-Étienne Cartier—made witty, rousing, and persuasive speeches. The corks kept on flying, men gathered warm confidence, and the hard-nosed Maritimers began to believe that, yes, some day a confederation of the colonies might actually come to pass. It was at this sunny, extravagant, mid-afternoon bash on the decks of a little steamship in Charlottetown's harbour that Confederation began to win down-east converts.

The Canadians finished their formal presentation on Tuesday, September 6, and the Maritimers abandoned all consideration of a mere Maritime Union. The partying continued. The Canadians entertained the island's lieutenant-governor and flocks of local ladies. The delegates spent a day at the beaches on the north shore, and everyone stayed up all night at a great ball, denounced by a local weekly as a "reeking slough of debauchery." Around 5 A.M., September 8, the nation-builders made their way through the warm island fog and climbed aboard the Queen Victoria for a trip to Nova Scotia.

They stayed in Halifax only long enough to adjourn to Saint John, agree to a further conference at Quebec City in October, and attend a banquet where the huge amounts of food seemed to reflect everyone's idea of the occasion's huge amount of importance. The Charlottetown Conference, for all the sniping it endured in the anti-Confederation press, had witnessed the first appearance in British North America of an authentic national spirit.

Thirty-odd Canadian and Maritime politicians met in Quebec City from

October 10 to 27 to hammer out a general agreement on the legal and financial basis for Confederation. The discussions were often tense and exhausting, but the Canadians again sponsored much tippling and dancing. In "The Life and Times of Confederation," P. B. Waite reported that one Maritime delegate called them "cunning fellows" who knew that if they could "dance their way into the affections of the wives and daughters of the country, the men will certainly become an easy target."[4]

"The [delegates] had nice times," A. J. Smith, leader of the Confederate-haters in New Brunswick would later joke. "Dinners, balls, champagne, suppers, and only when surrounded with such influences were they fit to form a new empire."

Yet form it they did. The seventy-two resolutions the Fathers of Confederation passed in Quebec became the foundation of the British North America Act, whose passage by the British Parliament in 1867 created the Dominion of Canada.

Throughout the northern colonies the debate over Confederation crackled and angrily see-sawed about, but nowhere was the antagonism toward the Quebec resolutions more fierce than in Nova Scotia. It obliterated even party lines. The whole colony wondered which side Howe would back. Before the rise of Tupper, Howe had often sounded like an advocate of the union of British North America. "If you had a circus," he supposedly complained, "and had got together a good show ... how would you like it if that fellow, Tupper, came and stood by the door and collected the shillings?" The temptation to settle old scores with Tupper must have been powerful, and Howe never enjoyed sitting on the sidelines.

His public assault on Confederation began in January 1865. In the "Botheration Letters" in the "Halifax Morning Chronicle," he ridiculed and damned the Quebec resolutions. He wrote the attacks anonymously, but their style was so recognizable everyone suspected he was the author. Howe was just warming up. In 1866, Tupper led the Nova Scotia delegation at a conference in London to iron out the final terms of Confederation. Howe and two anti-Confederate friends followed them across the Atlantic to oppose the union. He lobbied furiously all summer and winter and into the spring of 1867, but the men who ran Great Britain were either set on the Confederation scheme or bored by it. Howe sank into uncharacteristic gloom.

In March 1867, the British North America Act sailed through the British

Amherst-born, teacher, lawyer, and politician Jonathan McCully, Father of Confederation, took an active role in the Confederation debates both as editor of the Halifax newspapers, "Morning Chronicle" and the "Unionist," and as a delegate to the conferences.

Parliament with barely a ripple of debate. Howe's group sourly contrasted the uneventful passage of the BNA with the eagerness with which the British parliamentarians immediately plunged into a debate on a new dog tax. Confederation became a "fait accompli" on July 1. "With the first dawn of this gladsome summer morn," the "Toronto Globe" exulted, "we hail this birthday of a new nationality. A united British America takes its place among the nations of the world." Black crepe hung in the streets of Yarmouth and Halifax.

Nova Scotians had never voted on Confederation. The Tories gained power in 1863, and Premier Tupper, sensing that Confederation smelled bad to most Bluenose voters, avoided going to the people until after it had become a fact. But Howe, in a passionate and vicious election campaign, rallied the anti-Confederates to a repeal movement. In the nation's first federal election, September 18, 1867, Nova Scotia voted overwhelmingly for men who openly hated the federal dream. No separatist leader could have asked for more. Howe led his team to victory in every constituency but Tupper's, and Nova Scotia sent to Ottawa eighteen anti-Confederates and one Father of Confederation.

Armed with such a powerful expression of Nova Scotia's will, Howe sailed for England in February of 1868. He employed every lobbying trick he had ever known but gradually realized his cause was lost. When Tupper reached London in March, he and Howe sat down together alone. Tupper said, "Mr. Howe, you are here seeking a repeal of this union ... You will fail. What then?" Home in July, Howe spoke privately of a "sense of humiliation not easily described."

While some historians attributed Howe's attack on Confederation to his egomaniacal jealousy of Tupper, J. Murray Beck, the most authoritative Howe historian of the twentieth century, refuted their posthumous psychoanalysis. Beck argued that Howe opposed Confederation for three reasons: the deal was not as favourable to Nova Scotia as he thought it should be; it threatened his vision of a Nova Scotia within a magnificent federation of all the colonies in the British Empire; and the Canadians, the Bluenose Confederation-lovers, and Britain itself were forcing union on Nova Scotia without consulting the Nova Scotians. "Even French girls who would have no objections to being married don't like to be ravished," he complained.

MORNING CHRONICLE.

HALIFAX, JULY 1, 1867.

CANDIDATES OF THE NOVA SCOTIA PARTY.

COUNTY OF HALIFAX.

For the House of Commons of the Dominion of Canada:
A. G. JONES, Esq.,   P. POWER, Esq.
For the House of Assembly of Nova Scotia:
HENRY BALCAM, Esq., JAMES COCHRAN, Esq., JEREMIAH NORTHUP, Esq.

DIED.

Last night, at twelve o'clock, the free and enlightened Province of Nova Scotia. Deceased was the offspring of old English stock, and promised to have proved an honour and support to her parents in their declining years. Her death was occasioned by unnatural treatment received at the hands of some of her ungrateful sons, who, taking advantage of the position she had afforded them, betrayed her to the enemy. Funeral will take place from the Grand Parade this day, Monday, at 9 o'clock. Friends are requested *not* to attend, as her enemies, with becoming scorn, intend to insult the occasion with rejoicing.

Announcement of Confederation was grim news to many Nova Scotians.

By August 1868, Howe's allies were still howling against Confederation, but he knew Nova Scotia had no choice but to make the best of a bad situation. He managed to improve the financial terms of Nova Scotia's joining the new Canada, but Prime Minister John A. Macdonald warned that parliament would not approve these concessions unless Howe himself demonstrated that the repeal movement was dead. The beaten man would have to join the federal cabinet.

Howe was sworn in as president of the Privy Council in Ottawa in January 1869 and returned to face the whole issue in a brutal mid-winter by-election in Hants County. The provincial government and the anti-Confederate party hurled themselves into a campaign to defeat the man they now saw as an unspeakable traitor. The invective against him was like nothing he had known before, and his health sometimes appeared completely shattered. Yet he won the by-election, killing the very repeal movement he had once led.

Anti-confederate politician and publisher William Annand.

Howe served the Macdonald cabinet for four years, and they were not particularly good ones. He was accustomed to running things his own way. He had never been a pussyfooter, and his utterances sometimes embarrassed Macdonald. Moreover, his once-resilient constitution had lost its powers of recuperation. He was getting old.

On May 10, 1873, Howe was sworn in as lieutenant-governor of Nova Scotia, and came home from Ottawa by vessel. A crowd met him at the waterfront, but no one cheered. James A. Roy, one of his biographers, wrote, "There was something almost sinister about this silence ... It was the tragedy of his homecoming that killed Howe." Three weeks later, at age sixty-eight, he died.

Fewer than 30,000 people lived in Halifax, but some 20,000 lined the downtown streets to witness the funeral procession. The crowds filled even the trees, the minute guns boomed on Citadel Hill, and a remorseful writer for the "Morning Chronicle" confessed, "We feel one deep sensation of regret that perhaps at times we used harsher expressions regarding him than rigorous duty to the country appeared to demand."

A portrait of Joseph Howe in later years.

Anna Leonowens was instrumental in founding the Victoria School of Art and Design, (now the Nova Scotia College of Art and Design). It was incorporated through an act of the Nova Scotia government in 1888.

A celebration in the Halifax Public Gardens 1889.

CHAPTER 24

AS THE CENTURY TURNED

A severe international depression afflicted Nova Scotia in 1887. Young people left in droves to find work inland, and, as railways and steamships replaced sailing vessels, the economies of many Bluenose ports began to wither.

The telephone was a novelty. Halifax was lit by gas and oil, and horses pulled the tramcars. Business was sluggish, but cultural and spiritual affairs were vigorous. Repertory companies played the theatres, and military bands made magical music in the Public Gardens. On March 16, a newspaper trumpeted, "VICTORIA'S JUBILEE! Halifax Will Celebrate It By Contributing $3,000 Towards Establishing a School of Design and Spending $5,000 on a Grand Jollification ... "

In this time of Victorian respectability, Thomas H. Raddall wrote, Halifax prostitutes "hid themselves like guilty Eves behind the red blinds of their professions," and "sobriety and godliness went hand in hand."[1] A new law shrank the number of licensed drinking places in the city from 180 to 54, quite enough for a seaport of fewer than 40,000 people. Despite the depression, steamers kept arriving from London, Boston, Glasgow, Hamburg, and Antwerp. While the Age of Sail was doomed, sailing ships still brought goods from all over the world. The business community sniffed better times ahead.

Canada was twenty years old. The Northwest Rebellion had been crushed, Louis Riel had been hanged, and the Canadian Pacific Railway had reached

Shipping apples to Britain in 1881 from the Annapolis Valley.

the west coast. The European and American Railway, running from Halifax through southern New Brunswick to Maine, had been completed in 1871, and the Intercolonial, from Halifax to Quebec connections, in 1876. By the early 1900s, trains ran from Halifax to Yarmouth and Sydney.

The Annapolis Valley shipped to England so many Kings, Ribstons, Baldwins, Golden Russets, and Gravensteins—which a local politician called "the most splendid variety of apple yet produced"—that it was fast becoming "The Orchard of the British Empire." But increasingly, Nova Scotia's economic destiny lay not in foreign trade over the Atlantic Ocean, but in Canada. Cotton factories hummed in Windsor, Yarmouth, and Halifax. New Glasgow boasted a glass works, and Halifax a sugar refinery. J. Rhodes Curry & Company of Amherst manufactured the first Canadian-made railway cars. At Trenton and New Glasgow, the Nova Scotia Steel and Coal Company ran big mills. Coal mines had long thrived in both Springhill and Pictou County, and Sydney was a boom town.

American financiers merged coal companies and founded a steel industry in Sydney, and thus established the base for what would became the mighty Dominion Steel and Coal Corporation. The Americans sank hundreds of millions of dollars in plant and waterfront land. From Europe and all over Cape Breton, workers poured into town. "The Sydney Daily Record" predicted, "When Pittsburgh is a village and New York has got to be whistled for to stop a steamboat, Sydney will be the grand seaport of a continent."

"Canada's Century" lay just ahead, and Nova Scotia seemed determined both to contribute to it and to benefit from it.

A c. 1903 view of the coke oven plant at the Dominion Iron & Steel Company, Sydney.

The province had not been kind to Mi'kmaq. George Bryce, a Winnipeg professor, wrote, early in the 1900s, "A wretched band of Algonquins known as the Micmacs still flit about Nova Scotian waste places like returning ghosts of a departed people."[2] Bryce failed to acknowledge that his own race had reduced the Mi'kmaq to whatever wretchedness they were suffering. A more balanced view appeared eight decades later when historian Del Muise wrote, "Micmacs were pushed to the margins of society, increasingly confined to reserved lands where they became charges upon the dominant community. Natives, by and large, had cooperated with European settlers, who had responded to their openness by gobbling up available land and resources with utter disregard for their rights—usually with disastrous results for the 'People of the Dawn.' "[3]

An 1892 ad for Amherst's Rhodes, Curry & Co.

In 1840 Chief Paussamigh Pemmeenauweet decided to petition Queen Victoria directly. Five days later despatches were on their way to Lieutenant-Governor Falkland in Halifax, saying that the Queen was sympathetic, but wanted more information. The result: Joseph Howe was appointed Indian Commissioner. "Howe took up the task," Upton reports in "Micmacs and Colonists," "and in so doing he discovered an interest that was to stay with him for the rest of his life."[4] He did not last long; the job was unpaid, and far too big for one man, especially a man as busy as Howe. He resigned in 1842, and, after a three-year delay, was replaced by Abraham Gesner.

Trademark of the Nova Scotia Glass Company of New Glasgow. This company would be purchased and closed by out-of-province interests.

Both men worked hard, had excellent and very practical ideas for the betterment of the Mi'kmaq situation, and were frequently foiled, sometimes for lack of government financial support, sometimes from white antagonism. In the end, neither man achieved much in the way of improvement for the Mi'kmaq.

In an 1849 petition to the lieutenant-governor the Mi'kmaq revealed the pathos and injustice of their situation:

"Your people had not land enough, they came and killed many of our tribe and took from us our country. You have taken from us our lands and trees and have destroyed our game. The moose yards of our fathers,

Robb Engineering Company Ltd., Amherst.

where are they? White men kill the moose and leave the meat in the woods. You have put ships and steamboats upon the waters and they scare away the fish. You have made dams across the rivers so that the salmon cannot go up, and your laws will not permit us to spear them."[5]

After Confederation in 1867, the new regime proved much like the old, and most natives in the Maritime Provinces continued to eke out a marginal existence. Both before and after Confederation, the Mi'kmaq had reason to believe white authorities wanted them to assimilate—or die. As "wards of the crown," they had none of the ordinary rights of citizenship other Nova Scotians enjoyed. Governments denied their children a decent education, and when bands faced starvation, sometimes did little to help them. Weakened by malnutrition, many aboriginals succumbed to disease. By 1900, Nova Scotia's Mi'kmaq population had dwindled to about 2,000.

Blacks fared little better. Not only after the American Revolution, but during the War of 1812 Britain had promised land and liberty to escaped slaves from American plantations, and more than 2,000 "Chesapeake Blacks" arrived in Nova Scotia between 1813 and 1816. Like earlier black refugees, however, they soon felt betrayed. In 1841, more than a hundred blacks from Preston petitioned the lieutenant-governor. They said the government had placed them on lots of little more than four hectares. Some of these dinky holdings included swamps. Others were so barren that not even the most skilful and hard-working families could survive on them. Most of these people were desperately impoverished.

The government had never bothered to confirm the blacks' titles to holdings they had occupied for a quarter-century. They therefore could not sell their properties and move to better land. Since Nova Scotia restricted the franchise to property owners, they could not even vote, not without being harassed and cursed.

Like the Black communities, the schools that black children attended in nineteenth-century Nova Scotia were usually segregated. Communities that could afford to invest money to start a school were eligible for matching grants, but since many black settlements were too poor to qualify they had no schools at all. The abolition of legal segregation did not occur until 1954.

Blacks were the last to get jobs in good times, and the first to lose them in bad times. They endured humiliating rebuffs at restaurants, hostelries, and theatres, sometimes excluded by law, as well as by custom. The blatant discrimination continued long into the 1900s. Thousands joined the flood of white Nova Scotians to distant parts of Canada and the United States, and by 1901, the ones who remained totalled fewer than 6,000, the smallest black population in thirty years.

During the nineteenth century, Nova Scotia's Acadian population jumped from fewer than 4,000 to more then 45,000. Most Acadians lived in French-speaking villages on the province's western and Cape Breton coasts. Describing the Acadians in 1830, historian Brian Cuthbertson wrote in "Johnny Bluenose at the Polls," "Distinctive in language, religion, dress and customs, the Acadians had little intercourse with their English neighbours, but within less than a decade, would become an important electoral force and have their own representative in the Assembly."[6] It was in the 1830 election that an Acadian, Anselm Doucette of Clare, first ran for the Assembly. The 1836 Assembly saw the election of two Acadian members: Frederick Robichaud, a farmer and settler from Corberrie, and Simon d'Entremont, a self-educated farmer and fisherman, and the son of Benoni d'Entremont who had led the Acadians back to Pubnico after the expulsion.

St. Mary's Church at Church Point, Digby County, has the tallest wooden spire in North America.

In the late 1800s, a wave of Acadian nationalism swept through the Maritimes. The first French-language newspaper in the region, the "Moniteur Acadien," Shediac, N.B., began in the 1860s to arouse interprovincial Acadian patriotism. The "Moniteur" rebuked those who dreamed of a better life in the United States:

"To emigrate is to desert one's homeland. Our homeland is not only the ground that we walk on, but also and most of all the religion that we profess, the language that we speak, the laws by which we are governed, the institutions that we attend, the customs and habits that we observe as a people ... So to those of our compatriots who directly or indirectly encourage emigration, shame, contempt and infamy ... The United States needs mercenaries, slaves—and that is the right word—and such people are to be found among us."

Survival had not been easy. With the passing of the Free School Act of 1864, Acadian education was to be free, but in English only. Sally Ross and Alphonse Deveau describe the many years of the nineteenth century when children went to school speaking one language, but were expected to learn everything, including reading and writing, in another; they thus grew up knowing neither language well.[7] Improvements came slowly and with difficulty. The English barely tolerated the speaking of French; in 1879, when Isidore LeBlanc addressed his fellow members of the Legislature in French, the event was unique. He was pleading for the teaching of French in Acadian schools.

In 1881, roughly 5,000 people attended a national Acadian congress in Memramcook, N.B. More huge gatherings occurred in the following twenty-two years, and the sites included Church Point, Arichat, and Tidnish, in Nova Scotia. At Church Point, the Acadians set up sixty-metre tables outdoors and fed 4,000 people within two hours. Out of the congresses came a national day, not Saint-Jean-Baptiste Day, as in Quebec, but the Feast of the Assumption on August 15; a national flag, the French tricolour with a golden star to symbolize Acadia; a national anthem, "Ave Maria Stella"; and a national emblem with the motto "Strength Through Union." The Acadians could not have a state of their own, but they made sure they had a national spirit of their own.

Annie Isabella Hamilton was the first female medical student to graduate from Dalhousie University.

Throughout the 1800s women in Nova Scotia, like women elsewhere, were second-class citizens. For a while, if they owned property, they could vote, but Howe removed that privilege. Until 1884, wives could not even own property; they had to be unmarried or widowed. Women were wards of their husbands or fathers. Widows or unmarried daughters might work for the wealthy as servants, but society expected women to marry early, stay home, and run their households to please their husbands and children. An English-born widow, Susannah Oland of Halifax, ran a thriving brewery, but she was a spectacular exception to the rule that barred women from business, trade, and the professions. There was one other, less eminent exception. The enterprising Rose Fortune, a black woman of Annapolis Royal, trundled passengers' luggage, in her wheelbarrow, up from the steamer at the wharf to the hotel. She also kept order on the wharf, and her service later grew into a prosperous trucking business. But women normally strayed from domestic duties only to engage in do-gooding efforts such as the temperance movement and campaigns to curb prostitution.

A growing number of privileged women, however, worked for the right to vote. Historian Judith Fingard described their situation in "The Atlantic Provinces in Confederation": "A women's suffrage bill in 1893 almost slipped through the Nova Scotia legislature, arousing little more fuss than the passage of legislation allowing women the municipal franchise six years earlier ... Only by skilful manoeuvring did the attorney general, J. W. Longley, manage to delay and finally kill it near the end of the session."[8]

The women regrouped. Fingard reports that they "concentrated instead on fashioning a formidable, progressive social-reform network."[9] In the 1890s there emerged in Halifax a cadre of feminists and suffragettes: Anna Leonowens, who in 1887 founded the Victoria School of Art and Design, later the Nova Scotia College of Art and Design, and became known around world for her published accounts about working for the Siamese court, which would one day inspire others to write "Anna and the King of Siam" and "The King and I" for stage and screen; Eliza Ritchie, who received a Ph.D. at Cornell University in 1889 and may well have been the first Canadian woman to earn a doctorate; May Sexton, a graduate of the Massachusetts Institute of Technology, who campaigned to get Nova Scotia to welcome women to its pioneering program of technical education; Annie Isabella Hamilton, in 1894 the first woman to graduate as an M.D. from the Dalhousie Medical School; housewife Agnes Dennis, bearer of ten children, Commander of the Civil Division of the British Empire, and recipient of two honorary doctorates; and Edith Jessie Archibald, descendant of a Father of Confederation from Truro, daughter of a British diplomat, wife of the Bank of Nova Scotia's president, and relentless crusader for women's rights.

Eliza Ritchie may have been the first Canadian woman to receive a Ph.D.

In 1918, after four years of devoted service to the home front during the First World War, Nova Scotian women finally won the rights to vote and run for public office.

As the twentieth century approached, the occupational choices for women broadened. Some became salesclerks in the shops of the growing cities, and a few telephone operators. The luckier and more defiant attended university and became teachers or nurses. The unluckier ones, often from impoverished families, went to work in the needle trades or cotton mills. "Wages were low [in the mills], the hours of repetitive and boring work were long, and working conditions were poor—suffocating heat and dust, endless standing and draconian discipline, with fines for lateness and spoiled work."[10]

Edith Jessie Archibald was a crusader for women's rights.

For a province whose population in 1901 stood at fewer than 460,000, Nova Scotia had produced an extraordinary crop of military heroes, renowned scientists, and leaders in politics, business, and the professions. The names of Uniacke, McCulloch, Haliburton, Cunard, Howe, and Tupper would ring in

Captain Joshua Slocum, in his 37-foot sloop the Spray, was the first man to sail around the world alone.

William D. Lawrence launched his square-rigged vessel W. D. Lawrence at Maitland in 1874.

the ears of Bluenose schoolchildren, but they were far from being the only people of conspicuous talent who strode out of Nova Scotia in the 1800s, and onto bigger stages.

In Massachusetts, Donald McKay (1810–80), an immigrant from Shelburne County, Nova Scotia, constructed the fastest and most graceful clipper ships the world had ever seen, earning such admiration that the Louvre in Paris placed his bust between those of Raphael and Michelangelo. William Dawson Lawrence (1817–86), from Maitland, Hants County, built the biggest wooden ship in the history of the Maritimes, a 2,459-ton giant that he named after himself, and, ignoring gibes that it was too cumbersome to make money, he sailed with his family on a three-year adventure that earned the first of many handsome profits for the "Great Ship." Born and raised on Briar Island at the tip of Nova Scotia, Captain Joshua Slocum, a master of sail who detested steamships, sailed his little Spray around the world in 1895–98. No one before had circled the globe alone.

George Munro (1825–96), one of ten children of a Pictou County farmer, went to New York, reaped millions by publishing cheap reprints of good books, and, with fat donations, rescued Dalhousie University from financial disaster. Munro's generosity led to the birth of the Dalhousie Law School, the first in the British Empire to base its teaching on the common law.

Nova Scotians excelled in the British Army and Royal Navy. Halifax-born Provo William Parry Wallis (1791–1892) the twenty-two-year-old hero who brought both the Shannon and the conquered Chesapeake safely into Halifax, later climbed through the ranks to become Admiral of the Fleet. He died at the age of one hundred, still on full pay.

William Robert Wolseley Winniett (1793–1850), of Annapolis Royal, joined the Royal Navy, became governor of the Gold Coast, and journeyed to fabled African kingdoms to discourage the slave trade and human sacrifices. During the Crimean War, William Fenwick Williams

(1800–1883), also of Annapolis Royal, led the British defence of Kars (northeastern Turkey) against huge Russian attacks. Lionized in London, he reaped an honorary degree from Oxford, a pension from the British government, the Grand Cross of the Legion of Honour from France, and in 1865 an appointment as lieutenant-governor of his home province.

During the Indian Mutiny in 1857, Lieut.-Col. John Eardley Wilmot Inglis (1814–62) of Halifax took command of the garrison at Lucknow and, for three months, defended the governor's compound, full of terrified Englishwomen and children, against overwhelming odds. This performance earned him a promotion to major-general. Knighthoods came to Inglis, Wallis, Winniett, and Williams, but not to William Edward Hall (1826–1904). Born near Wolfville, this son of a black slave from Virginia fought so furiously at the relief of Lucknow that Queen Victoria awarded him the Victoria Cross. He was the first Canadian sailor and the first black to win this supreme award for valour. But when he died in 1904 Hall was buried without any military honours, and it was not until 1937 that he began to receive recognition.

Sir Arthur Lawrence Haliburton (1832–1907), a son of Thomas C. Haliburton, reached the exalted position of under secretary of war for Britain and became the first native-born Canadian to sit in the House of Lords. His brother, lawyer Robert Grant Haliburton, helped found the Canada First Party, turned to anthropology, and discovered a race of pygmies in the North African mountains.

William Edward Hall was the first Black and the first Canadian to be awarded the Victoria Cross.

Nova Scotia spawned more than its share of eminent professors and inventors. In 1846, author, physician, geologist, and chemist Abraham Gesner (1794–1864) of Annapolis County distilled oil from coal and tested it in a lighthouse in Halifax Harbour. His kerosene found its way into millions of homes. Simon Newcombe (1835–1909), a poor farmboy from Wallace Bridge, became a math professor for the US navy, a world authority on the astronomy of the solar system, a rear admiral, president of the American Association for the Advancement of Science, recipient of seventeen degrees from American and European universities, and an officer of the Legion of Honour in France.

The geologist and paleontologist, Sir John William Dawson (1820–99) of Pictou and a student of Pictou Academy was the first Canadian scientist whose reputation spread throughout the world. He was the beloved principal of McGill University for thirty-eight years and turned it into one of North America's most admired universities. Dawson was the only person ever to

Internationally recognized geologist Abraham Gesner.

George Monro
Grant.

Sir John William
Dawson.

Simon Newcombe.

preside over both the American and British associations for the advancement of science. The map-making genius of his Pictou-born son, the geologist George Mercer Dawson (1849–1901), helped determine the route of the Canadian Pacific Railway in British Columbia and open up the Canadian west and northland for lumbering, mining, ranching, and farming. Another Pictou County boy, George Monro Grant, was principal of Queen's University from 1877 until his death in 1902. He turned a tiny and financially shaky college into a major university. "Principal Grant" was a legend in the life of Queen's.

Nova Scotia blacks shone at prizefighting. George Dixon (1870–1909), of Halifax, nicknamed "Little Chocolate," was the first boxer ever to win world titles in three weight divisions. Many fight fans considered Sam Langford (1884–56), "The Boston Tar Baby" from Weymouth, N.S., the uncrowned heavyweight champion of the world; he was a fighter so devastating that title-holders hid from him.

Among amateur athletes, William Alexander Henry, Jr., son of a Father of Confederation, had no equal anywhere in Canada. He played football for Harvard, and after one battle against Yale, the "New York Times" reported, "The feature of the games was the playing of Henry of Halifax, the equal of which has never been seen in American college football." Henry excelled at cricket, lacrosse, baseball, hockey, golf, track and field, and as he got older, admiralty law.

Nova Scotia also boasted two pioneers of chloroform. In February 1848, only three months after doctors in Edinburgh employed the liquid as an anesthetic for the first time in medical history, Dr. William Johnson Almon (1816–1901) of Halifax, later the first physician to enter Canada's Senate, put a woman to sleep with it before amputating one of her thumbs. Pictou chemist J. D. B. Fraser (1807–69) not only made chloroform, but in March 1848 administered it to his wife during the birth of their seventh child.

In the Black community, the early leaders were mostly churchmen. Richard Preston made his way to Nova Scotia around 1814, with the black refugees of the War of 1812. In "Blacks," Dr. Bridglal Pachai wrote: "He became a strong member of the Baptist church in Halifax and in 1831 was sent to London to prepare for the ministry ... and returned to Halifax to assume charge of the African United Baptist Church, Cornwallis Street, which was constituted on April 14, 1832."[11] Preston inspired 12 black Baptist churches from around the province to form the African United Baptist Association, and until his death in 1861 was the chief spokesman for the black Baptists in Nova Scotia.

By the end of the nineteenth century, the Black community was beginning to take a more prominent role in the life of the province. James Johnston graduated from the Dalhousie Law School in 1898, the first black lawyer in Nova Scotia. The Rev. William White, chaplain to the 2nd Construction Battalion in World War I, was the only black chaplain in the British armed forces. He was pastor for many years at the Cornwallis Street Baptist Church in Halifax. The most famous of his thirteen children was Portia White, internationally renowned opera singer.

William Harvey Golar (1846–1939), Halifax, moved to Boston as a bricklayer, earned a theology degree at Lincoln University in Pennsylvania, and later, at Livingstone College in North Carolina, became the only black Nova Scotian ever to serve as a college president.

Nova Scotians also shone in the legal community. Sir William Johnston Ritchie (1813–1892) of Annapolis Royal joined the new Supreme Court of Canada as a judge in 1875, gave it stability during its troubled infancy, and presided as chief justice from 1879 to 1892. No judge ever served the Supreme Court longer. Sir George Bourinot (1836–1902), born in Sydney, served as Clerk of the Commons for twenty-two years, became a world authority on parliamentary procedure and constitutional law, and collected honorary degrees from almost all the Canadian universities of his time.

Sir John Sparrow David Thompson (1845–94) of Halifax became premier of Nova Scotia, a judge on the Supreme Court of Canada, a cabinet ally of Sir John A. Macdonald, and in 1892 prime minister. He had the talent and character to become one of the greatest leaders in Canadian history but in 1895, after Queen Victoria swore him in as a member of the Imperial Privy Council, he died of a heart attack in Windsor Castle. Charles Tupper ascended to the prime ministership in 1896, but quickly lost the job when the Conservatives suffered a shocking defeat at the polls. From 1911 to 1920, Sir Robert Laird Borden (1854–1937) of Grand Pré was the prime minister of Canada. He led it through all the crises of World War I and later promoted both the British Empire's becoming the British Commonwealth of Nations and international recognition of the autonomy of the dominions. The last of the Nova Scotian prime ministers, Borden was an international statesman.

Sir John Sparrow David Thompson.

Portia White.

Sir Robert Laird Borden.

Right: A map showing the extent of the devastation (marked in black), caused by the Halifax Explosion.

Below: An eastward view of the Richmond area of Halifax with the harbour in the background after the 1917 explosion.

CHAPTER 25

JOHNNY CAME
MARCHING HOME—
TO AN ANGRY
NOVA SCOTIA

The year 1901 launched a turbulent century in dramatic fashion. Wall Street panicked. The Boer War raged, with Bluenose soldiers and nurses valiantly serving the British cause. An anarchist assassinated American President William McKinley with a pistol. Vice-President Theodore Roosevelt suggested the United States "Speak softly and carry a big stick." Prime Minister Wilfrid Laurier urged, "Let us keep in our hearts this thought: Canada first, Canada forever, nothing but Canada." Nova Scotia joined the entire British Empire in mourning the death of Queen Victoria. She had been on the throne since 1837, the year Joseph Howe introduced to the House of Assembly in Halifax a devastating, twelve-point attack on the Council of Twelve.

Throughout the first two decades of the century, spectacular, disastrous, or historic events kept occurring in the province, or sideswiping it. In 1902, at Table Head near Glace Bay, Cape Breton Island, Guglielmo Marconi set up North America's first transocean wireless station. In 1905, the British Army handed the entire Halifax fortress over to the Canadian government, and in 1906 the Royal Navy gave to Canada the Halifax Dockyard. The last imperial troops left the city, ending an occupation of more than a century and a half.

Marconi and the wireless station at Table Head, Cape Breton, in 1904.

In 1907, telephone inventor Alexander Graham Bell and American aviation pioneer Glenn Curtiss met with others in Halifax to form one of the world's first flying clubs. In 1909, at the spot Bell loved most—the village of Baddeck on the shores of Lake Bras d'Or, Cape Breton Island—local boy J. A. D. McCurdy, a member of the club, piloted the Silver Dart, in the first controlled flight in the British Empire.

In 1912, on April 15, news of the Titanic disaster flowed from Halifax around the world. The steamship Mackay Bennett brought into the city a cargo of 190 of the liner's 1,503 drowned men, women, and children. In 1917, Leon Trotsky, bound from New York to the Russian Revolution, was stopped in Halifax and briefly incarcerated at a prisoner of war camp in Truro. By then, a fever of military recruitment had been sweeping Nova Scotia for three years.

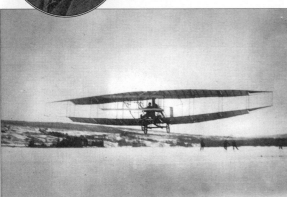

Dr. Alexander Graham Bell (above) and the Silver Dart at Baddeck, 1907, which made the first controlled flight in the British Commonwealth.

After World War I broke out, Bluenose preachers turned their sermons into pep talks for enlistment, and Nova Scotia's school system hurled itself into the war effort. Lt.-Col. Allison H. Borden asked schoolchildren to deliver recruitment pitches to "your fathers and big brothers, or any men who are strong and well in your section between the ages of eighteen and forty-five." He warned that if Nova Scotian men failed to fight "the faithless Germans" in France, they might "come to Nova Scotia and take or destroy our farms and houses." Nova Scotia's "Journal of Education" pressed teachers to help conquer "the cancer of Hohenzollern absolutism" by advocating dieting. This would liberate "full rations for our hard-working, weather-beaten, shell-pounded soldiers, who must always be ready to move at the 'double' with bayonet and bomb." Teachers were urged to persuade youngsters "that every particle of food wasted should be looked upon as withheld from starving men, women and children in Europe."

Warfare was once again a fine thing for parts of Nova Scotia. The Trenton steel works made more shells than any other plant in the Empire, outside England. "Men and women toiled in the munitions plants seven days a week ... Ships, armour plate, shells from the smallest to the largest calibre used by the British forces,"[1] all came from Pictou County.

The tons of shipping that Halifax handled, the value of its exports, and its bank clearings all sky-rocketed. The racket of hammers and saws echoed throughout the city. With the Royal Navy back in town, Thomas H. Raddall wrote, "the picnickers at Point Pleasant watched Britannia's lean, gray ships come and go."[2] Bedford Basin was crammed with merchant vessels preparing to join transatlantic convoys. The greatest steamships of the White Star and Cunard lines arrived in the harbour to take Canadian troops aboard.

Halifax was the major embarkation point for Canada's fighting men, and trains moved hundreds of thousands of soldiers from Montreal to Halifax for shipment overseas. Flocks of prostitutes, led by a contingent from Montreal, descended on the city from across Canada. After the province imposed prohibition on Halifax in 1916, blind pigs sprung up, and many doubled as brothels.

Nova Scotia boasted one of the highest enlistment rates in Canada. The Nova Scotia Highlanders, for instance, started as one battalion, but after attracting enough recruits for four, blossomed as a whole brigade. The recruits came from "every walk of life, professional and industrial and commercial, with farmers and manufacturers amongst the officers, while clergymen, college professors and teachers paraded shoulder to shoulder in the rank and file," wrote M. S. Hunt in "Nova Scotia's Part in the Great War."[3] When the Highlanders, bound for Europe, trooped aboard the Olympic at Pier Two, Halifax, in May 1916, tens of thousands of weeping and cheering Bluenosers lingered on the waterfront for hours.

A troop ship in Halifax Harbour during World War I, during which time the port played a central role in the war effort.

British military authorities called the brigade "the finest body of troops sent over from Canada." While the Nova Scotia Highlanders excelled in many battles, nothing better exemplified their valour than the way Captain Ross M. MacKenzie led the Cape Breton Islanders of D Company, the 85th Battalion, at Passchendaele in Western Flanders. Hunt told the story: "The Huns were advancing in great force ... Captain MacKenzie ordered his Company to drop all kit, and to fix bayonets and advance in true Highland fashion. With huzzas they made for the enemy—dashing upon the Huns with such a rush and momentum that the Huns became bewildered, next were seized with panic, broke and 'beat it.' "

Having routed the charging Germans, the Cape Breton soldiers advanced into heavy gunfire. "Then it was that the ancient fighting spirit of his Gaelic ancestors shone brilliantly in Captain MacKenzie ... [He] was shot through the abdomen—some say he was literally riddled—with machine-gun bullets, and he fell. But he struggled to his feet and kept on with his Company, bleeding to death, and commanded his men, encouraging them, until he dropped exhausted into a shell hole. Even then, though undone, he would not be attended to, but kept encouraging his Company. Eventually, he permitted himself to be placed on a stretcher, and while being borne away, he died—like Cuchullain [a legendary Gaelic hero], unconquerable in death."[4]

Many Mi'kmaq enlisted, and fought heroically, but the federal government decided Blacks might be a source of trouble in the ranks, and ruled they could not join the armed services. Outraged, the feisty Colonel Dan Sutherland of River John recruited several hundred Blacks, trained them himself on the Pictou waterfront, and sent them to France as the 2nd Construction Battalion, to work in forestry. While important for the French war effort, their toil created no heroes.

The Imo after the explosion in Halifax Harbour, 1917.

Back home, explosions took a hideous toll. In the fall of 1917, a blast in a coal mine in New Waterford, Cape Breton Island, killed sixty-five men and boys. On December 6, the Belgian relief steamer Imo struck the Mont Blanc, a French munitions ship, in Halifax Harbour, causing a fire that set off the most hideous man-made explosion the world had ever known. It flattened a large section of the city's North End, killed some two thousand Haligonians, and injured so many more that, even decades later, one of Halifax's most distinctive features was the number of scarred faces on the streets. It was in the Halifax of this grisly calamity that Cape Breton–born novelist Hugh MacLennan set his "Barometer Rising," a landmark in Canadian literary history.

Forty-eight days after the explosion in Halifax, a coal shaft blew up in Stellarton, killing eighty-eight miners. Nova Scotia, the "New Glasgow Evening Chronicle" said, was "in the path of a cyclone of death. Death from explosions at home and death from explosions abroad have given us a terrible punishment. What for?"

In its Peace and Reconstruction Number of December 1919, "The Busy East," a magazine for the Maritimes, exulted, "The eastern provinces are waking from their dream, and yet—and this is the best part of the story, for this is what makes and keeps the real flame of patriotism alive—waken as they may, they will always remain, ALONE AND DISTINCTIVE, THE MARITIME PROVINCES. When factories thunder in every city and town and skyscrapers touch the heavens, men will still be found in these provinces by the sea, eating their beans on Saturday night. For that, if you get the picture rightly, is just the kind of men they are down here."

While this was a passionate expression of a growing sense of common culture among the seaside provinces, it was also whistling in the dark. With respect to industrial growth, profit, per-capita income, and standard of living, the rest of Canada was roaring ahead of the Maritimes and leaving them, alone, distinctive, and choking in the exhaust fumes.

The most painful symptom of the region's economic torpor was the exodus of its young. Wave after wave of Nova Scotians left their homeland, rolling inland again and again to seek jobs in New England, New York, the American midwest and far west, Quebec, Ontario, the Prairies, British Columbia, and the northern territories. For generations, the streets paved with gold supposedly lay in "the Boston states." Later, they were in the Canadian west, then Toronto, and later still the west again. As part of Nova Scotia's heritage, leaving home would long outlast the Age of Sail.

Most of those who left were young sons and daughters of farmers, fishermen, carpenters, blacksmiths, shipwrights, coopers, carriage-makers, and merchants. Many were the children of jacks-of-all trades. To raise a family in rural Nova Scotia, a man often had to be not only a farmer-fisherman but also a house-builder, boat-builder, furniture-maker, barrel-maker, pulpwood-cutter, and a bit of a blacksmith, too. His wife had to be no less versatile. All over Nova Scotia, the young who left their parents' farms for good took with them a matter-of-fact willingness to try their hand at anything.

The qualities that gave Nova Scotia able pioneers later gave Canada lawyers, judges, premiers, and lieutenant-governors, bank presidents and university presidents, scientific wizards and financial wizards, mariners and missionaries. The Nova Scotians who rattled west on Harvest Excursion trains—and often settled out there—were treasured on the Prairies not simply because they were willing to sweat twelve hours a day for a couple of dollars, but also because they could handle horses, and swing axes like lumberjacks.

Premier William S. Fielding held office from 1884 to 1896, when he resigned to become minister of finance and receiver general in Sir Wilfrid Laurier's Liberal government.

Teachers' salaries in that distant land were triple what they were in Nova Scotia, and doughty schoolmarms from the Maritimes once taught half the youngsters in the Canadian west.

As early as 1870, more than 6,000 Nova Scotians had already settled in Boston alone, where they routinely greeted fresh loads of hopeful Bluenosers who came by scheduled steamships from Halifax and Yarmouth. In the next thirty years, a quarter-million Maritimers, 40 per cent of all those in the region in 1870, moved away, mostly to the United States. In the half-century between 1881 and 1931, more than 600,000 people left the region, a huge proportion of them Nova Scotians.

Immigration did little to take up the population slack. Though Canada welcomed more than four million immigrants between 1901 and 1931, those who disembarked at Halifax quickly boarded trains and shot through the dark forests of Nova Scotia and New Brunswick en route to Ontario and the Prairies. One result of the exodus, and the feebleness of the immigration flow to Nova Scotia, was that in the first eight decades of the twentieth century, the population of those who stayed in the province did little better than double (from 459,600 to 847,400) while the population in Canada as a whole almost quintupled (from 5,371,000 to 24,343,000).

Long before World War I, Nova Scotians grimly recognized that the more their share of Canada's population shrank, the tougher it would be for their factories to survive against central Canadian competitors. A small population also meant small local markets, which prevented many industries from adopting the new technologies for large-scale production. Low family incomes in Nova Scotia and the stubborn survival of household production of goods also limited nearby markets. On the whole, Nova Scotian industries simply were not big enough for maximum efficiency. They were less productive than their rivals in Ontario, and less profitable. The wages they paid were much lower.

Geography, too, penalized Nova Scotia. It would never have enough hydroelectric power to exploit the new industrial technologies thoroughly. Its soil was mostly poor, and its growing season short. Bluenose farmers had no major urban market nearby. As prices for their produce plummeted in the late nineteenth century, many gave up. Forests reclaimed their fields.

Nova Scotia also lacked an easily accessible hinterland. The Intercolonial Railway trundled over a long and inefficient route and, for access to markets beyond Montreal, had to rely on the cooperation of other lines. Since Nova

Scotia perched north of the great east–west railways of the United States, and south of the St. Lawrence waterway to the interior, it derived little benefit from the burgeoning trade between central North America and Europe. Moreover, it was too far from the Prairies to exploit the wheat boom that began in the late 1890s and thus missed out on what may well have been the biggest boom in Canadian history. In the late nineteenth century, the United States replaced Britain as a supplier of iron, fuel, and machinery for Canadian manufacturers, and this, too, gave Ontario a decided advantage over Nova Scotia.

For the Bluenose coal and steel industries, rising costs of extraction and decreased demand drained profits, but so did the distance to markets. By 1911, Yarmouth, Amherst, and Sydney Mines had simply stopped growing. And the decline of wooden shipbuilding, the dominance of steamships, the damage that beet sugar had inflicted on the West Indian economy, and the shriveling of markets for dried fish had all helped shove Nova Scotia into the doldrums. But so had voracious industries in the provinces that dominated the nation. Distance from major markets and a shortage of capital made Bluenose manufacturers vulnerable to cut-throat competition from Canadian companies out to destroy them.

As early as the 1880s, Nova Scotia believed the real source of all its economic problems lay in the greedy way central Canadians manipulated the Confederation deal to line their pockets at Maritimers' expense. The National Policy, a system of tariff protection that the government of Sir John A. Macdonald had introduced in 1879, favoured manufacturers in Ontario and Quebec and hamstrung Nova Scotia's foreign trade. The Halifax "Morning Chronicle" described the typical commercial traveler from Ontario or Quebec as a self-important, condescending loudmouth who "saps our resources, sucks our money and leaves a lot of shoddy behind him. He has been able ... to have laws passed that compel us to buy his wares or submit to a tremendous fine if we purchase [elsewhere]."

That was in 1886, the year Premier W. S. Fielding and his Liberals swept the province with an election campaign that promoted but one cause: "Secession!" More than three decades later, as the Roaring Twenties got under way, the continuing and deepening resentment over Canada's oppression of its down-east provinces gave birth to the Maritime Rights protest movement. As the most populous and proud of the Maritime Provinces, Nova Scotia was right in the thick of it.

The Halifax "Morning Chronicle" featured Robert Chambers' first published cartoon on May 2, 1923, addressing the Maritime Rights movement that was fuelled by regional disparity.

CHAPTER 26

THE ROARING TWENTIES JUST DIDN'T ROAR

Bewailing a decades-old trend, the Halifax "Chronicle-Herald" complained in 1957, "Industry after industry here has been acquired by Central Canadian interests, and closed down to [strengthen] the purchasing companies' operations in Toronto, Montreal, and elsewhere. There have been cotton mills, boot and shoe factories, the once-bustling Rhodes Currie plant at Amherst, the sugar refinery at Dartmouth and many others." Central Canada's gift to Nova Scotia was "a trail of empty buildings."

Remembering the 1880s, a ninety-year-old man, M. Poirier of Chéticamp, Cape Breton Island, then wrote to the editor, "Nova Scotia was equal or better than any province in Canada, commercially and financially. We had two cotton factories, two of tobacco, one cigar factory, one skate factory, a boot and shoe factory, and so on ... Now we have none of those industries; the Upper Provinces smothered us." Pictou County historian James M. Cameron complained in 1960 that the brain drain from Nova Scotia was "a practical means of circumventing the strangling clutch ... of political association with central Canada ... Ninety-three years after Confederation, Nova Scotia has declined from the wealthiest per capita province to almost the poorest."[1]

The pre-Confederation "golden age" in the seacoast province, however, was partly a myth. At the time of Confederation, Nova Scotia was already poorer than Ontario, just as it is today. Scholars still debate whether or not Confederation sabotaged the economy of the Maritimes, but what is indisputable is that it failed to conquer regional disparity. Indeed, the region has suffered the lowest personal income and highest unemployment rates for as long as anyone can remember. Many Nova Scotians agree with New Brunswick economist William Y. Smith that, ever since Canada's infancy, "Ontario has been big and powerful enough to impose its concept of federalism on the whole country, a form of federalism geared, of course, to the interests of Ontario rather than to balanced growth across the country."[2]

By the 1920s, the Maritime Rights movement was loudly demanding justice. As the Maritimes' share of Canada's population had declined, so had their influence in the federal parliament. (During the 1870s, Nova Scotia had twenty-one seats in the House of Commons, but by 1925, even though the total of Commons seats had increased, its representation had shrunk to a mere fourteen.) The Maritimes' federal subsidies were now far smaller than those of the Prairies. Moreover, Central Canada and the west had ganged up on policies of the Intercolonial Railway that favoured the Maritimes. Desperate to counteract these trends, the down-east provinces joined hands to fight for Maritime Rights.

Their case went like this: Canada had needed Confederation for its very survival. Maritimers had been doing fine without it. They were now Canadians not out of choice, but because politicians from Ontario and Quebec had seduced down-east leaders, and Britain had pushed the region into Confederation. Maritime Rights spokesman Alexander Paterson from New Brunswick claimed that later propaganda had persuaded Canadians to believe a monstrous lie: "That, in 1867, Canada permitted Nova Scotia and New Brunswick to join her, and that, ever since, she has found these Provinces a very heavy burden. In the hazy distance, beyond the blue hills of Quebec, such people see in the Maritimes a strange folk who, when not fishing or lumbering, are insistently clamouring for financial aid from the Federal Government."[3]

Another lie was that the Maritimes were in debt to the rest of Canada. In truth, they had contributed much more to "the Confederation Scheme" than they had received from it. The federal government had pumped tens of millions of Maritimers' dollars into projects from Quebec to British Columbia, while allowing down-east industries to die. "The whole tragic circumstance is the direct outcome of a self-centred disregard for the sacred interests of three Provinces by the political dominance of Central Canadian financial and commercial interests," Paterson wrote.

"Consequently they have denied the Maritimes the right to participate in the general progress and prosperity of Canada."

While the British North America Act was "an Agreement," Paterson continued, Canada had "shattered sacred pledges" to the Maritimes. One pledge had been to run the Intercolonial Railway not as a commercial line, but as "a National Work" to enable Maritime goods to flow profitably into Upper Canadian markets and to bring the foreign trade of the new nation through Maritime ports. Sir John A. Macdonald himself had said Canada would "cheerfully contribute to the utmost extent ... to make that important link." Macdonald had promised: "Build the road and Halifax will soon become one of the great emporiums of the world. All the great resources of the West will soon come over the immense railways of Canada to the bosom of your harbour." Half a century after Confederation, Macdonald's pledge struck Nova Scotians as a cruel joke.

For central and western Canadians had insisted the Maritimes pay freight rates sufficiently high to make the Intercolonial a commercial success, and the result, Alexander Paterson insisted, was that "the old I.C.R.—'The People's Road'—ceased to exist as such." In 1918, the federal government moved the railway's headquarters from Moncton to Toronto and forced its absorption by a national system. Another round of brutal increases in Maritime freight rates soon followed.

The Maritime Rights movement inspired rare unity among the often fractious groupings in the down-east provinces. While the Maritime Board of Trade became a major "channel of agitation," the campaign had the support of the Maritime Division of the Canadian Manufacturers Association, chambers of commerce, merchants' alliances, Acadian conventions, lumber barons, farmers, fishermen, railway workers, longshoremen, lawyers, priests, professors, and journalists. The movement sponsored economic conferences, pamphleteering, cross-Canada speaking tours, and the arrival in Ottawa of delegation after delegation.

In 1926, Prime Minister Mackenzie King appointed Sir Andrew Duncan, a

A 1925 Nova Scotia Conservative party election poster, designed to urge women voters to support Maritime Rights, encouraged job restoration in the province.

Where's My Boy?

Vote Him Back Home

Vote Against The Government That Drove Him Into Exile
Vote For a change that will give A Good Living For All Nova Scotians

On Thursday, June 25th, Place the Interests of Your Province ABOVE Party
—DO IT FOR NOVA SCOTIA.

lawyer from Britain, to investigate the myriad grievances of the Maritimes. The government later implemented Duncan's recommendations for freight-rate reductions and certain increases in subsidies, but not his proposals to base subsidies on fiscal need and to use transportation to hasten regional development. The Great Depression crushed whatever hopes Duncan's report aroused, and "regional resentment and vestiges of cooperation remained the movement's legacies."4

World War I had given Nova Scotia some market advantages, but after a brief boom in 1919, the return of normal trading conditions plunged it into a depression. In world markets, the competition got hotter. Prices for fish and lumber plummeted. Disease hit the orchards of the Annapolis Valley, and a depression in the United Kingdom also hurt the apple business. The coal and steel industries languished. Employers hacked at the wage increases the unions had so recently achieved. As wages fell, strikes proliferated. In 1920, they broke out among railways, street railways, shipyards, and mines. In the Sydney coalfields alone, the years 1920 to 1925 saw some sixty strikes. The worse conditions got, the more the exodus grew. Roughly 122,000 Maritimers moved away during the 1920s, and Nova Scotia's population actually dropped, from 523,800 to 512,800.

An advertisement depicting Nova Scotia's United Fruit Companies booth at a United Kingdom trade show in the 1930s.

Nowhere in the province was life tougher than in industrial Cape Breton, where the gigantic, callous, and foreign-owned British Empire Steel Corporation (BESCO) ran the coal mines and steel mill. The cruelty and niggardliness of its management style helped arouse some of the most bitter labour strife in Canadian history. Three times within four years, soldiers poured into industrial Cape Breton, ostensibly to keep order. A local war veteran complained to Prime Minister Mackenzie King that Sydney and Glace

Bay looked like an occupied part of Germany during World War I.

By 1920, Cape Breton's miners, led by the Scottish-born James B. McLachlan, had won recognition for District Twenty-Six, the United Mine Workers (UMW) of America. A miner from boyhood, McLachlan was a fiery orator and, in his struggle against BESCO, a crafty tactician. Indeed, he may well have been the most talented Communist in Canadian history. He believed that, while battling BESCO, the miners were simply fighting for "a living wage, home and children—against stocks, bonds and dividends." McLachlan was a major reason why it was that, "At a time when organized labour across Canada was often in retreat following the defeat of the Winnipeg General Strike of 1919, the Nova Scotia coal miners found themselves at the vanguard of the class struggle in Canada."[5]

Kings County-born Ernest Howard Armstrong was premier of Nova Scotia 1923–1925 and held the portfolio of public works and mines from 1911 until the end of his career.

In January 1922, after market conditions and BESCO's own corporate strategies had sabotaged the company's financial health, it slashed miners' wages by a third. In response, the miners cut production by a third, a ploy borrowed from British unions. As winter turned to spring and spring to summer, the tension increased. BESCO's president, Montreal financier Roy Wolvin, openly hoped to break the union, and a federal cabinet minister denounced its members as "un-British, un-Canadian and cowardly."

Living conditions were notoriously poor among company houses, such as these at New Waterford.

When the desperate miners launched a strike on August 15, 1922, Wolvin demanded military protection for BESCO, and County Court Judge Duncan Finlayson, invoking the Militia Act, called up troops. Hundreds of Royal Canadian Artillery soldiers, equipped with eighteen-pound field guns and gas-driven machine guns, poured into Glace Bay. Lieutenant-Governor MacCallum Grant approved the immediate

DOMINION NO. 14 COLLIERY. NEW WATERFORD N.S. CANADA

recruitment of up to 1,000 more men for a violent "special force" of provincial police. On August 26, the union caved in. "The wage schedule was accepted by miners under the muzzle of rifles, machine guns and gleaming bayonets," McLachlan said, "with further threatened invasions of troops and marines, with warships standing to. The miners, facing hunger, their Dominion and Provincial governments lined up with BESCO ... were forced to accept the proposals."

Less than a year later, it was the steelworkers' turn to suffer at the hands of Canada's biggest industrial consortium and its allies. Long negotiations had led only to BESCO's bluntly refusing to shorten the workers' shifts, increase their wages, or grant them the union recognition they had sought for nearly twenty years. On June 28, 1923, the steelworkers went on strike. On June 30, the first of more than 1,100 troops arrived in Sydney. On July 1, a squad of the special police—now nicknamed "Armstrong's Army," after Premier E. H. Armstrong—showed up on Victoria Road in the steelworkers' ghetto at Whitney Pier, Sydney.

To teach striking workers a lesson during the 1923 BESCO steelworkers' strike in Sydney, "Armstrong's Army" virtually attacked church-goers who were on their way home

Strikers and corporation men had already had ugly confrontations, and the police wanted to teach the workers a lesson they would not forget. Recruited from the Montreal and Halifax waterfronts, the men of Amstrong's Army included thugs and boozers and, though employed by the province, served as company goons. Riding horses and swinging three-foot clubs on this black Sabbath in 1923, they galloped into a crowd of worshippers strolling home from church. They knocked down fences, smashed windows, shot a dog, split open the heads of young and old, and charged into houses in search of more victims. "Bloody Sunday" would remain one of the most infamous days in the history of labour strife in Nova Scotia. "No miner or mine worker can remain at work while this Government turns Sydney into a jungle," McLachlan stormed. "To do so is to sink your manhood and allow Armstrong and his miserable bunch of grafting politicians to trample your last shred of freedom on the sand." At his bidding, 8,500 miners downed tools. McLachlan now lost both his job and his freedom. Since the sympathy strike violated a UMW policy, John L. Lewis, the American boss of the international union, fired him as head of District Twenty-six. Convicted of seditious libel for his tongue-lashings of authorities, McLachlan spent seventeen months in jail. By March 1924, he was back on Cape Breton Island, editing the "Maritime Labour Herald."

A year later, a health officer in Glace Bay reported that 2,000 unemployed miners and their families were on the verge of starvation. BESCO responded by closing the company food stores, and the miners who were still getting a shift or two per week walked out. A mysterious fire destroyed McLachlan's print shop. The strike was only four days old when BESCO executive J. E. McClurg set new standards for insensitive management gloating. "Things are getting better every day they stay out," he told a reporter. "Let them stay out two months or six months, it matters not. Eventually they will come crawling to us. They can't stand the gaff." And what did he mean by "the gaff?" McClurg replied, "The privation—and attendant hunger."

James B. McLachlan was an outspoken advocate of workers' unions.

On June 11, 1923, with the strike entering its fourth month, BESCO goons on horseback, wielding pistols and nightsticks, attacked a demonstration of unarmed miners at a power plant near New Waterford. Thirty BESCO men wound up in hospital, but the company police wounded half a dozen miners, and one of them killed miner William Davis, age thirty-seven, with a bullet through the heart. Davis had not even participated in the demonstration. Two of his eleven children had played hooky, and he had gone to the plant to find them. Some 2,000 troops once again arrived in industrial Cape Breton, but they could not stop the enraged miners from looting and burning BESCO buildings. Before the month was out, they had set twenty-two fires, causing damage totalling hundreds of thousands of dollars.

In a provincial election just twenty-five days after Davis died, the Conservatives whipped the Liberals for the first time since 1882, winning forty out of forty-three seats. A court acquitted the man accused of shooting Davis. BESCO drifted into bankruptcy, only to rise again as the Dominion Steel and Coal Company. The miners, however, "did not regain the elusive wage scale of 1920 until World War II." But Billy Davis Day on June 11 remains sacred as a public holiday in mining communities in Nova Scotia.

The March 25, 1929, edition of the "Halifax Herald," headlined the I'm Alone incident.

Feeling Running High Over Sinking Of I'm Alone

INDEPENDENT, Impartial And Progressive. No entangling Alliances.

THE HALIFAX HERALD

"The People's Paper—For Nova Scotia First"

IF it will help Nova Scotia THE HALIFAX HERALD is for it.

VOLUME 54, NO. 71   (PHONE SACKVILLE 2381)   HALIFAX, CANADA, MONDAY, MARCH 25, 1929   The Weather:—Fair   18 PAGES

JUSTIFIES SINKING OF SCHOONER

Trouble For United States Is Now Forecast

EMBASSY IS ASKING FOR INFORMATION

Hundreds Land At Halifax From Liners

Coastguard Claims Lunenburg Vessel Was Law-Violator

DICTATOR ENJOYS HIMSELF

RECORD SET AT OCEAN TERMINALS

"Colonel" Found To Be A Woman

34 DROWN IN WATERS ON RAMPAGE

Captain Says Attack Was Cowardly

Crew Landed at New Orleans — "I'm Alone" Gave Cutters Day-Long Chase —

A Wallace MacAskill photo of Lunenburg Harbour in the 1930s. Schooners enjoyed renewed popularity in the rum-running trade which brought fortunes to some along Nova Scotia's South Shore during prohibition. Lunenburg was the port of registry for the most famous rum-running vessel, I'm Alone.

CHAPTER 27

RUM-RUNNING: "EMPLOYER OF THE LAST RESORT"

A continuing uproar over the evils of drink in Nova Scotia accompanied the continuing uproar over the evils of Upper Canada. Temperance groups had first blossomed in the province in the 1820s and were among the earliest in North America. Their leaders were not just busybodies and religious zealots; most were responsible people reacting to a gigantic social ill. Rum was everywhere. Guzzlers found it not just in taverns, dives, and brothels, but in every general store, at every building bee, and as a daily allowance for workers in forests, shipyards, and construction. In household cellars, rum kegs were as commonplace as barrels of fish. "A member of my congregation," the Rev. George Patterson recalled in his history of Pictou County in 1877, "told me, of himself and others working at a job for a fortnight in the heat of summer drinking each their quart bottle of rum a day, and not at the time feeling the worse of it, though they felt unfit for work of any sort for the following week or two. Men would sometimes drink half a pint at a time, or even a pint, and I knew of one who undertook to drink a whole quart at once, and did so, but it nearly cost him his life."[1]

By 1900, prohibition in Nova Scotia, once a matter of personal salvation, was a major goal of a movement that saw Christ as the greatest social reformer of all time. Since he had died to save not only souls but society, leaders of the "social gospel" urged sweeping public reforms. They battled against everything from political corruption and marketplace dishonesty to prizefights and racetracks, from child labour and child cigarette-smoking to the drug trade and prostitution, from sweatshops for workers to what a committee of the Methodist Church in 1903 called "any forms of commercial or industrial oppression affecting our people." And booze. It bred alcoholics, and caused accidents, poverty, disease, household violence, and abandonment by drunken fathers of their wives and children. Indeed, as a Baptist publication told Nova Scotians in 1903, "That monster iniquity, the liquor traffic [gathers] under its banner all the supreme ills that afflict the people [and] stalks forth to challenge Christianity to mortal combat."

A Methodist conference in 1905 urged church-goers to forget "the curse of blind [political] partisanship," and "by the exercise of that God-given privilege—the Ballot—smite the liquor traffic to the death." For the next decade, the battle between the church-led prohibitionists and the governing Liberals dominated provincial politics. The premier was George Henry Murray, a politician so wily he stayed in power for twenty-seven consecutive years, longer than anyone in the history of the British Empire and Commonwealth.

Slowly and reluctantly, Murray gave in to the forces of the social gospel. In 1910, Nova Scotia outlawed the sale of intoxicating beverages—except for certain special purposes—everywhere but in Halifax. One of the special purposes was medicinal. Sick people could drink legally. Doctors wrote prescriptions for spirits, to be filled at drugstores. Notorious abuse of this system saw "veritable epidemics" occurring in the Christmas season.

By the middle of World War I, even hard-drinking Halifax was officially bone-dry. In 1918, the federal government used the War Measures Act to prohibit the manufacture and sale of intoxicating liquor throughout Canada, and two years later the Bluenose enemies of booze could claim total victory. In a plebiscite, Nova Scotians approved prohibition by a vote of 82,573 to 23,953.

George Henry Murray, born in Grand Narrows, Cape Breton, served as premier of Nova Scotia from 1896 to 1923, holding office longer than anyone in the British Commonwealth.

Prohibition brought not so much a new age of social justice as a new age of rum-running. Ten months before the plebiscite, the Volstead Act had outlawed the sale of alcoholic beverages in the United States, and many Nova Scotian fishermen, war veterans, and boat-owners promptly became smugglers. The life was exciting, and the money good. The smugglers picked up liquor, often at St. Pierre and Miquelon, and ran it to the coastal waters of the United States. Keeping a sharp eye out for the Coast Guard and sometimes vanishing behind smokescreens, they off-loaded bottles and kegs to American boats while still in international waters. When they could get away with it, they took the booze right to US shores. As "total" prohibition descended on Nova Scotians, the rum-runners happily applied their newly acquired expertise to a domestic market.

Nova Scotia's anti-liquor forces were no more effective at crushing the illicit trade at the local level than American authorities were at the international level. One inspector-in-chief wearily reported in 1925 that bootleggers with automobiles were spreading so much liquor throughout Nova Scotia that shutting down speakeasies and blind pigs was having little effect on total consumption. Local inspectors failed to control smuggling, "or even check it to any appreciable extent." The federal government's tiny staff of customs officers could not possibly police every cove and inlet. (Stretching for 7579 km, Nova Scotia's coastline is longer than Canada is wide.) Moonshiners thrived, and the disillusioned inspector-in-chief reported that, owing to home brewing, beer drinking in some rural neighbourhoods had actually increased during prohibition.

With Bluenose rum-runners supplying both the United States and home markets by sea, the schooner enjoyed its last fling. "The Maritime Merchant" reported in 1925 that no fewer than half of Lunenburg's hundred vessels were rum-runners. American syndicates leased many schooners, and paid as much as $4,000 a month for a good one. Particularly on the South Shore, smuggling brought fortunes to some Nova Scotians. "Their bank accounts and beautiful homes are evidence of this even today (1984)," Ted Hennigar wrote in "The Rum Running Years." "Many prominent Nova Scotian families can attribute their wealth to the sale of liquid gold."[2] Lunenburg was the port of registry for the most famous rum-running schooner of them all. Built for a Bostonian who named it the I'm Alone, because he had broken away from a smuggling gang to operate by himself, it was thirty-eight metres long and eight metres in beam. It boasted twin 100-horsepower diesel engines. The I'm Alone moved fast and carried a lot of booze, and in September 1928, a jolly, hulking American, Big Jamie Clark, arrived in Lunenburg and, as agent for New York bootleggers, acquired it for $18,000. He set up a fake corporation to own and operate the I'm Alone as a Canadian rather than an American vessel. Big Jamie now found the skipper he wanted: Captain Thomas Randell, an ex-Newfoundlander living in Liverpool, N.S., who had earned medals for bravery in the British Navy during the recent war. A dark, swaggering, middle-aged playboy, Randell carried aboard the I'm Alone a dinner jacket, tailcoat, six dress shirts, a dozen dress collars, eighteen pairs of silk socks, and a collapsible opera hat. As skipper of the I'm Alone, he delivered several cargoes of liquor from British Honduras to inky meetings off the Louisiana coast. He outsmarted the United States Coast Guard throughout the winter of 1928–29.

On March 22, however, after a long high seas chase—during which the reply of the pistol-waving Randell to an American captain's demand that he surrender was, "I'll see you in hell first"—the Coast Guard cutter Dexter sent such a barrage of shells into the Canadian schooner that Randell ordered his crew to put boats over the side. When the I'm Alone's bow was six metres underwater and its stern three metres in the air, he jumped. The schooner dove and took with it not only Randell's wardrobe, not only 2,800 cases of rum, brandy and whisky, but the life of one crewman.

Randell and his seven surviving crew were under heavy guard and wearing manacles when they came ashore at New Orleans. A few days later the American authorities decided their case was weak and quietly released the prisoners. Nasty diplomatic notes flew between Ottawa and Washington. Canada demanded that the United States prove the Coast Guard had not committed an act of piracy. By now a Canadian hero, Randell declared, "I did not stop because I knew I was entitled to freedom of the sea. This is the most cowardly attack on a merchant ship since the submarine warfare." Six years later a pair of judges, one American and one Canadian, agreed that the sinking of the I'm Alone was unlawful. The US State Department formally apologized to Canada and awarded the men of the I'm Alone compensation totaling $25,666.50.

When prohibition hit Halifax, blind pigs sprouted like crocuses in April. "This Dauphinee family were famous bootleggers," Alex Nickerson, a seventy-nine-year-old ex-newspaperman remembered in 1987. "They ran booze in from Sambro and the mouth of the Northwest Arm, and there was a whole bunch of them. Right in the middle of downtown, they had an old frame house with iron doors, and when you went in, you walked upstairs for your shot of beer or rum. They were always being raided. They built a lookout. It projected from the front of the house, upstairs, and the fellow on duty could look up and down the street, and if he saw the police coming, he would give a warning. By the time the law got through the metal doors, the rum was flushed down the toilet."

Some bootleggers had "ingenious hides" for liquor. While demolishing a building on Water Street in the 1930s, a wrecking crew found a sink inside the front door. A hidden pipeline ran through the house, up a backyard slope and into another building on Hollis Street. "The bootlegger on Water Street could turn a tap on," Nickerson said, "and rum would come down the pipe from Hollis and into a pitcher in the sink. But he could also shut it off and turn another valve, and then out came only water. Just to tell you how smart they were." Bootleggers were smart not just in Halifax but throughout Nova Scotia.

Since women found jobs even harder to get than men did in the Nova Scotia of the 1920s, many of them, especially single mothers, turned to bootlegging. Temperance inspector Clifford Rose, in 1980, wrote harshly about Mrs. Delores Nicholson, a Pictou County bootlegger whose place he had repeatedly raided more than half a century before. During one raid, someone had clouted his head with a bottle, and in "Four Years with the Demon Rum" (1980), Rose described Mrs. Nicholson as cruel and foul-mouthed. But a Mrs. Bernice Masson of Trenton placed an ad in the "New Glasgow Evening News" to explain that Mrs. Nicholson had done her job "the only way she knew how," and "fought rotten government, cops and crooked politicians." Mrs. Masson remembered Mrs. Nicholson's "tears when her children went hungry and the nights when the three, mother and children, cuddled with arms around each other to keep warm ... Well, I too lived in that dive beside the railway tracks. I am the very proud daughter of that savage, cruel, profane-tongued Delores on page 42 of the book." In the illegal booze traffic, there were two sides to every story.

Smuggling and bootlegging provided so many jobs that, as historian E. R. Forbes wrote, "It was rum more than the fisheries which became the true employer of the last resort."[3] If the illicit trade provided employment, so did the hopeless effort to squelch it. Towns hired extra police. The province appointed its own inspectors. The federal government founded a Preventive Force, with officers on land and sea. The number of Crown prosecutors and defence lawyers increased. Bureaucracies expanded, offering hundreds of new posts. Then, as a new decade began, the Nova Scotia government gave up. Prohibition would last for another three years in the United States, but in 1930, Nova Scotia repealed it and, in keeping with the growth of bureaucracy, opened government-run liquor stores.

In the fall of 1929, just as the Bluenose economy had begun to revive, the crash hit the New York Stock Exchange. A month later an earthquake sent tremors through the whole province. They would later seem like a signal of the bad times to come.

From its earliest days, the Bluenose was symbolic of Nova Scotian pride and heritage.

CHAPTER 28

HOPE SHINES
THROUGH THE
DIRTY THIRTIES

While Canada's population climbed from 4.8 million to 10.4 million between 1891 and 1931, that of the seven easternmost counties of Nova Scotia dropped from 131,886 to 105,279. The one-family farms of the pioneers had not been big enough to support the grown children of later generations. The promise of urban excitement and regular wages had lured the rural young far westward or to the mines and mills of Cape Breton and Pictou County. Hard-up parents scrimped, and even mortgaged their homes, to make sure at least one of their children, usually a boy, got an education to help him move upward in a distant and wealthier society. This "skimming process," as Father Moses Michael Coady called it, long robbed eastern Nova Scotia of its "natural leaders."

Coady was among the activist priests who saw that, for those who stayed behind—many of them middle-aged or old—life was changing for the worse. Automobiles, trucks, and improved roads drained the countryside of people. Rural stores vanished. Country lawyers and doctors moved into the growing towns. Back in the hills where the dirt roads remained skinny and families still used privies and kerosene lamps, grain fields succumbed to the advancing wilderness, community spirit faded, and church congregations got smaller and older.

As subsistence farming gave way to market-based economies, farmers became less independent than their forebears and more deeply in debt. Inshore fishermen were in a similar fix: "The farmers and fishermen owed their souls and their livelihood to the middlemen who bought their products, extended credit, and supplied them with such little luxuries as tea and sugar,"[1] wrote Halifax author Jim Lotz in "The Nova Scotia Historical Review." Many rural folk came to believe they were losers and failures.

Out of these depressing conditions sprang a miraculous social movement. Its leaders were Cape Breton-born priests who aimed not only to restore the pride of farmers, fishermen, and miners, but also to show them how to become masters of their own destiny. When St. Francis Xavier University of Antigonish founded its Extension Department in 1928, it gave official birth to the Antigonish Movement. This was an unusual phenomenon. Conservatism dominated the Catholic church, yet here was a Catholic, liberal, social-action movement.

It had three formidable champions. "The prophet, [Father John James Tompkins], who cried out for years in the wilderness, came from the Margaree Valley," Lotz explained. "The messiah [also from Margaree country] was Father Coady, a cousin and protégé of Father Jimmy, and a man of great physical presence. The organizer was Angus B. MacDonald who did the careful planning and administrative work that every social movement needs."[2] As far back as 1920, Father Jimmy Tompkins published his "Knowledge for the People," urging St. Francis Xavier University to plunge into adult

Dr. J. J. Tompkins was an influential member of the Antigonish Movement that restored pride to rural workers in the 1930s.

A National Film Board of Canada photo of Dr. Coady with international students at St. Francis Xavier University.

education as a way to achieve social and economic justice. A short man, he was energetic, abrasive, pushy, and inspiring. One admirer said, "When that little father starts talking, he turns on a queer light back of his eyes, and the first thing I know I find myself wanting to go out and do something about the evil in the world."

Then there was Coady. The first head of the Extension Department, he dominated its adult education programs for almost three decades. "Antigonish had a fantastic history of social action," journalist Margaret Daly wrote in 1970. "It was here that Moses Michael Coady walked out of the Margaree Valley to found the co-op movement that spread throughout the world." Lotz called Coady "a charismatic figure, a big, rough-hewn man with a transcendental vision of the good life." He was also a dramatic orator, "and no one who met him ever forgot him."

By organizing public meetings to air problems and then study groups to hash out solutions, and by providing instruction on everything from keeping a set of books to setting up a library, the Antigonish Movement inspired "the little people" to found their own credit unions, buying clubs, co-ops for the marketing of fish and farm produce, and co-op grocery stores and housing projects.

Father Moses Michael Coady was founder of the co-op movement and first head of the adult education Extension Department at St. Francis Xavier University.

During the grim 1930s the movement, helped by organizations with similar goals, flourished throughout the Maritimes. In 1938, no fewer than 19,600 Maritimers belonged to 2,265 study clubs. Three hundred and forty-two Maritime credit unions were doing business, as well as 162 other kinds of co-op organizations. Eleven full-time and seven part-time staff worked at the Extension Department, and dozens more were out in fishing villages. The movement's Rural and Industrial Conference in 1938 attracted a thousand people, and the subsequent Co-operative Institute brought together 200 clergymen, social workers, and teachers from every province and thirty American states. That was the year the Antigonish Movement won papal approval.

By the early 1960s, the number of Maritime credit unions had climbed to 434, with 100,000 members and assets of $14 million. Co-op wholesale organizations boasted a turnover of $30 million. Retail co-op stores totaled 150, and housing projects fifty. Moreover, village leaders in the West Indies, Central America, and South America were all employing techniques they had learned in Antigonish. After Father Coady died in 1959, St. Francis Xavier

University founded the Coady International Institute, which has since given training to thousands of community organizers from Africa, Asia, and Latin America. To this day, the institute helps the Third World to help itself.

A myth has it that Nova Scotia, along with New Brunswick and Prince Edward Island, somehow suffered less than the rest of Canada during the Dirty Thirties. A bigger proportion of Maritimers than other Canadians did live on farms where they grew their own food and cut their own firewood, but Maritimers as a whole endured more misery than any other part of the nation except the drought-ridden Prairies. Their governments were too poor to gain a fair share of federal relief programs. The federal government gave the nine provinces $463,667,018 during the 1930s, but the Maritimes got only $15,151,475, a piddling 3.3 per cent.

Wallace MacAskill's photograph of the Margaree Valley—home of Father Coady—as featured in a 1930s government travel guide.

With respect to aid for the jobless, the Maritimes were the stingiest provinces in Canada. Officials in Nova Scotia tried to weasel out of their responsibility for relief, and, according to E. R. Forbes in "Challenging the Regional Stereotypes," "The record abounds with examples of elderly and destitute refused assistance, deaf and blind cut off from their schools, seriously ill denied hospitalization, and moral offenders savagely punished."[3]

The authorities were short of money, to be sure, but they were often short of compassion, too. While people with steady jobs benefited from rock-bottom prices for everything from food to maid services, many of them denounced the destitute as lazy and undeserving folk who had only themselves to blame for their troubles. The official cause of the death of a Sydney man was "malnutrition," but Bill Boyd, a CBC producer from industrial Cape Breton remembered a fellow worker of the dead man saying, "He died of starvation and Christian sympathy. That's what killed him."

In industrial Cape Breton and Halifax, conditions were not just tough, but horrifying. Three-hundred-and-seventy families lived in 192 condemned houses in Halifax, "As many as seven families would save money by crowding into quarters designed for far fewer, using a common sink in the hallway and climbing several flights of stairs to get water," Pierre Berton wrote in "The Great Depression." "More than 11,000 men, women, and children were exposed to substandard sanitary conditions."[4]

With the steel mill closed in Sydney, many families faced starvation. At a meeting of the unemployed, men were so desperate they passed a motion that they take their guns to city hall and demand an increase in relief. (After further debate, they rescinded the motion.) The city council refused help for a tubercular mother who could afford but one pint of milk per day for her nine children. Many people died of outright starvation or of diseases that struck bodies enfeebled by hunger.

A view of Sydney in the 1930s. One of many Nova Scotia industrial towns that suffered greatly during the Depression.

In Glace Bay, the miners lived almost as slaves to Dominion Coal, a company so heartless it used company bullies to stop men with freezing children from dipping into its mountains of stored coal. The miners were proud, and only when their families faced starvation did they furtively seek scraps of food from the distributors of relief. Bill McNeil, a CBC producer who grew up near the collieries, wrote, "Many children died during the Depression in Glace Bay. Nobody said they starved to death but that was actually the reason."

Michiel Horn's book, "The Dirty Thirties, Canadians in the Great Depression," published a letter that an old New Glasgow man sent to Prime Minister R. B. Bennett in 1934. "There is a great deal more destitution here than we have ever known. My house is besieged front door, back door and side door from early in the morning till long past the dewy eve. A couple of evenings ago I had a visit from three different widows who have boys between the ages of sixteen and twenty without employment and who are absolutely destitute."[5] His daughter had given away every scrap of spare clothes they had. He himself now owned but one pair of trousers.

"Around 1933, there wasn't a day went by that somebody wasn't fed at our house," recalled Alex MacIntosh, a Stellarton-born corporation lawyer in Toronto. His mother, a widow who ran a small farm outside the coal-mining town, fed the drifters as they "popped off the trains." Stellarton had not only despairing drifters but also hundreds of despairing Stellartonians. "In the year 1933," MacIntosh said, "I don't think the mine whistle blew once in Stellarton."

Pictou County miners, like other destitute Nova Scotians, endured the humiliation of going to the town hall to prove they were so poor they deserved "direct relief." They got no cash. The town issued them orders, which they then traded with merchants for food and clothing. Since the town reimbursed the merchants for the orders, and since merchants dominated the municipal councils, the system guaranteed that unless a whole town went bust, the shopkeepers got their money. Taxpayers who did not need relief squealed about giving it to those who did. Councillors got it in the neck from the hungry for being cruel, and from the well-fed for being wastrels.

Pictou County was the scene of perhaps the only tar-and-feathering—actually a tar-and-graveling—in Canada during the Depression. The victim was a landlord who tried to raise the rent of a widow with five small children

Captain of the Bluenose for eighteen years, Angus Walters poses with the "Halifax Herald" trophy.

from five dollars a month, which she could not afford, to eight dollars. Unemployed miners dragged him down his driveway, tore off his clothes, and covered him with warm tar. Decades later, in "Ten Lost Years: 1929–39," Barry Broadfoot quoted one of them: "One lad put a rope around this bastard's feet and another under his arms and they rolled him back and forth, pulled him up and down in the loose gravel and dust ... You never, never saw such a mess ... I got down on one knee and I said, close to his face, 'Don't you raise that widow's rent one red cent. You got that?' He never did."[6]

During these times of bread lines, soup kitchens, and hobo jungles, Nova Scotia boasted a beautiful asset that no other province could match: the *Bluenose*. By 1919, the tough schoonermen of Nova Scotia and New England had grown so scornful of the tenderness displayed by the delicate yachts competing for the America's Cup off New York that they campaigned for a series of races between "real" sailing vessels. They meant the working schooners from Lunenburg and Gloucester that headed for the Grand Banks off Newfoundland in the sort of breezes that sent the America's Cup boats scurrying for cover. W. H. Dennis, owner of the "Halifax Herald," offered an International Fisherman's Trophy, and it was for this competition that William J. Roue of Halifax designed the Bluenose, and Smith and Rhuland of Lunenburg built it.

Hugh MacLennan at Oxford University in 1931. Ten years later he would receive rave reviews for his book "Barometer Rising," inspired by his boyhood memories of the Halifax Explosion.

The Bluenose slid into the water on March 26, 1921. Its overall length was more than forty-three metres, and its beam eight metres. The mainmast soared twenty-five metres above the deck. The vessel could carry 929 square metres of sail. It was "a witch to windward," and under Captain Angus J. Walters, suffered defeat in only one series. The Boston schooner Gertrude L. Thebaud beat the Bluenose for the Lipton Cup in 1930, but the Nova Scotia schooner won the International Fisherman's Trophy in 1921, 1922, and 1923, and again in 1931 and 1938, beating its nemesis, the Thebaud, in both of these later series. Walters became a national hero, and Halifax newspaperman Andrew Merkel spoke for nearly 600,000 Nova Scotians when, in 1948, he called the Bluenose "the fleetest fisherman ever to sail the Seven Seas."

The vessel was a seagoing boost to the pride Nova Scotians took in their history and distinctiveness. Not even the Great Depression could squelch that provincial patriotism. It was in the 1930s that Cape Breton–born novelist Hugh MacLennan heard a customs inspector in Halifax tell disembarking steamship passengers, "Nova Scotians in Aisle A. Aliens and Canadians in Aisle B."

Victory Loan Parade
Barrington Street,
Halifax, June 1941.

NOVA SCOTIA GOES TO WAR—AGAIN

After twenty years of depression, Halifax in 1939 was a derelict and somewhat puritanical town of 70,000 people, but on September 10, when Canada declared war on Nazi Germany, the city became what British Rear Admiral S. S. Bonham-Carter called "probably the most important port in the world." It had neither pubs nor nightclubs, only nine movie theatres, few good restaurants, and little professional entertainment, but it still boasted the natural harbour that, 190 years before, had so impressed Governor Edward Cornwallis. In any season, on any tide, the world's biggest vessels could dock beside the 600-metre-long New Quay, and for the assembling of convoys no body of water anywhere was better than Bedford Basin.

On a scale unimaginable in previous centuries, Halifax again fulfilled its destiny as an instrument of war. Britain's survival depended on the Allied convoys sent from Halifax, whose identity military censors routinely obscured as "An East Coast Port." It was from here, little more than 3200 kilometres from Europe, that the convoys sailed into waters infested with U-boats—by the winter of 1942–43, the Nazis had 212 submarines at sea—and wallowed across the Atlantic with food, lumber, steel, shells, tanks, guns, and highly explosive aviation fuel.

On a raw, foggy Sunday in December 1939, five liners sat on the Halifax waterfront, "their former dazzle erased by the camouflage of war, their prows now as grey as the ocean itself."[1] Already on board were 7,400 men, half of the Canadian First Division. Commenting on how easy it was for spies to report troopship movements to the Nazis, H. B. Jefferson, regional censor of publications during the war, wrote, "Even the veriest landlubber can tell at a glance that the leviathans towering above nearby buildings are no ordinary vessels." Four Canadian destroyers shepherded those first five troopships out to sea, where they met a Royal Navy escort for the voyage to Britain. By year's end, 16,000 Canadian soldiers had sailed from Halifax for the United Kingdom. As Nova Scotia vanished astern, many climbed high in each vessel's rigging for a last view of Canada.

Rear Admiral Leonard Warren Murray, commander-in-chief of Canadian Northwest Atlantic.

Fearing that if Britain did fall, the Nazis would turn on east-coast Canada, the Canadian navy installed anti-submarine defences at Sydney, Halifax, and Shelburne, and the air force built bases at Sydney, Debert, Yarmouth, Shelburne, and Eastern Passage at Halifax-Dartmouth. Army training bases sprung up at Debert and Aldershot, and for the navy, at Cornwallis. By the spring of 1940, the war seemed so close that Nova Scotians "worried lest one electric light serve as a target for enemy aircraft. Increasingly the region took on the appearance and feeling of an armed camp; rumours of spies and saboteurs, black-outs and air-raid drills fed the sense of fear ... "[2]

No city in Canada was more "in the war" than Halifax.

"Right up to early 1945 when ships were mined or torpedoed sometimes within gunshot of outer Halifax forts, and the distant thud of depth charges could be heard through the open windows of the Nova Scotian Hotel," Thomas H. Raddall wrote, "the sight of the grey ships plodding out to face such music all the way to Britain ... was something to catch the heart."

Even closer to Europe than Halifax, Sydney, too, was a key port in the Battle of the Atlantic. In October 1940, U-boats sank twenty of the thirty-four ships in a convoy from Sydney. By January 2, 1941, nearly a thousand vessels in forty-eight convoys, "slow and vulnerable, but packed with supplies, had sailed [from Sydney] for Britain, in desperate need and surviving its darkest hour."[3] Canadian naval officer James B. Lamb remembered, "The oldest, slowest boats were sent here, which created enormous problems of maintenance, and so on, much more difficult than the Halifax convoys. Sydney did a splendid job and made you welcome."

In both Sydney and Halifax, the crew of the merchantmen hailed from around the world. "Make no mistake," said Rear Admiral Leonard Warren Murray, a native of Pictou County, "the real victors in the Battle of the Atlantic were ... the Allied merchant seamen." Murray knew what he was talking about. As commander in chief, Canadian Northwest Atlantic, he was the only Canadian to boss an entire theatre of war.

Commander Ewart Simpson, convoy routing officer in Sydney during the early 1940s, recalled, "They [the merchant seamen] were worn out. They knew the losses, yet there were no desertions. There was sickness and there was trouble. There were tough men—some would certainly finish up in Sydney jail before making passage. Some needed psychiatric treatment, which they could not get, so they just had to sweat it out. We could always get recruits from the mines in Cape Breton, until they put a stop to it [because coal was so important to the war effort]. The miners loved to go aboard the ships."

In Nova Scotia and Newfoundland, nothing brought the war home more horribly than the sinking of the best-loved ferry that had ever sailed between North Sydney and Newfoundland, the Caribou. In the deepest part of the Cabot Strait, before dawn on October 14, 1942, a Nazi torpedo struck the ferry on the starboard beam, and charged right on through the port side. Among the 137 people who died on that black morning off southwestern Newfoundland were fifty-six military personnel from Canada, Newfoundland and the United States; forty-eight civilians, including women and children; and thirty-one of the ferry's crew.

"If there were any Canadians who did not realize we were up against a ruthless and remorseless enemy," said Angus L. Macdonald, Canada's navy minister and the once-and-future premier of Nova Scotia, "there can be no such Canadians now."

During the next month, Nazi submarines sank 119 Allied ships. They were destroying vessels almost twice as fast as Allied yards could build replacements. In March 1943, they sent 108 vessels to the bottom. Two convoys, during three hideous days, lost twenty-two of their eighty-eight ships, and 360 people, including two women and two children.

"The only thing that ever really frightened me," Winston Churchill later wrote, "was the U-boat peril ... Here was no field for gestures or sensations; only the slow, cold drawing of lines on charts, which showed potential strangulation."

Thanks to the convoys, the strangulation never occurred. U-boats continued to sink ships off Halifax till the end of the war, but well before that, the tide in the Battle of the Atlantic had turned in the Allies' favour. In July

1944, a convoy of 167 merchant ships—nineteen columns of vessels covering 78 square kilometres—crossed the Atlantic, under the protection of Canadian warships, without encountering a single U-boat.

All in all, Desmond Morton said in "A Military History of Canada," "Vast tonnages crossed the ocean unscathed. Training and hard experience in [the Royal Canadian Navy and Royal Canadian Air Force] paid off as Canadians extended their role closer to British waters."[4] By war's end, convoys from Halifax had included 17,593 ships.

Until 1942, troopships crossed the Atlantic in small convoys, but after that they sailed singly, relying on their speed to escape U-boats. The Queen Elizabeth carried 14,000 soldiers per voyage. During the whole war, about 100 troopships made more than 300 sailings, all but one of which arrived safely, and carried across the Atlantic 368,000 men and women of the Canadian Army. Almost all sailed from Halifax.

The war gave Nova Scotia the economic boost it had long and desperately needed. Men willing to risk their lives could now join an exciting mission and earn a living wage. Unemployed, underemployed, and bored Bluenosers rushed to join the armed services.

Mills hummed as they had not hummed in decades. Trenton Industries Ltd., in Pictou County, hired hundreds of workers to assemble and ship four-inch guns for the Royal Navy. Trenton Steel Works manufactured nuts, bolts, gun mountings, and more than two million shells for Canadian and British forces. Shipbuilding boomed in Halifax and Pictou town, and Canada's Tribal class destroyers, pocket cruisers really, with a reputation as the hardest-hitting destroyers in the world, were made from Nova Scotia steel. The Dominion Coal and Steel Company's Sydney steel plant churned out more than a third of the nation's entire output of regular ships' plates.

When shipyard tradesmen joined the armed services, women became welders, sheet-metal workers, crane drivers, pipefitters, electricians, and warehouse hands. More than a third of Nova Scotia's female workers were domestic servants as the 1940s began, but hundreds rushed into jobs, at thrice their old wages, in the new wartime industries.

The war was a godsend to Halifax's previously quiet and decrepit waterfront. The world's biggest floating dockyard arose at the Halifax Shipyard. Long-declining harbourside industries hired hundreds of workers to cope with the crippled ships that crept into port, and all along the waterfront men and women worked even at night—"under the cluster of flood lights ... and the intense violet flare of arc-welders."[5] By war's end, Halifax-Dartmouth yards had repaired 7,000 vessels damaged in the Battle of the Atlantic.

Halifax resented ignorance in the rest of Canada—and especially among federal bureaucrats—about its sacrifices and importance. "I expect anything from [federal] officials who solemnly inquired, on the occasion of the [1939] visit of the king and queen, whether Halifax Harbour was big enough for their ship to turn around in," Mayor William E. Donovan scornfully complained.

As early as 1941, magazine writer Frederick Edwards called Halifax "a cross section of the Empire." He said, "You may hear within the space of one block Cockney, Yorkshire, Lancashire and Scottish accents. Royal Navy and Royal Canadian Navy officers and ratings mingle with men of the merchant marine. Egyptian, Malayan and Hindu seamen wait in line before theatre box offices with airmen from Australia and New Zealand, Canadian soldiers, and sailors of Allied countries: Free French, Norwegians, Dutchmen, Poles. After nightfall, a civilian on Barrington Street looks as though he didn't belong."

As in every war in Halifax's history, this one brought not only money, drama, and men in uniform, but also prostitutes, bootleggers, administrative headaches, and tension between townsfolk and the military. Far more than inland cities, Halifax endured shortages of food, clothing, housing, gasoline, and even kitchen utensils. Trains jam-packed with airmen, soldiers, and sailors steamed into Union Station, and the population shot from 69,000 to more than 100,000. No other Canadian city had to cope with such a sudden and overwhelming increase in population.

A view from Africville of a World War II convoy assembly in Bedford Basin in 1941.

Soldiers and sailors slept in tents, an immigration shed, and sidelined railway cars. Hotels were so crowded some filled their public rooms with beds. In a wartime article magazine Eric Hutton wrote: "Your greeting at the hotel [in Halifax] is a look of weary regret from the room clerk. He holds up a two-inch stack of wires and letters. 'Reservations,' he explains. 'Perhaps in two or three days ...' However it turns out that he can let you have a bed. With all the ceremony of a pukka guest you are escorted to a large ground-floor room, once the ladies' lounge, now occupied by a score of beds. This dormitory is popularly—or unpopularly—known as the 'dog house' or 'bull pen.' It costs $2.25 a night to join the chorus of snores."[6]

As wives and children followed their men to Halifax, the shortage of accommodation became a blueprint for inflation. The more crowded the city got the easier it was for landladies and landlords to charge high rents for slummy rooms. As many as ten people sometimes shared a room, and the 1941 census reported that Halifax had an average of five per room. On the outskirts, colonies of grubby, ramshackle sleeping huts arose and spread into the woods.

HMS Queen Elizabeth—the Cunard Liner (QE I) converted to a troop carrier—arrived in Halifax with joyful returned soldiers at Pier 21, 1945.

Halifax seemed almost like one of Europe's refugee-crowded cities and got noisier as the war continued. Dozens of vessels in a American convoy would spend an entire night creeping past the city towards Bedford Basin, and if fog happened to enshroud the harbour, each ship blew its own warning every few seconds. Accompanying this din were loud signals to summon pilot launches, medical boats, and coal barges; the racket from bell-buoys and shore-based fog whistles; and the regular and vigorous ringing of bells aboard every ship lying at anchor. "The whole thing," regional censor H. B. Jefferson, complained, "was a bedlam which made sleep almost impossible."

Recalling July of 1943, Jefferson continued, "Motorcycles, army and commercial trucks roar through the streets, dozens of locomotives shunt day and night with the usual bell-ringing and whistling, and ... the streetcars pound over the dilapidated rails with a clatter that makes conversation almost impossible. Overhead there is the continuous, monotonous droning of all kinds of planes ... Every evening sees swarms of drunks reeling, singing or fighting on all the principal thoroughfares." After complaining about standing in line at everything from restaurants to railway ticket windows, and the near impossibility of finding a taxi, he concluded, "All this is very hard on the nerves."

The Halifax waterfront was dotted with clubs and canteens for men from assorted nations. Thousands of Bluenose men and women, acting as both individuals and members of service clubs, fraternal organizations, and churches, did their generous best to make strangers in uniform feel good about being in Nova Scotia. To take just one example of wartime do-gooding, women set up "Mothers' Corners," where they mended, pressed, and otherwise looked after the clothing of men they had never seen before and would never see again. At just three of the bigger hostels, Mothers' Corners tended to the uniforms of more than 20,000 men.

"During the calendar year 1941," a pamphlet from the provincial government boasted, "more than 6,650,000 men ... were provided with comforts, educational facilities and entertainment by the people of Nova Scotia. This does not mean that so large a number of different men were thus served. Men of the Navy may visit the hostels twice or a dozen times yearly and a record of their visit is made on each occasion. As men of the Army or Air Force move from one section of the Province to another their attendance at hostels is recorded at each place. It should be pointed out, however, that the work involved is the same as if the various needs of nearly seven million individuals had been supplied."

In Halifax, relations between civilians and the military gradually deteriorated. "There were hundreds of kindly Halifax people whose hospitality and generosity won't be forgotten," William H. Pugsley remembered in "Saints, Devils and Ordinary Seamen." "And there were hundreds of women who gave unstintingly to make the canteens a haven of enjoyment for the sailor. Unfortunately ... they seemed to be outnumbered by citizens who were, at best, indifferent."[7] At worst, they were greedy and insolent, like so many taxi-drivers, salesclerks, and proprietors of grubby diners.

Thousands of lonely young soldiers and sailors wandered the streets with little to do. The more snobbish young women of Halifax, preferring naval officers, refused to go out with mere sailors. While the officers gathered over rum in their messes, ratings could get liquor only at a government store. Forbidden from drinking it on any base, they gulped it down in alleys and parks. When Winston Churchill passed through Halifax on his way to the Quebec Conference in August 1943, he climbed out of a car at the Citadel to view the harbour, and whom did he see pulling a case of beer out of some bushes but a Canadian sailor? "The sailor went to attention in a sort of squatting position," a newspaper reported, "one hand in salute, the other firmly grasping the beer."[8]

"As the war dragged on, there was an increasing ennui among servicemen, a steady decline in shore discipline," Thomas H. Raddall wrote. "Four out of five men were well behaved, but theft, robbery with violence, malicious damage and assault upon women by men in uniform became matters of daily occurrence."

News that Germany had surrendered reached the world on May 7 and, in Halifax, ignited the most spectacular riots in the city's history. They lasted two nights and a day. Soldiers, sailors, airmen, and thuggish civilians all participated in the anarchy that saw wholesale window-smashing, public fornication in broad daylight, and the theft of at least 150,000 bottles of beer, liquor, and wine. The consensus among sober Haligonians who had witnessed the destruction was that the chief culprits were sailors from the navy's main Halifax base, HMCS Stadacona.

A mob scene of Victory Day riots in Halifax, May 1945. The calamity lasted for two nights and a day.

Novelist Hugh Garner called the "$5 million spree" an orgy of looting and boozing, "probably unequalled since the revelries of the Roman Empire." The head on a front-page editorial in the "Halifax Mail" on May 9 read, "Reign Of Terror Disgrace To The Whole Dominion," and the main story began:

"Commercial Halifax ... lies in wreckage today; acres of plate grass are strewn in the streets and looted store stocks are mangled and trampled on floors and pavements sticky with rain and debris, aftermath of Victory Day riots that raged unchecked for hours and cost the city a sum running well into the millions. Dartmouth also was involved ... as crazed men tried to set the ferries afire, smashed into business places and added rape to the list of crimes ... In the jails are a few score of the many thousands of drunken and hysterical men and women— service and civilian alike—youths and calculating vultures who flocked to the scene to reap what others had sowed in destruction ... In a morgue is the body of a sailor who drank himself to death on Monday night." Another navy man died from a skull fracture.

One witness to the riots said he believed the grudges sailors and others held against merchants who had gouged them and treated them "like animals" simply exploded on VE Day "when they let out the long-held-back feelings of hate, in conjunction with the exhilaration of going home soon. It was like a great thunderstorm or cyclone that came up suddenly."[9]

The federal government commissioned Judge Roy L. Kellock of the Supreme Court of Canada to investigate the riots, but as war correspondent Douglas How later wrote, "The commissioner was a judge who had never seen war service, a puritanical man who detested liquor, and sat in judgment on perhaps the biggest drunk in Canadian history."

Finding the navy chiefly responsible for the mayhem and the damage to 564 Halifax businesses, and blaming the command of Rear Admiral Leonard Warren Murray for failing to prepare adequate celebrations or quell the disorders, Judge Kellock ruined the previously distinguished career of the best naval officer Canada had ever produced. Crushed, disgraced, embittered and forgotten, Murray spent his last twenty-five years in England. Naval veterans would later see Kellock's ruling as a tragic injustice.

One sweaty evening in July 1945, an eerie footnote to the war in Europe rattled all of Halifax-Dartmouth. With peacetime had come ships loaded with newly redundant explosives. They deposited their cargo at a naval magazine on the Dartmouth side of Bedford Basin, and at suppertime on the 18th, an explosion there smashed windows and shook buildings up and down both sides of the harbour. The blast ignited fires that soon licked at the magazine's open ammunition dumps. All night, the din continued—the rumblings, pop-pop-crack of minor explosions, deafening blams of bigger ones, and fireworks above Bedford Basin.

Fearing a gigantic blast yet to come, the navy urged half the people of Halifax to evacuate their homes. An enormous parade of trucks and cars, loaded with bedding, furniture and food, inched westward on the St. Margaret's Bay Road. The scene looked like Movie Tone news footage of refugees in war-torn Europe. On everyone's mind was the horror that had struck the city on December 6, 1917.

The danger, however, passed within twenty-four hours. When Halifax learned that navy volunteers had risked their lives to extinguish the magazine fires, it forgave the navy for the VE Day riots. Indeed, the explosions, Thomas H. Raddall asserted, "blew away in a night and a day what might have been years of bitterness between Halifax and the service to which it [was] bound."

The Canso Causeway between Cape Breton and the
mainland opened on August 13, 1955.

CHAPTER 30

THE POSTWAR BUST. WEATHERING A CRISIS

As so often in the past, Nova Scotia's wartime boom did not survive the peace. Facing big cuts in defence spending, the Bluenose economy was perhaps even less fit to cope with the world after the war than before. The federal government had imposed on the Maritimes a policy not just to let them slide backward, but to shove them backward. At the time it seemed right to celebrate Munitions and Supply Minister C. D. Howe as the strong man who put Canadian industry on a war footing and reconstructed the postwar economy, but New Brunswick historian Ernest R. Forbes has shown that Howe was so determined to fatten central Canadian industry with taxpayers' money—while starving Maritime industry—that he did so even at the cost of bungling parts of the war effort.

The Dominion Steel and Coal Company (DOSCO) was the biggest industrial employer in the Maritimes and one of Canada's "big three" steel producers. The others were the Steel Company of Canada, in Hamilton, and Algoma Steel, in Sault Ste. Marie. While granting these Ontario firms juicy subsidies to modernize and build mills, the federal government was so tight-fisted with DOSCO that the company's president, Arthur Cross, complained to Howe in 1941 that his was "the only primary steel producer in this country which is receiving no government assistance."

As Ottawa concentrated steel-making, shipbuilding, and even the repair of fighting vessels in central Canada, skilled workers flowed inland from the Maritimes. Having caused a labour shortage in the Maritimes, the federal government then used it as an excuse not to bolster Maritime industries. Howe's anti-Maritimes and anti-DOSCO bias, along with Montreal's political clout, forced hundreds of warships to go for repairs not to convoy headquarters in Halifax, but all the way up the St. Lawrence.

"The navy," Forbes explains, "was reduced to the desperate expedients of leaving some vessels frozen in St. Lawrence ports for the winter, routing others to British Columbia, and sending still others on the dubious gamble of breaking into refit schedules at American ports."[1]

As early as 1940, British naval authorities objected to Canada's policy of building vessels at inland yards. Ice barred the new ships from the ocean for almost half the year, and winter damaged them even before they could be launched. The British asked the Canadian government to build a superior repair centre at Halifax, with graving docks for their biggest vessels. Investigators from the United States found Halifax's repair facilities so inadequate they told their government to send tugboats to rescue the vessels of many nationalities that languished in the Canadian port while awaiting repairs. The American report irritated Howe, but it did not get Halifax the repair centre the Allies needed.

Angus L. Macdonald, premier of Nova Scotia 1933–1940 and 1945–1954, was a much loved politician whose popularity in the province was perhaps second only to Joseph Howe's.

If Nova Scotia industry did not receive its share of government investment during arrangements for war, neither did it get a fair share during arrangements for peace. In 1944, Howe took charge of the Department of Reconstruction, which used a formula to make sure government assistance went only to profitable companies that might make a successful transition to peacetime production. By July 1, 1945, Ontario had received 48 per cent of the funds, Quebec 32 per cent, British Columbia 15 per cent, and the six Maritime and Prairie provinces a total of only 5 per cent.

Nova Scotia industries such as DOSCO survived the war, but, thanks to government-fuelled expansion and modernization of Ontario competitors, found themselves badly weakened in the marketplace. During the next quarter-century, DOSCO would be taken over by British interests, milked of its capital, and dismantled. In the long run, the impact on Nova Scotia of the government's wartime policies was bad. They accentuated and consolidated all the old trends toward regional disparity.

The 1950s in Nova Scotia saw the advance of electricity, indoor plumbing, refrigerators, television, road-building, the family car, and mass consumer culture—and the retreat of an older order based on a belief in thrift and hard work to conquer scarcity. The elderly got their first pension cheques, and as consolidated schools replaced one-room schoolhouses, the young got their first daily bus rides. The Angus L. Macdonald Bridge in Halifax-Dartmouth and the Canso Causeway, both of which opened in 1955, stood as "monuments to the development ethic of the dynamic decade," Margaret Conrad wrote in "The Atlantic Provinces in Confederation."[2] As the peninsula of Halifax was rapidly becoming full, the bridge gave a tremendous spurt to the construction of suburbs on the Dartmouth side of the harbour.

The decade, however, was not as dynamic as it sometimes appeared. Indeed, pessimism enshrouded Nova Scotia in the mid-fifties. The war seemed to have been only an interlude in a decline that had begun long ago. Nova Scotia heard only faint echoes of the postwar boom happening in distant parts of Canada. Between 1949 and 1956, Nova Scotia's per-capita spending on new and durable physical assets such as factories and housing was only 58.8 per cent of Canada's. "We just weren't an industrial province," Yarmouth businessman Seymour Kenney remembered in 1980. "If you drove for fifty miles along the whole French Shore, you'd see hardly a gallon of paint on the buildings."

In 1946 personal income, per capita, in Nova Scotia was $678, or 80 per cent of the figure for all Canada; ten years later it was only $971, or a mere 71 per cent. Canadian wages averaged $66.44 a week in 1956. Nova Scotian wages, at $52.90, lagged even behind those in New Brunswick and Newfoundland. To make the picture even less promising, it had mostly been federal government money that had kept the province from plummeting even further.

The stagnation and outright decline of industries left the economy increasingly dependent on the incomes of construction labourers, pulpwood-cutters, farm hands, fishermen, and other seasonal workers. Thousands of skilled Nova Scotians moved inland, leaving behind a disproportionate number of the very young, the elderly, the illiterate, the unemployed, and others who contributed little to the province's income and often needed government help.

Owing to questionable management by absentee directors, outdated plant, and competition from oil and gas, the future of the miners and steelworkers of Cape Breton looked shaky at best, and hopeless at worst. Disasters in DOSCO collieries at Springhill in 1956 and 1958 riveted the attention of television watchers around the world, killed 113 Bluenose miners, and closed down the mines.

As the fifties ended, Nova Scotia's political leaders had come to believe that the answer to economic backwardness lay in state planning and that the success of state planning lay in federal aid. Moreover, the federal government now recognised that its national policy must include a commitment to regional equality. Both Ottawa and Halifax believed in the interventionist state.

Liberal Premier Angus L. Macdonald, the most popular and eloquent Bluenose politician since Joseph Howe, died on April 13, 1954. In 1956, the shy, bony, decent Robert Stanfield led the Tories to victory in the closest election in Nova Scotia history. "We felt we had to run very hard just to stand still," he later told journalist Geoffrey Stevens. "In agriculture we had a system of small farms, which people were constantly leaving ... The so-called inshore fisherman was pretty well disappearing ... The forest industry had to be reorganized substantially. The coal-mining industry was failing rapidly."

To promote the growth of a more diversified economy with secondary industries, the Stanfield government founded Industrial Estates Limited, a provincial Crown corporation with total government financing. "IEL" would become the most familiar acronym in Nova Scotia, the tag for an outfit the national business press hailed as Canada's most imaginative effort to revitalize a provincial economy. The glamour of IEL, as its agents circled the world to lure investment to Nova Scotia, helped propel Stanfield to the national leadership of the Progressive Conservative party. He later earned high respect for his integrity as the Leader of the Opposition in the House of Commons.

During the 1960s, IEL spent $123,004,328 to help dozens of industries establish themselves or expand their plants on Nova Scotian soil. In direct employment, IEL money in this period helped create more than 5,000 jobs, but what most Nova Scotians would remember was its two spectacular flops. The collapse of Clairtone Sound Corporation Ltd., which aimed to pioneer the manufacturing of colour television sets in Stellarton, left the province owing close to $25 million. A total of roughly $250 million in public monies, $135 million of it from the province, would eventually vanish in the engineering and marketing fiasco of the heavy-water plant at Glace Bay, Deuterium of Canada, Ltd.

The sun shone briefly on the Nova Scotia economy in the mid-1960s; by 1966 average incomes had risen 40 per cent over their 1956 level. In 1967, however, costs, unemployment, and government deficits were all rising ominously. The British-controlled Hawker Siddeley Canada abandoned the

Cape Breton coal industry, and, with largely federal funding of nearly $100 million, the Cape Breton Development Corporation took over the mines. "This is the first time the government has ever nationalized an industry," said Mines and Energy Minister Jean-Luc Pepin. On October 13, 1967—known thereafter as Black Friday in Cape Breton—DOSCO made a brutal announcement: it would shut down the Sydney steel mill for good. By 1968, a provincial Crown corporation, the Sydney Steel Corporation (Sysco), owned and operated the steel works. Sysco would be a huge drain on provincial revenue for decades to come.

Chamber's cartoon of Stanfield. He became national leader of the Conservative party in 1967.

A big success story came at the end of the sixties. Announced with great fanfare, it was the establishment of two Michelin tire plants, one at Granton and the other at Bridgewater. Of the $150 million in projected costs, $100 million would come from government sources. The government of Nova Scotia did everything it could to please Michelin, including drafting controversial labour legislation to make it difficult for unions to enlist members. Michelin did not like unions. A third plant, at Waterville, opened in 1979, and Michelin now employs more than 5,000 Nova Scotian workers. Some still question the price the province paid for those jobs.

The late 1950s and early 1960s had seen dramatic changes on the national political scene. In 1958, with John Diefenbaker as the Tory prime minister, the Liberals chose Lester Pearson as their leader, and in the elections of 1963 and 1965, he led them to power in minority governments. In 1961, the relatively leftist Cooperative Commonwealth Party (CCF) became the New Democratic Party (NDP). (The only CCF member of Parliament east of Ontario, Clarie Gillis, who represented the mining towns of Cape Breton, had sat in the Commons from 1940 to 1957.) In 1964, after furious debate in parliament and the media, a new flag, with a red maple leaf against a white background, replaced the Union Jack as Canada's official flag. A strong defender of regional development, Prime Minister Pearson began to call for national unity. And on July 1, 1967, our national medical plan came into being.

As premier of Nova Scotia 1956–1967, Robert L. Stanfield, revived the Conservatives' popularity among Nova Scotians.

This was Centennial year, the proudest and most luminous year for Canada since its Confederation in 1867. All over Nova Scotia—and indeed all across the nation—Canadians celebrated Confederation by building theatres, concert halls, schools, and community centres. Families invented their own centennial projects, painting houses, planting gardens, making the countryside blossom as never before. At the Nova Scotia pavilion at Expo 67, the world's fair in Montreal, David Stevens, one of the province's supreme builders of wooden boats, constructed the schooner Atlantica—just to show the world exactly how it was done. Expo 67 was not only the culmination of a century of national history, but an international triumph, and for Canadians the source of a deep sense of achievement.

But 1967 was also the year that Charles de Gaulle of France made his inflammatory cry to hundreds of thousands of Montrealers: "Vivre le Quebec libre!" Though Quebec had always harboured separatists, many Canadians would look back on the end of that triumphant year as the beginning of the relentless surge towards Quebec's independence that still threatens to unravel the very Confederation that 1967 celebrated.

Fearing John Diefenbaker had become an embarrassment to them, the Tories dumped him in 1967, and chose Nova Scotia's Robert Stanfield as their national leader. Led by Pierre Trudeau, the Liberals won the 1968 election. By 1970, separatist fanatics had bombed the Montreal stock exchange; kidnapped the British trade commissioner in Montreal, James Cross; and murdered Pierre Laporte, a cabinet minister in the Quebec government. Trudeau had invoked the War Measures Act. Nova Scotia, like every province, began to worry about its future in a troubled Canada. Campaigning for independence, the Parti Quebecois easily won the Quebec election of 1976, arousing more anxiety in Nova Scotia, particularly since Ottawa sometimes seemed to view the Ontario border as the beginning of Canada.

By 1971 the per-capita personal income in Nova Scotia stood at only $2,261, compared to $4,015 in Ontario. Nonetheless, optimism flourished for a while. The Trudeau government had founded the Department of Regional Economic Expansion in 1969, and its purpose was to invest federal money in the reduction of regional disparities.

When Nova Scotia entered the 1970s with a new Liberal government under Premier Gerald A. Regan, it was reaping more benefits from federal funds than ever before. With transfer payments and money from other federal programs, the province had expanded its health care, education, and welfare serviccs. Living standards, in the 1970s, were higher than they had ever been. The discovery of offshore oil and gas excited the whole province. Tourism was

an important growth industry, and the decade saw Nova Scotians take a fresh and rising interest in protecting the environment.

Some things, however, did not change. As the seventies rolled to a close, and the Tories, under Premier John Buchanan, took power, unemployment was high, skilled Nova Scotians were still leaving the province, and personal incomes remained far below the national average. "None of the great hopes of the 1970s had been fully realized," said John Reid in "The Atlantic Provinces in Confederation," and "whatever remaining faith Atlantic Canadians had, in 1970, that economic disparities could be easily eliminated through government action was now gone."[3]

In 1963 Volvo established in Halifax the first European auto assembly plant in postwar North America.

The Michelin Tire Plant at Granton is one of three tire manufacturing facilities in the province.

By the beginning of the twentieth century, some 45,000 Acadians were in Nova Scotia, about 10 per cent of the population, still living in the old rural, isolated, and traditional fashion. The period of the Second World War brought change. By the 1950s it was easy to adopt English ways in the new world of radio, television, and paved roads. Acadian educators now fought for the restoration of French schools as their best protection against assimilation.

In 1969 Trudeau proclaimed the Official Languages Act, and New Brunswick became officially bilingual. The rise of Quebec nationalism also strengthened Acadian aspirations, and in 1981 the Nova Scotia legislature passed Bill 65 to amend the Education Act. This long-awaited amendment gave "legal status to Acadian schools, set guidelines for the ratio of instruction in French and English schools, and ensured the development of a cur-

riculum that would include the history and heritage of the Acadians."[4]

The ethnic origin of almost 80 per cent of the people of Nova Scotia lay in Great Britain and Ireland, and the mother tongue of more than 93 per cent was English. Those of Acadian descent numbered nearly 40,000. Most still lived on the French Shore, the most westerly part of the province, and in pockets of Cape Breton Island. On the whole, they claimed French as their mother tongue, but only about 22,000 still used it in their daily lives. While some worried about the death of their culture, Father Anselme Chiasson of Chéticamp was less pessimistic. More than two centuries after the great expulsion in the 1700s, he wrote that the Acadian people were "a tree pulled up by its roots, fragmented by the hurricane ... Is this the end? Is the tree going to die? We know it is not. All the fragments have taken root and today are in a magnificent state of bloom."[5]

The aboriginal population, almost entirely Mi'kmaq, had made an impressive recovery by the mid-1990s. It stood at nearly 22,000, roughly 10,000 of whom were registered with the federal government as status Indians. Six thousand lived on reserves. Mi'kmaq no longer exhibited the docility of a defeated people. They had recovered their pride and become assertive. White society found them increasingly difficult to ignore or abuse. In 1968, for instance, at the Eskasoni reserve on Cape Breton Island, their public demonstrations while demanding better housing and medical and sanitation services launched an era of confrontation in relations between government and the Nova Scotia Mi'kmaq. As the century wore on, high unemployment, low incomes, and even poverty still afflicted some native communities, but, in the opinion of historian John Reid, Nova Scotia Mi'kmaq nevertheless "revealed the achievements that were possible even for peoples whose numbers were small, when efforts for self determination were strongly pursued."[6]

The Mi'kmaq are focusing on education to solve problems among their young. The high drop-out rate for native students in the public school system led some bands to conclude there's a better way to educate their children. At Eskasoni, Chapel Island, Whycogamagh, Wagmatook, and Pictou Landing, bands have their own schools and programs of native studies. Children from the Milbrook band go to schools in nearby Truro, but also attend classes on the reserve. The reserve schools add a Mi'kmaq perspective to the content of courses, but they have their own teaching methods as well. Spelling bees and other competitive activities remain a big part of schooling for white children, but they're not part of traditional Mi'kmaq culture.

Blacks, too, endured steeper rates of joblessness, lower incomes than most whites, a lack of educational opportunities, and overt racial discrimination. Still, their lives had improved since World War II. The province in 1954 dropped legislation that sanctioned separate schools for Blacks; in 1955 outlawed discrimination based on colour (as well as race or national origin) in employment and union membership; and in 1967 established the Nova Scotia Human Rights Commission (NSHRC).

In 1964 that the city of Halifax demolished Africville, which sat in the North End on the shore of Bedford Basin. Dating back to the early 1800s, it was the oldest, urban, Black community in Canada. Its 400-odd people had their own church, school, and post office, but despite paying taxes to the city, no running water and no electric power. Bitter debate swirled around their repeated demands for a water system and electricity, but in the end, the city promised them new houses elsewhere, declared everyone would be happy, and sent in the bulldozers. No one—except the Blacks—understood the folly of destroying a cohesive and beloved community. The construction of a container port at what was once Africville long angered the people who had lived there.

By the late 1960s Nova Scotia Blacks were openly denouncing racial prejudice and demanding social justice and, after the birth of the Black United Front (BUF), became more confrontational. The creation of BUF, and the rising number of complaints Blacks took to the NSHRC, "represented a

Africville in North End Halifax was completely demolished in 1964, despite the strong opposition of its residents.

major effort to seize the initiative in combatting the problems faced by Nova Scotia's approximately 20,000 Black people."[7]

Among the modern Nova Scotian Blacks who've earned recognition for their contributions not only to their own people but to the province as a whole are: journalist and black activist Carrie Best; Pearleen Oliver, a tireless worker for the Black community; her husband, Rev. William Oliver, Baptist pastor and adult educator; Daureen Lewis, the first woman mayor of Annapolis Royal; filmmaker Sylvia Hamilton; Burnham "Rocky" Jones, controversial youth leader and now a legal aid lawyer; Wayne Adams, a cabinet minister in the Nova Scotia government; George Boyd, a former CBC broadcaster, now a playwright; and George Elliot Clarke, poet, newspaper columnist, and lecturer at Duke University.

A portrait of Carrie Best, human rights crusader, poet, journalist, and broadcaster from her autobiography, "That Lonesome Road." Her many awards include an Honorary Doctor of Laws Degree from St. Francis Xavier University and the Order of Canada.

The 1980s opened with a severe recession, and the prospect of fundamental changes in Ottawa's treatment of the poorer provinces. To make matters worse, Nova Scotia soon faced double-digit inflation, the highest interest rates ever, and the apparent collapse of the anticipated development of offshore oil and gas. When the Conservatives, with Brian Mulroney as their leader, won a landslide victory in the federal election of 1984, the country heard increasing talk of federal decentralization and the government's abandonment of national responsibility for social services.

"Never have Canadians found in so short a time such a bewildering array of initiatives of fundamental importance," historian E. R. Forbes said in "The Atlantic Provinces in Confederation."[8] East-coast Canada had gained the most from the growth of federal programs, and now felt it had the most to lose from their dismemberment. Changes in transportation policy were at least as troubling. As unprofitable railways closed, more and more freight moved by truck. As highways deteriorated, the provinces endured a transfer of transportation responsibilities to their own shoulders, without any accompanying transfer of federal funding.

After long negotiation, Canada and the United States agreed on a free trade treaty in 1987, but the Canadian Senate refused to sanction it, forcing the Tory government to seek public approval in an election. Led by Prime Minister Mulroney, the Conservatives won the election—but not with a lot of votes from the Atlantic Provinces. This may have weakened their political ability to combat the draconian budget cuts the government planned for the region. Facing a deficit crisis, the government announced the cancellation of railway subsidies for the shipment of flour and grain from Halifax and Saint John, a 50 per cent reduction in railway passenger subsidies, and the shrinking or elimination of military bases.

"In the past," Forbes states, "the Maritime provinces had often been successful in influencing national policies to their advantage ... The one factor common to virtually all the region's past gains was the province's ability to co-operate in their pursuit. The divisions among the four provinces have seldom been more pronounced that they were in the 1980s."[9]

Divided though they were, they all faced a calamitous decline in fish stocks. The federal fisheries department finally admitting it had been recklessly optimistic about cod and haddock quantities, took action. A ban on fishing endangered stocks closed fish plants up and down the coasts of Nova Scotia. No one knows if the fish will return in abundance, or if the growing tourist trade will replace the cod and haddock industries of the past.

As the end of the millennium drew near, federal funding for Nova Scotia was drying up. Some claimed Nova Scotia would have been better off without it, and that Bluenose business conditions had actually improved since its shrinkage, but many still saw it as having been the underpinning of the province's whole economy. Facing a monumental crisis of debt, the federal government was considering the "devolution" of many of its responsibilities to the provinces, and thereby weakening its enforcement of national standards and promotion of national unity. Moreover, the provincial government, having run up enormous deficits, found itself with little choice but to impose painful cutbacks in spending, and contemplate reductions in social services.

To make matters worse, the prospect of Quebec's separation from Canada became more serious. The words Joseph Howe had uttered in 1866 now seemed alarmingly appropriate: "Two-fifths of the [Canadian] population are French and three-fifths are English. They are therefore perplexed with an internal antagonism which was fatal to the unity of Belgium and Holland, and which, unless the fusion of races becomes rapid and complete, must ever be a source of weakness ... They are at the mercy of a powerful neighbour whose population already outnumbers them by more than eight to one ... A more unpromising nucleus of a new nation can hardly be found on the face of the earth."

In the mid-1990s, the future of Nova Scotia and its neighbouring provinces seemed so uncertain that their leaders once again considered the dream of 1864: Maritime Union. Some Bluenosers contemplated the unpalatable possibility that, if Canada fell apart, the Maritimes might have to join the nation whose birth arose from the American Revolution that Nova Scotia had rejected more than two centuries ago.

Those who first saw Halifax during the Second World War would scarcely recognise it now. Province House and Government House remain two of the most beautiful public buildings in Canada, but a new city, with a population of nearly 300,000, has swallowed the shabby little wartime port. Halifax now boasts gleaming office towers, bookstores, concert halls, theatres, fine hotels and restaurants, and several universities.

It has become multicultural, too. In 1940 Haligonians spoke English, and a little French, but on the streets of the city today you hear German, Greek, Italian, Swahili, Arabic, Oriental languages, and a dozen others. Like other cities, Halifax has its homeless, unemployed, and lineups at food banks, but it has nevertheless become a vibrant and fascinating blend of the old and the new.

Whatever the future holds for Nova Scotia, it remains a beautiful and

An aerial view of downtown Halifax and the harbour puts the centrality of Citadel Hill in perspective.

friendly corner of the world. In June 1995, while Halifax was host to the twenty-first G-7 economic summit, thousands of foreign bureaucrats and journalists, as well as millions of television viewers, got a taste of the province's unusual charm. More often than not, the leaders of Canada, France, Germany, Italy, Japan, the United Kingdom, and the United States—called the G-7—come together in Tokyo, London, Paris, or some other gigantic city. This time, however, they gathered in little old Halifax, and the presidents of the European Commission and Russia joined them.

Behind closed doors, the leaders talked about economic growth, international trade, the global information highway, controlling the spread of nuclear weapons, protecting the environment; when they stepped outside they met the cheering folks of Nova Scotia.

Halifax, knowing it could not compete with the big host of cities of the past, offered no lavish banquets or fleets of limousines, and rationed pomp and circumstance. Some leaders walked to and from their hotels. Haligonians, and other Nova Scotians who had come to town to sniff history in the making, got close enough to the presidents of great nations to shake their hands. Nova Scotians, Greg McCune wrote for the Reuters news agency, "were genuinely excited by the summit, and the streets filled with singing, dancing people every evening."

Among the happy crowds, the chancellor of Germany and the presidents of France, the United States, and Russia appeared as relaxed as if they were enjoying a house party with friends, and relatives. On the night the conference ended, tens of thousands of Nova Scotians gathered on Citadel Hill for a concert that both honoured and said farewell to all the visitors from away. The performers included the Rankin Family, the Barra MacNeils, and other groups whose musical heritage was Scottish, Irish, or Acadian. According to Ray Conlogue in "The Globe and Mail," "The result was a massive concert that had the energy of a rock show but the sentiment of a family gathering." The music evoked "a world that made sense, the kind of world that most people wish we lived in."

"Even a few cynical journalists seemed, for a brief moment, to be touched by the hospitality," wrote Greg McCune of Reuters. Perhaps he had read Conlogue. For "The Globe and Mail's" man ended his review with these words, "The G-7 summit may be a cynical event, but hospitality, at least in [Nova Scotia], is a sacred thing. This concert was as much for the hosts as the guests—a testimony that they had honoured their own traditions."

In a time of extraordinary change in technology, political thought, the economy and relations among governments in Canada, Nova Scotia must identify and pursue its own course. To quote E. R. Forbes once more, "Here a starting point might be the reflection on past experiences, on those policies and strategies that worked and those that did not."[10] For the most notable achievements in this part of Canada have long rested primarily on the persistence and ingenuity of the people of Nova Scotia and its neighbouring provinces.

The G-7 economic summit in June 1995 brought world leaders to Halifax.

NOTES

CHAPTER 1

1. George MacDonald, "Debert: A Paleo-Indian Site in Central Nova Scotia," Anthology Papers no. 16 (Ottawa: National Museum of Man, 1968).

2. James A. Tuck, "Maritimes Provinces Prehistory" (Ottawa: Archaeology Survey of Canada, 1984).

CHAPTER 2

1. R. A. Skelton, "John Cabot," "Dictionary of Canadian Biography" (Toronto: University of Toronto Press, 1966–) 1:146–58.

2. Leslie Hannon, "The Discoverers" (Toronto: McClelland and Stewart, 1971).

3. Ibid.

4. Ibid.

5. Thomas B. Costain, "The White and the Gold: The French Regime in Canada" (New York: Doubleday & Co., 1954).

6. Hannon, "The Discoverers."

7. Skelton, "John Cabot," "DCB."

CHAPTER 3

1. Costain, "The White and the Gold."

2. Hannon, "The Discoverers."

3. Alfred G. Bailey, "The Conflict of European and Eastern Algonkian Cultures, 1504–1700" (Toronto: University of Toronto Press, 1969).

Chapter 4

1. Hannon, "The Discoverers."

CHAPTER 5

1. Beamish Murdoch, "A History of Nova-Scotia or Acadie," Volumes I, II, III (Halifax: James Barnes, 1865).

2. "John Quinpool," "First Things in Acadia" (Halifax: First Things Publishers, 1936).

CHAPTER 6

1. André Vachon, "Jessé Fléché," "Dictionary of Canadian Biography" (Toronto: University of Toronto Press, 1966–) 1:307.

2. Huia Ryder, "Jean de Biencourt de Poutrincourt," "Dictionary of Canadian Biography" (Toronto: University of Toronto Press, 1966–) 1:96–99.

3. George MacBeath, "Claude Saint-Étienne de La Tour," "Dictionary of Canadian Biography" (Toronto: University of Toronto Press, 1966–) 1:596–98.

CHAPTER 7

1. George MacBeath, "Isaac de Razilly," "Dictionary of Canadian Biography" (Toronto: University of Toronto Press, 1966–) 1:567.

2. M. A. MacDonald, "Fortune & La Tour: The Civil War in Acadia" (Toronto: Methuen, 1983.)

CHAPTER 8

1. Jean Daigle (ed.), "The Acadians of the Maritimes: Thematic Studies" (Moncton: Centre of Acadian Studies, 1982).

CHAPTER 9

1. Daigle, "The Acadians."

2. John Clarence Webster, "Acadia at the End of the 17th Century" (Saint John, N.B.: New Brunswick Museum, 1934, reprinted, 1979).

3. Alfred G. Bailey, "The Conflict of European and Eastern Algonkian Cultures, 1504–1700" (Toronto: University of Toronto Press, 1969).

4. Ibid.

5. Bruce G. Trigger, "The Indians and the Heroic Age of New France" (Ottawa: Canadian Historical Association Booklets, No. 30, 1977.)

6. Daigle, "The Acadians."

CHAPTER 10

1. René Baudry, "Daniel d'Auger de Subercase," Dictionary of Canadian Biography (Toronto: University of Toronto Press, 1966–) 2:35–39.

2. "Encyclopedia Britannica" (11th edition, 1910)

3. Donald Creighton, "Dominion of the North: A History of Canada" (Toronto: Macmillan of Canada, 1957).

4. "Chronicle of Canada" 1990.

CHAPTER 11

1. Creighton, "Dominion of the North."

2. Maxwell Sutherland, "Richard Philipps," "Dictionary of Canadian Biography" (Toronto: University of Toronto Press, 1966–) 3:515–18.

3. Beamish Murdoch, "History of Nova-Scotia," Vol. II.

4. T. A. Crowley and Bernard Pothier, "François Du Pont Duvivier," "Dictionary of Canadian Biography" (Toronto: University of Toronto Press, 1966–) 4:251–55.

5. G. C. Campbell, "The History of Nova Scotia" (Toronto: The Ryerson Press, 1948).

6. Creighton, "Dominion of the North."

7. Christopher Moore, "Louisbourg Portraits: Life in an Eighteenth-Century Garrison Town" (Toronto: Macmillan of Canada, 1982).

8. Ibid.

9. Raddall, Thomas H., "Halifax: Warden of the North" (Toronto: McClelland and Stewart, 1971).

10. Creighton, "Dominion of the North."

CHAPTER 12

1. Raddall, "Warden of the North."

2. Campbell, "History of Nova Scotia."

3. Raddall, "Warden of the North."

4. Ibid.

5. Dominick, Graham, "Charles Lawrence," "Dictionary of Canadian Biography" (Toronto: University of Toronto Press, 1966–) 3:361–66.

CHAPTER 13

1. C. P. Stacey, "The British Forces in North America during the Seven Years' War," "Dictionary of Canadian Biography" (Toronto: University of Toronto Press, 1966–) 3:xxiv–xxx.

2. Raddall, "Warden of the North."

3. Creighton, "Dominion of the North."

4. Barry M. Moody, "John Winslow," "Dictionary of Canadian Biography" (Toronto: University of Toronto Press, 1966–) 4:774–75.

5. Father Anselme Chiasson, "Cheticamp: History and Acadian Traditions" (St. John's, Nfld.: Breakwater, 1986).

6. John Fortier, "Augustin de Boschenry de Drucour," "Dictionary of Canadian Biography" (Toronto: University of Toronto Press, 1966–) 3:71–74.

CHAPTER 14

1. Chiasson, "Cheticamp."

2. Henri Blanchard, "Île du Prince Édouard: History of the Acadians of Prince Edward Island" (Moncton: 1927).

3. Dominick, "Charles Lawrence," "DCB."

4. John Bartlet Brebner, "The Neutral Yankees of Nova Scotia" (Toronto: Carleton Library No. 45, McClelland and Stewart, 1969).

5. Campbell, "History of Nova Scotia."

6. Brebner, Neutral Yankees .

7. Rev. George Patterson, "A History of the County of Pictou, Nova Scotia" (Montreal: Dawson Brothers, 1877).

8. Charles Bruce, "Channel Shore" (Toronto: Macmillan, 1951).

CHAPTER 15

1. "Columbia Encyclopedia." 5th edition, 1993.

2. Creighton, "Dominion of the North."

3. Ibid.

4. Brebner, "Neutral Yankees."

5. Raddall, "Warden of the North."

CHAPTER 16

1. Creighton, "Dominion of the North."

2. W. S. MacNutt, "The Loyalists: A Sympathetic View." "Acadiensis," Autumn 1976.

3. Brian C. Cuthbertson, "The Loyalist Governor: Biography of Sir John Wentworth" (Halifax: Petheric, 1983).

4. Neil MacKinnon, "This Unfriendly Soil: The Loyalist Experience in Nova Scotia 1783–1791" (Kingston, Montreal: McGill-Queen's University Press, 1986).

CHAPTER 17

1. Daniel N. Paul, "We Were Not the Savages" (Halifax: Nimbus, 1993).

2. Leslie F. S. Upton, "Micmacs and Colonists: Indian-White Relations in the Maritimes, 1713–1867" (Vancouver: University of British Columbia Press, 1979).

3. Paul, "We Were Not the Savages."

4. Upton, "Micmacs and Colonists."

5. Walter Stewart, "True Blue: The Loyalist Legend" (Toronto: Collins, 1985).

6. MacKinnon, "Unfriendly Soil."

7. Dorothy Duncan, "Bluenose: A Portrait of Nova Scotia" (New York: Harper & Brothers, 1942).

8. Cuthbertson, "Loyalist Governor." ??

CHAPTER 18

1. Cuthbertson, "Loyalist Governor."

2. Ibid.

3. Ibid.

4. Ibid.

5. Mollie Gillen, "Thérèse-Bernardine Mongenet," "Dictionary of Canadian Biography" (Toronto: University of Toronto Press, 1966–) 6:516–18.

6. Cuthbertson, "Loyalist Governor."

7. Ibid.

8 Ibid.

9. Judith Fingard, "John Wentworth," "Dictionary of Canadian Biography" (Toronto: University of Toronto Press, 1966–) 5:848–52.

CHAPTER 19

1. Brian C. Cuthbertson, "The Old Attorney General: A Biography of Richard John Uniacke" (Halifax: Nimbus, 1980).

2. John Leefe, "The Atlantic Privateers (1749–1815)" (Halifax: Petheric, 1978).

3. Ibid.

4. Raddall, "Warden of the North."

5. H. F. Pullen, "The Shannon and the Chesapeake" (Toronto: McClelland and Stewart, 1970).

6. Raddall. "Warden of the North."

7. C. H. J. Snider, "Under the Red Jack" (Toronto: Musson Book Company, 1928).

8. Ibid.

9. Pullen, "Under the Red Jack."

10. Raddall, "Warden of the North."

11. Robert Collins, "Canada 1812–1871: The Formative Years," edited by James Knight, (Toronto: Imperial Oil Review, July 1967).

12. Ibid.

CHAPTER 20

1. J. Murray Beck, "Joseph Howe," "Dictionary of Canadian Biography" (Toronto: University of Toronto Press, 1966–) 10:362–370.

2. Longley, J. W., "The Makers of Canada: Joseph Howe" (Toronto: Morang & Co., 1904).

3. Beck, "Joseph Howe," "DCB."

4. James Morris, "Heaven's Command: An Imperial Progress" (London: The Folio Society, 1992).

CHAPTER 21

1. Campbell, "History of Nova Scotia."

2. Marjory Whitelaw, "Thomas McCulloch: His Life and Times." (Halifax: Nova Scotia Museum, 1985).

3. Ibid.

4. Morris, "Heaven's Command."

5. D. A. Muise in "The Atlantic Provinces in Confederation," edited by Ernest R. Forbes and D. A. Muise (Toronto: University of Toronto Press, 1993).

CHAPTER 22

1. James Marsh, s.v. "Royal William," "The Canadian Encyclopedia," 1st ed.

2. Duncan, "Bluenose."

3. Rev. George M. Grant, "Ocean to Ocean: Sandford Fleming's Expedition Through Canada in 1872" (Toronto: James Campbell & Son, 1873).

4. Raddall, "Warden of the North."

5. Ibid.

CHAPTER 23

1. Creighton, "Dominion of the North."

2. Arthur R. M. Lower, "Colony to Nation: A History of Canada" (Toronto: Longmans, Green, 1957).

3. Creighton, "Dominion of the North."

4. P. B. Waite, "The Life and Times of Confederation" (Toronto: University of Toronto Press, 1962).

CHAPTER 24

1. Raddall, "Warden of the North."

2. George Bryce, "A Short History of the Canadian People" (Toronto: William Briggs, 1914).

3. Muise, "The Atlantic Provinces."

4. Upton, "Micmacs and Colonists."

5. Mi'kmaq Fisheries, Netukulimk: Towards a Better Understanding (Mi'kmaq Grand Council, the Union of Nova Scotia Indians, the Native Council of Nova Scotia, Department of Fisheries and Oceans of Government of Canada, 1993).

6. Brian C. Cuthbertson, "Johnny Bluenose at the Polls, Epic Nova Scotian Battles. 1758–1848" (Halifax: Formac, 1995).

7. Sally Ross and Alphonse Deveau, "The Acadians of Nova Scotia, Past and Present" (Halifax: Nimbus, 1992).

8. Judith Fingard in "The Atlantic Provinces in Confederation," edited by Ernest R. Forbes and D. A. Muise (Toronto: University of Toronto Press, 1993).

9. Ibid.

10. Ibid.

11. Bridglal Pachai, Blacks (Halifax: Nimbus Publishing, 1997).

CHAPTER 25

1. James M. Cameron, "Industrial History of the New Glasgow District" (New Glasgow, N.S.: Hector Publishing, 1960).

2. Raddall, "Warden of the North."

3. M. Stuart Hunt, "Nova Scotia's Part in The Great War" (Halifax: Nova Scotia

Veteran Publishing, 1920).

4. Ibid.

CHAPTER 26

1. Cameron, "Industrial History of the New Glasgow District."

2. William Y. Smith, "How Ontario Achieved Its Imperial Position." "Acadiensis," Autumn 1976.

3. Alexander P. Paterson, "Confederation's True Story." Six-part series reprinted in Halifax "Chronicle-Herald," July 23, 25, 26, 27, 28, 29, 1977.

4. "The Canadian Encyclopedia." 1985

5. David Frank in "The Atlantic Provinces in Confederation," edited by Ernest R. Forbes, and D. A. Muise (Toronto: University of Toronto Press, 1993).

CHAPTER 27

1. Patterson, "History of the County of Pictou."

2. Ted. R. Hennigar, "The Rum Running Years" (Windsor, N.S.: Lancelot Press, 1984).

3. E. R. Forbes, "Prohibition and the Social Gospel in Nova Scotia," "Acadiensis," Autumn 1971.

CHAPTER 28

1. Jim Lotz, "The Historical and Social Setting of the Antigonish Movement," "The Nova Scotia Historical Quarterly," June 1975.

2. Ibid.

3. E. R. Forbes, "Challenging the Regional Stereotype: Essays on the 20th Century Maritimes" (Fredericton: Acadiensis Press, 1989).

4. Pierre Berton, "The Great Depression: 1929–1939" (Toronto: McClelland & Stewart, 1990).

5. Michiel Horn, "The Dirty Thirties: Canadians in The Great Depression" (Toronto: Copp Clark, 1972).

6. Barry Broadfoot, Ten Lost Years: 1929–39 (Toronto: Doubleday Canada Ltd., 1973).

CHAPTER 29

1. Berton, "Great Depression."

2. Carman Miller in "The Atlantic Provinces in Confederation."

3. Pamela Newton, "Sydney 1785–1985" (Sydney, N.S.: City Printers, Leon Doublet, 1985).

4. Desmond Morton, "A Military History of Canada" (Edmonton: Hurtig, 1985).

5. Miller, "The Atlantic Provinces."

6. "An East Coast Port ... Halifax at War 1939–1945," edited by Graham Metson

(Toronto: McGraw-Hill Ryerson, 1981).

7. William H. Pugsley, "Saints, Devils and Ordinary Seamen. Life on the Royal Canadian Navy's Lower Deck" (Toronto: Collins, 1946).

8. "An East Coast Port … Halifax at War 1939–45," op. cit.

9. Hal Brown in "An East Coast Port … Halifax at War 1939–45," op. cit.

CHAPTER 30

1. Forbes in "The Atlantic Provinces in Confederation."

2. Margaret Cannon in "The Atlantic Provinces in Confederation."

3. John Reid in "The Atlantic Provinces in Confederation."

4. Ross and Deveau, "Acadians."

5. Chiasson, "Cheticamp."

6. Reid, "The Atlantic Provinces in Confederation."

7. Della Stanley in "The Atlantic Provinces in Confederation."

8. Forbes, "The Atlantic Provinces in Confederation."

9. Ibid.

10. Ibid.

BIBLIOGRAPHY

BOOKS

Allen, Ralph. "Ordeal By Fire: Canada 1910-1945." Toronto: Doubleday Canada, 1961.

Bailey, Alfred G. "The Conflict of European and Eastern Algonkian Cultures, 1504-1700." Toronto: University of Toronto Press, 1969.

Beck, J. Murray. "The Government of Nova Scotia." Toronto: University of Toronto Press, 1957.

_____. (ed.). "Joseph Howe: Voice of Nova Scotia." Toronto: Carleton Library No. 20, McClelland and Stewart, 1964.

_____. "Joseph Howe, Volume II, The Briton Becomes Canadian 1848-1873." Kingston, Montreal: McGill-Queen's University Press, 1983.

Bell, John (ed.). "Halifax: A Literary Portrait." Lawrencetown Beach, N.S.: Pottersfield Press, 1990.

Bercuson, David J., and Grantstein, J. L. "The Collins Dictionary of Canadian History: 1867 to the Present." Toronto: Collins, 1988.

Berton, Pierre (ed.). "Historic Headlines." Toronto: The Canadian Illustrated Library, McClelland and Stewart, 1967.

_____. "The Great Depression: 1929-1939." Toronto: McClelland & Stewart, 1990.

Blakeley, Phyllis Ruth. "Nova Scotia: A Brief History." Toronto: J. M. Dent & Sons (Canada), 1955.

Blanchard, Henri. "Île du Prince Édouard: History of the Acadians of Prince Edward Island." Moncton: 1927.

Borrett, William Coates. "Historic Halifax in Tales Told under the Old Town Clock." Toronto: Ryerson, 1948.

_____. "Tales Retold under the Old Town Clock." Toronto: Ryerson, 1957.

Bourinot, Sir John G. "Builders of Nova Scotia." Toronto: Copp Clark, 1900.

Brebner, John Bartlet. "The Neutral Yankees of Nova Scotia." Toronto: Carleton Library No. 45, McClelland and Stewart, 1969.

Broadfoot, Barry. "Ten Lost Years: 1929-39." Toronto: Doubleday Canada Ltd., 1973.

Bruce, Charles. "Channel Shore." Toronto: Macmillan, 1951.

Bruce, Harry. "Lifeline: The Story of the Atlantic Ferries and Coastal Boats." Toronto: Macmillan of Canada, 1977.

_____. "R. A.: The Story of Roy Jodrey, Entrepreneur." Toronto: McClelland and Stewart, 1979.

_____. "The Man and the Empire: Frank Sobey". Toronto: Macmillan of Canada, 1985.

_____. "Down Home: Notes of a Maritime Son." Toronto: Key Porter, 1988.

Bryce, George. "A Short History of the Canadian People." Toronto: William Briggs, 1914.

Bumsted, J. M. (ed.). "Canadian History Before Confederation: Essays and Interpretations." Georgetown, Ont.: Irwin-Dorsey, 1979.

_____. "The Peoples of Canada: A Pre-Confederation History." Toronto: Oxford University Press, 1992.

Calder, J. William. "Booze & a Buck." Antigonish, N.S.: Formac, 1977.

Cameron, James M. "Industrial History of the New Glasgow District." New Glasgow, N.S.: Hector Publishing, 1960.

_____. "Pictou County's History." Pictou County Historical Society, 1972.

Campbell, D., and MacLean, R. A. "Beyond the Atlantic Roar: A Study of the Nova Scotia Scots." Toronto: The Carleton Library No. 78, McClelland and Stewart, 1974.

Campbell, G. C. "The History of Nova Scotia." Toronto: The Ryerson Press, 1948.

Campbell, Lyall. "Sable Island: Fatal and Fertile Crescent." Windsor, N.S.: Lancelot Press, 1974.

"The Canadians at War, 1939/45," Volume 1, Volume 2, and supplementary "The Tools of War." Montreal: Reader's Digest Association (Canada) Ltd., 1969.

Chiasson, Father Anselme. "Cheticamp: History and Acadian Traditions." St. John's, Nfld.: Breakwater, 1986.

Collins, Louis W. "In Halifax Town." Halifax: privately printed, 1975.

Condon, Ann Gorman. "The Envy of the American States: The Loyalist Dream for New Brunswick." Fredericton: New Ireland Press, 1984.

Costain, Thomas B. "The White and the Gold: The French Regime in Canada." New York: Doubleday & Co., 1954.

Creighton, Donald. "Dominion of the North: A History of Canada." Toronto: Macmillan of Canada, 1957.

Cuthbertson, Brian C. "The Old Attorney General: A Biography of Richard John Uniacke." Halifax: Nimbus, 1980.

_____. "The Loyalist Governor: Biography of Sir John Wentworth." Halifax: Petheric, 1983.

Daigle, Jean (ed.). "The Acadians of the Maritimes: Thematic Studies." Moncton: Centre of Acadian Studies, 1982.

Dennis, Clara. "Down in Nova Scotia." Toronto: Ryerson Press, 1934.

_____. "More About Nova Scotia." Toronto: Ryerson Press, 1937.

Doane, Frank A. "Nova Scotia Sketches." Truro, N.S.: Truro Printing and Publishing, 1949.

Duncan, Dorothy. "Bluenose: A Portrait of Nova Scotia." New York: Harper & Brothers, 1942.

Dunn, Charles W. "Highland Settler: A Portrait of the Scottish Gael in Nova

Scotia." Toronto: University of Toronto Press, 1953.

Eccles, W. J. "Frontenac: The Courtier Governor". Toronto: McClellland and Stewart, 1959.

Elliott, Shirley B. (ed.). "Nova Scotia Book of Days: A Calendar of the Province's History." Halifax: Nova Scotia Communications & Information Centre, 1979.

Fergusson, Bruce, and Pope, William. "Glimpses into Nova Scotia History." Windsor, N.S.: Lancelot Press, 1974.

Fingard, Judith. "Jack in Port: Sailortowns of eastern Canada." Toronto: University of Toronto Press, 1982.

Forbes, Ernest R. and Muise, D. A. (eds.). "The Atlantic Provinces in Confederation." Toronto: University of Toronto Press, 1993.

Forbes, Ernest. R. "The Maritime Rights Movement, 1919-1927." Montreal: McGill-Queen's University Press, 1979.

_____. "Challenging the Regional Stereotype: Essays on the 20th Century Maritimes." Fredericton: Acadiensis Press, 1989.

Gramling, Oliver. "AP: The Story of News." New York: Farrar and Rinehart, 1940.

Grant, Rev. George M. "Ocean to Ocean: Sandford Fleming's Expedition Through Canada in 1872." Toronto: James Campbell & Son, 1873.

Hamilton, William B. "The Nova Scotia Traveller." Toronto: Macmillan of Canada, 1981.

Hannon, Leslie. "The Discoverers." Toronto: McClelland and Stewart, 1971.

Hardy, W. G. "From Sea Unto Sea: The Road to Nationhood 1850-1910." New York: Doubleday & Company, 1960.

Hennigar, Ted. R. "The Rum Running Years." Windsor, N.S.: Lancelot Press, 1984.

Horn, Michiel. "The Dirty Thirties: Canadians in The Great Depression." Toronto: Copp Clark, 1972.

Hunt, M. Stuart. "Nova Scotia's Part in The Great War." Halifax: Nova Scotia Veteran Publishing, 1920.

Innis, Harold. "The Fur Trade in Canada." Toronto: University of Toronto Press, 1956.

Inwood, Ken (ed.). "Farm, Factory and Fortune: New Studies in the Economic History of the Maritime Provinces." Fredericton: Acadiensis Press, 1993.

Jenness, Diamond. "The Indians of Canada." Toronto: University of Toronto Press, National Museum of Man, 1932.

Longley, J. W. "The Makers of Canada: Joseph Howe." Toronto: Morang & Co., 1904.

Lotz, Pat and Jim. "Cape Breton Island." Vancouver: Douglas, David & Charles, 1974.

Lower, Arthur R. M. "Colony to Nation: A History of Canada." Toronto: Longmans, Green, 1957.

MacDonald, M. A. "Fortune & La Tour: The Civil War in Acadia." Toronto: Methuen, 1983.

_____. "Rebels and Royalists: The Lives and Material Culture of New Brunswick's

English-Speaking Settlers 1758-1783." Fredericton: New Ireland Press, 1990.

Macgillivray, Don, and Tennyson, Brian (eds.). "Cape Breton Historical Essays." Sydney, N.S.: University College of Cape Breton Press, 1985.

MacKinnon, Neil. "This Unfriendly Soil: The Loyalist Experience in Nova Scotia 1783–1791." Kingston, Montreal: McGill-Queen's University Press, 1986.

Martin, Chester. "Empire and Commonwealth." Toronto: Oxford University Press: 1929.

McGee, H. F. "The Native Peoples of Atlantic Canada. A History of Ethnic Interaction." Toronto: Carleton Library No. 72, McClelland and Stewart, 1974.

Merkel, Andrew. "Schooner Bluenose." Toronto: The Ryerson Press, 1948.

Metson, Graham (ed.). "An East Coast Port...Halifax at War 1939-1945." Toronto: McGraw-Hill Ryerson, 1981.

Moore, Christopher. "Louisbourg Portraits: Life in an Eighteenth-Century Garrison Town." Toronto: Macmillan of Canada, 1982.

Moorsom, Captain W. "Letters from Nova Scotia; comprising sketches of a young country." London: Henry Colburn and Richard Bentley, 1830.

Morris, James. "Heaven's Command: An Imperial Progress." London: The Folio Society, 1992.

Morton, Desmond. "A Military History of Canada." Edmonton: Hurtig, 1985.

Murdoch, Beamish. "A History of Nova-Scotia or Acadie," Volumes I, II, III. Halifax: James Barnes, 1865.

Parker, John P. "Sails of the Maritimes: The story of the three- and four-masted cargo schooners of Atlantic Canada 1859-1929." Halifax: The Maritime Museum of Canada, 1960.

Patterson, Rev. George. "A History of the County of Pictou, Nova Scotia." Montreal: Dawson Brothers, 1877.

Paul, Daniel N. "We Were Not the Savages." Halifax: Nimbus Publishing Ltd., 1993.

Pugsley, William H. "Saints, Devils and Ordinary Seamen. Life on the Royal Canadian Navy's Lower Deck." Toronto: Collins, 1946

Pullen, H. F. "The Shannon and the Chesapeake." Toronto: McClelland and Stewart, 1970.

"Quinpool, John." "First Things in Acadia." Halifax: First Things Publishers, 1936.

Raddall, Thomas H. "The Path of Destiny: Canada from the British Conquest to Home Rule 1763-1850." Toronto: Doubleday Canada, 1957.

_____. "Halifax: Warden of the North." Toronto: McClelland and Stewart, 1971.

Rawlyk, George A. (ed.). "Joseph Howe: Opportunist? Man of Vision? Frustrated Politician?" Toronto: Copp Clark, 1967.

Rose, Clifford. "Four Years With the Demon Rum, 1925-1929." Fredericton: Acadiensis Press, 1980.

Rutledge, Joseph Lister. "Century of Conflict: The Struggle Between the French and British in Colonial America." Toronto: Doubleday Canada, 1956.

Saunders, S. A. "The Economic History of the Maritime Provinces." Fredericton:

Acadiensis Press, 1984.

Schull, Joseph. "The Salt-Water Men: Canada's Deep-Sea Sailors." Toronto: Macmillan, 1957.

Seary, V. P. "The Romance of The Maritime Provinces." Toronto: W. G. Gage & Co., 1937.

Sherwood, Roland H. "Atlantic Harbours." Windsor, N.S.: Lancelot Press, 1972.

Snider, C. H. J. "Under The Red Jack." Toronto: Musson Book Company, 1928.

Spicer, Stanley T. "Masters of Sail." Halifax: Petheric Press, Nova Scotia Museum, 1968.

Stevens, Geoffrey. "Stanfield." Toronto: McClelland and Stewart, 1973.

Stewart, Walter. "True Blue: The Loyalist Legend." Toronto: Collins, 1985.

Waite, P. B. "The Life and Times of Confederation." Toronto: University of Toronto Press, 1962.

_____. "The Man from Halifax: Sir John Thomson, Prime Minister." Toronto: University of Toronto Press, 1985.

Upton, Leslie F. S. "Micmacs and Colonists: Indian-White Relations in the Maritimes, 1713–1867." Vancouver: University of British Columbia Press, 1979. 243 p.

Webster, John Clarence. "Acadia at the End of the 17th Century." Saint John, N.B.: New Brunswick Museum, 1934 (reprinted, 1979).

Whitehead, Ruth Holmes. "Elitekey: Micmac Material Culture from 1600 AD to the Present." Halifax: The Nova Scotia Museum, 1980.

Wright, Esther Clark. "The Loyalists of New Brunswick." Fredericton, 1955.

PAMPHLETS, BOOKLETS

Anon. Loyalist Souvenir: One Hundred and Fiftieth Anniversary of the Landing of the Loyalists in the Province of New Brunswick. New Brunswick Historical Society, 1933.

Anon. Nova Scotia Helps the Fighting Man. Halifax: Government of Nova Scotia, 1942.

Anon. The Fort of Beauséjour. Canadian Parks Service, 1993.

Archibald, Mary. Loyalists of Nova Scotia. Halifax: Petheric Press, 1982.

Barkhouse, Joyce. Abraham Gesner. Don Mills, Ont.: Fitzhenry & Whiteside, 1980.

Beck, J. Murray. Joseph Howe and Confederation: Myth and Fact. Transactions of the Royal Society of Canada, June, 1964.

_____. Joseph Howe, Anti-Confederate. The Canadian Historical Association Booklets., No. 17, 1965

Bumstead, J. M. Understanding the Loyalists. Sackville, N.B.: Centre for Canadian Studies, Mount Allison University, 1986.

Chittick, Hattie. Hantsport on Avon. Hantsport Women's Institute, 1968.

Condow, James E. The Deportation of the Acadians. Ottawa: Environment Canada, undated.

Finley, A. Gregg. The Loyalists. Saint John: New Brunswick Museum, undated.

Grant, John. Black Nova Scotians. Halifax: Nova Scotia Museum, Nova Scotia Department of Education, 1984.

Historic Nova Scotia. Halifax: Government of Nova Scotia, undated.

"Journal of Education." Supplement to report of Superintendent of Education for Nova Scotia, October, 1917.

Knight, James (ed.). "Canada 1812–1871: The Formative Years." Toronto: Imperial Oil Review, July, 1967.

Leefe, John. The Atlantic Privateers (1749–1815). Halifax: Petheric, 1978.

Mi'kmaq Fisheries Netukulimk: Towards a Better Understanding. Mi'kmaq Grand Council, the Union of Nova Scotia Indians, the Native Council of Nova Scotia, Department of Fisheries and Oceans of Government of Canada, 1993.

Newton, Pamela. Sydney 1785-1985. Sydney, N.S.: City Printers, Leon Doublet, 1985.

Perkins, Charlotte. The Romance of Old Annapolis Royal. Historical Association of Annapolis Royal, 1952.

Stephens, David E. Iron Roads: Railways of Nova Scotia. Windsor, N.S.: Lancelot Press, 1972.

Trigger, Bruce G. The Indians and the Heroic Age of New France. Ottawa: Canadian Historical Association Booklets, No. 30, 1977.

Whitehead, Ruth Holmes, and McGee, Harold. The Micmac: How Their Ancestors Lived Five Hundred Years Ago. Halifax: Nimbus Publishing Limited, 1983.

Whitelaw, Marjory. First Impressions. Halifax: Nova Scotia Museum, 1987

_____. Thomas McCulloch: His Life and Times. 1985.

REPORTS, PAPERS

Atlantic Canada Today. Halifax: Atlantic Provinces Economic Council, Formac Publishing, 1987.

MacDonald, George. Debert: A Paleo-Indian Site in Central Nova Scotia. Anthropology Papers, no. 16. Ottawa:. National Museum of Man, 1968.

Tuck, James A. Maritimes Provinces Prehistory. Ottawa: Archaeology Survey of Canada, 1984.

Whitehead, Ruth Holmes. Nova Scotia: The Protohistoric Period, 1500-1630. Halifax: Curatorial Report Number 75, Nova Scotia Museum, Nova Scotia Department of Education, 1993.

ARTICLES

Anon. "Petition of Coloured People at Preston." "Dalhousie Gazette," March 9, 1995.

Beck, J. Murray. "Joseph Howe: Opportunist or Empire-builder?" "The Canadian Historical Review," September 1960.

Bruce, Harry. "Here Lies Joseph Howe." Special edition, The 4th Estate, Halifax, June 1973.

_____. "Making a tourist buck from Joe Howe's bones." "Saturday Night," July 1973.

_____. "Raise a glass, if you please, to the Dalhousie Law School!" "Atlantic Insight," September 1983.

_____. "The news of the world flashed through Nova Scotia." "Atlantic Insight," July 1984.

Ells, Margaret. "Loyalist Attitudes." "Dalhousie Review," October 1935.

Forbes, E. R. "Prohibition and the Social Gospel in Nova Scotia." "Acadiensis," Autumn 1971.

_____. "The future receding into the past." "Telegraph Journal," Saint John, N.B., February 2, 1995.

_____. "Maritimes were left without resources." "Telegraph Journal," Saint John, N.B., February 3, 1995.

_____. "An uneasy place in Confederation." "Telegraph Journal," Saint John, N.B., February 6, 1995.

How, Douglas. "A Career Run Aground." "Legion," May 1980.

Inness, Lorna. "The Baronets of Nova Scotia: A living link with our province's history." Halifax "Chronicle-Herald," September 10, 1971.

Lotz, Jim. "The Historical and Social Setting of the Antigonish Movement." "The Nova Scotia Historical Quarterly". June 1975.

MacMechan, Archibald. "The Great Ship." "Dalhousie Review", Summer 1928.

MacNutt, W. S. "The Loyalists: A Sympathetic View." "Acadiensis," Autumn 1976.

Miller, Carman. "The Atlantic Provinces and the Problem of 'Regionalism.' " "Acadiensis," Spring 1982.

Paterson, Alexander P. "Confederation's True Story." Six-part series reprinted in Halifax "Chronicle-Herald," July 23, 25, 26, 27, 28, 29, 1977.

Regan, John W. "The Inception of the Associated Press." Nova Scotia Historical Society Collections, Vol. 18-20, 1914-1921.

Smith, William Y. "How Ontario Achieved Its Imperial Position." "Acadiensis," Autumn 1976.

Thornton, Patricia A. "The Problem of Out-Migration from Atlantic Canada, 1871-1921: A New Look." "Acadiensis," Autumn, 1985.

ENCYCLOPEDIAS

"Dictionary of Canadian Biography." Toronto: University of Toronto Press, 1966–.

"Encyclopedia Canadiana." Grolier Society of Canada, 1963

"Canadian Encyclopedia." Hurtig Publishers, Edmonton, 1985.

"The Columbia Encyclopedia." Columbia University Press, New York, 5th edition, 1993.

"The Oxford Companion to Canadian History and Literature." Oxford University Press, Toronto, 1967.

"Encyclopedia Britannica." 11th edition, 1910.

ILLUSTRATION SOURCES

Art Gallery of Nova Scotia = AGNS
British Museum = BM
Communications Nova Scotia = CNS
Canadian Heritage (Parks Canada) = CH
Colonial Society of Massachusetts = CSM
Dalhousie University = DAL
Halifax Herald Limited = HH
Halifax Regional Library = HRL
Hector Centre = HC
Heritage Trust of Nova Scotia = HTNS
L. B. Jenson = LBJ
Library of Congress = LC
Legislative Library of Nova Scotia = LLNS
Maritime Command Museum = MCM
McCord Museum = McCM
The Louvre = L
National Gallery of Canada = NGC
National Library of Canada = NLC
National Portrait Gallery = NPG
New Brunswick Museum = NBM
Private Collection = PC
National Archives of Canada = NAC
National Film Board of Canada = NFB
Nova Scotia Museum = NSM
Public Archives of Nova Scotia = PANS
University College of Cape Breton = UCCB
University of King's College = UKC
Universitatsbibliothek Heidelberg = UBH
Saint Mary's University = SMU
Victoria and Albert Museum = V&A
Volvo Canada = VC
Yarmouth County Historical Society = YHS

Location of image on page:
Top location = (T)
Middle location = (M)
Bottom location = (B)
Left location = (L)
Right location = (R)

Front cover/CH, Back cover/CH, Title pg/CH, 8/PANS, 10/DAL, 11/NSM, 12/PANS, 13(T)/DAL, 13(B)/HT, 14(T)/DAL, 14(B)/DAL, 15/UBH, 16/DAL, 17/DAL, 18/DAL, 19/PC, 20/DAL, 22/NAC, 23/L, 25/NAC, 26/NAC, 27(T)/NAC, 27(BL)/NAC, 27(BR)/SMU, 28/DAL, 30/SMU, 31/SMU, 32/DAL, 34/DAL , 36/NAC , 38/DAL ,40(T)/CH, 40(B)/CH, 41/PANS, 42/NLC, 43(T)/NAC, 43(B)/CH, 44/NAC, 45/CNS, 46(T)/CNS, 46(B)CNS, 47/CH, 48(L)/PANS, 48(R)/DAL, 50(T)/DAL, 50(B)/DAL, 51/DAL, 52(T)/CNS, 52(B)/PC, 53/NAC, 54/CNS, 55/PC, 56/DAL, 58/NAC, 60/NBM, 61/SMU, 62/DAL, 64/NBM, 65/DAL, 66/DAL, 68/CH, 70/PC, 71/CH, 73/NGC, 74/DAL, 75/CSM, 76/CSM, 77/PC, 78(T)/CSM, 78(B)/DAL, 80/SMU, 81/NAC, 83/CH, 84(T)/NAC, 84(M)/NAC, 84(B)/NAC, 85/DAL, 86/CH, 87(T)/DAL, 87(B)/PANS, 88(T)/DAL, 88(B)/SMU, 90(T)/NBM, 90(B)/CH, 91/PC, 92/DAL, 92/DAL, 93(T)/HM, 93(B)/PANS, 94/PANS, 95/NAC, 96/DAL, 97/DAL, 98/(T)PANS, 98(B)/NAC, 100/PANS, 101/PANS, 102/PANS, 103/NAC, 104/NPG, 105, PANS, 106(T)/PANS, 106(B)/PANS, 107/PANS, 108(T)/DAL, 108(B)/PANS, 110(T)/NAC, 110(B)/NAC, 111/NAC, 112/CH, 113/CH, 114/PANS, 115(T)/DAL, 115(B)/DAL, 116(T)/NAC, 116(B)/DAL, 117(TL))/PANS, 117(TR)/PANS, 117(B)/PANS, 118(T)/PANS, 118(M)/NSM, 118(B)/UKC, 120/NSM, 121/CH, 122(T)/DAL, 122(B)/PANS, 123(T)/LLNS, 123(B)/PANS, 124/PANS, 125/HC, 126/UCCB, 127/NBM, 128(TL)/PC, 128(TR)/NSM, 128(B)/PANS, 130/DAL, 131/LC, 132/DAL, 133(T)/UKC, 133(B)/NAC, 134/LC, 135/PANS, 136(T)/DAL, 136(B)/LC, 138(T)/PANS, 138(B)/PANS, 139/NSM, 140/LC, 141/NAC, 142/NSM, 143/PANS, 144(T)/UCCB, 144(B)PANS, 145/SMU, 146(T)/NSM, 146(M)/HRL, 146(B)/PANS, 149/UKC, 150/NSM, 152/PC, 153/CNS, 154(T)/DAL, 154(B)/PANS, 156/PANS, 158/DAL, 159/PC, 160/NSM, 161(T)/DAL, 161(B)/UKC, 162/CNS, 162/CNS, 163/CNS, 164(T)/NGC, 164(M)/DAL, 164(B)/DAL, 166/NSM, 167/CNS, 168/DAL, 170/DAL, 171/MCM, 172/PANS, 173/NAC, 174/MCM, 175(T)/NGC, 175(B)/PANS, 176(T)/PANS, 176(B)/SMU, 178(T)/PANS, 178(B)/DAL, 179/PANS, 180/NSM, 181/PC, 182/SMU, 183/DAL, 184(T)/PANS, 184(B)/PANS, 186/PANS, 187/PANS, 188/YHS, 189/NSM, 190(T)/DAL, 190(B)/McCM, 191/PANS, 192(T)/PANS, 192(B)/LBJ193/PANS, 194(T)V&A, 194(B)/PANS, 195(T)/PANS, 195(B)/DAL, 196(TL)/PANS, 196(TR)/NAC, 196(B)/SMU, 198/DAL, 199/NAC, 200/PANS, 201/PC, 202(T)/PANS, 202(B)/MCM, 203/MCM, 204(T)/DAL, 204(B)/UKC, 208/SMU, 209/SMU, 210(T)/SMU, 210(B)/SMU, 211/SMU, 212/PANS, 213(T)/PANS, 213(B)/UKC, 214(T)/AGNS, 214(B)/PANS, 216(T)/PANS, 216(B)/SMU, 217(T)/NSM, 217(M)/NSM, 217(B)/PANS, 219/CNS, 220/DAL, 221(T)/UKC, 221(B)/UKC, 222(T)/PANS, 222(M)/MSN, 222(B)/NSM, 223(T)/PANS, 223(B)/PANS, 224(T)/DAL, 224(M)/McCM, 224(B)/LC, 225(T)/ PANS, 225(M)NSM, 225(B)/PC, 226(T)/DAL, 226(B)/MCM, 227(T)/SMU, 227(B)/SMU, 228(T)/NAC, 228(B)/NAC, 229/MCM, 230/MCM, 232/MCM, 234/PANS, 237/UKC, 238/UCCB, 239(T)/PANS, 239(B)/UCCB, 240/UCCB, 241/UCCB, 242(T)/SMU, 242(B)/PANS, 244/PANS, 248/NAC, 250(T)/NFB, 250(B)/NFB, 251/UCCB, 252/PC, 253/SMU, 254/PANS, 255/DAL, 256/MCM, 258/MCM, 261/NAC, 262/MCM, 264/MCM, 266/PANS, 268/PANS, 271(T)/HH, 271(B)/PANS, 273(T)/VC, 273(B)/CNS, 275/PANS, 276/PANS, 278/NIMBUS, 280/CNS.

09/98